Mac® OS X
Illustrated

A Design Graphics Field Guide

DESIGN GRAPHICS

WILEY

Wiley Publishing, Inc.

Mac® OS X Illustrated

A Design Graphics Field Guide

Published by

Wiley Publishing, Inc.

909 Third Avenue

New York, NY 10022

www.wiley.com

ISBN: 0-7645-3915-9

Manufactured in the United States of America

10 9 8 7 6 5 4 3 2 1

1K/TQ/RS/QS/IN

Published by Wiley Publishing, Inc., Indianapolis, Indiana

Published simultaneously in Canada

For general information on our other products and services or to obtain technical support, please contact our Customer Care Department within the U.S. at 800-762-2974, outside the U.S. at 317-572-3993 or fax 317-572-4002.

Wiley also publishes its books in a variety of electronic formats. Some content that appears in print may not be available in electronic books.

Library of Congress Cataloging-in-Publication Data

Mac® OS X Illustrated
A Design Graphics Field Guide

Conceived and produced by DG Books Pty Ltd
2 Sherbrooke Road
Sherbrooke VIC 3789
Australia

DG Books is a member of the Xandia group of companies.

From the Xandia Group, Design Graphics publishes:

Design Graphics magazine (monthly)
Art & Design Education Resource Guide (annual)
Oz Graphix (annual)

Acknowledgments

Mac® OS X Illustrated
A Design Graphics Field Guide

Concept and Art Direction
Colin Wood

Project Editor & Design Coordinator
Colleen Bate

Associate Editor
Daniel Wade

Technical writer
Steven Noble

Indexing & proofreading
Daniel Wade

Contributors
Colleen Bate
Daniel Wade
Steven Noble
Paul Hellard

Designers
Stuart Colafella
Shannon Nation
Lauren Stevens

Pre-production
Stuart Colafella

Cover design
Colin Wood

Contents summary

Contents

1 Transition to OS X

2 Getting started

3 Help, where am I?

4 Mac OS Finder

10 | Cool new things

11 | 3rd party hardware & software

12 | The network

13 | The Internet

This is a guide for people who don't read manuals. Apple's Mac OS X is a significant leap forward in operating systems and is the biggest change for users in the history of the Macintosh.
This guide aims to make your transition to OS X as painless as possible. It should also increase your levels of fun and productivity as you bring out the best in you and your Mac. There are loads of new features and new ways of

doing things. Some things will be familiar; some won't. Some things have moved and are not where you'd expect them to be.

This guide will help you find all your favorites and introduce you to all the new features. Find out how to make your Mac a digital hub and use all the new apps and utilities. Let 'Mac OS X Illustrated' be your constant companion as you settle in and get comfortable with your new working environment.

How to use this guide

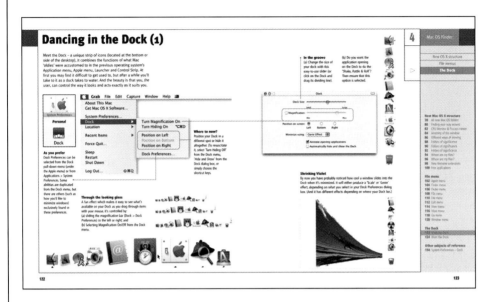

Browse
Before you get stuck into details, browse through the book. You'll be surprised what you'll pick up.

Subject groups
The book is divided into six *subject groups*. (See the Contents summary on page 6.)

Chapters
Chapters are grouped within the six *subject groups*. (See page 6.)

Macro subjects
Each chapter contains related *macro subjects*. Macro subjects contain several *individual subjects*.

Individual subjects
So that you're not swamped with too much information at once, each spread is devoted to a single subject. Related subjects may be nearby.

Contents summary
The contents summary shows the six *subject groups* with their chapters. (See page 6.)

Contents
Every subject is listed, together with page numbers. (See page 8.)

Start with the easy stuff
The front part of the guide has the easy stuff. We've placed the more technical subjects at the back.

Index
See page 310 for the comprehensive index.

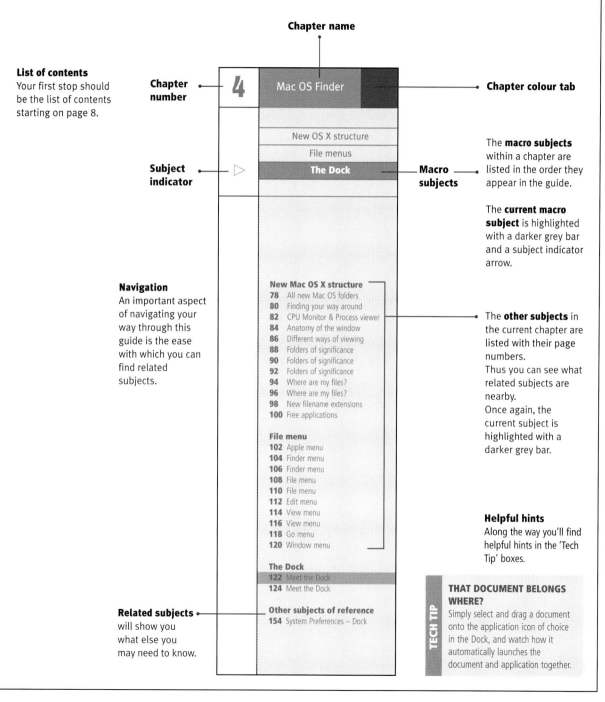

Chapter name

List of contents
Your first stop should
be the list of contents
starting on page 8.

**Chapter
number**

4

Mac OS Finder

Chapter colour tab

New OS X structure

File menus

**Subject
indicator**

▷

The Dock

**Macro
subjects**

The **macro subjects**
within a chapter are
listed in the order they
appear in the guide.

The **current macro
subject** is highlighted
with a darker grey bar
and a subject indicator
arrow.

Navigation
An important aspect
of navigating your
way through this
guide is the ease
with which you can
find related
subjects.

The **other subjects** in
the current chapter are
listed with their page
numbers.
Thus you can see what
related subjects are
nearby.
Once again, the
current subject is
highlighted with a
darker grey bar.

Helpful hints
Along the way you'll find
helpful hints in the 'Tech
Tip' boxes.

Related subjects
will show you
what else you
may need to know.

TECH TIP

**THAT DOCUMENT BELONGS
WHERE?**
Simply select and drag a document
onto the application icon of choice
in the Dock, and watch how it
automatically launches the
document and application together.

The Macintosh advantage

With every new Mac you purchase, you receive a library of free
software covering all of the major areas you're likely to use with your
new 'digital hub'. iPhoto lets you manage your digital photos; iMovie
lets you edit digital movies and add effects; iDVD lets you create your
own Hollywood-style DVDs; iTunes manages your MP3 collection; iCal
lets you schedule your time; Address Book keeps track of your
contacts; iSync syncs your contacts and schedules with your iPod,
Palm PDA, or Bluetooth phone; or iChat lets you chat with friends;
and Mail lets you manage e-mail and avoid spam.

iPhoto
Transfer images from your digital camera and manage, edit and share your digital photos. See pages 132-133.

iMovie
Transfer digital video from your DV camera, edit the footage, add effects, titles and music. See pages 134-135.

iDVD
Take edited digital movies from iMovie, add backgrounds, menus, slideshows, and music, then burn your DVD. See pages 136-137.

iTunes
Convert your music CDs to MP3, manage your MP3 collection, create playlists, and transfer music to your iPod. See pages 138-139.

iSync
Sync your Address Book contacts, iCal calendars and To Do lists with your Palm PDA or Bluetooth mobile phone. See pages 140-141.

iCal
Create calendars, share them online with your .Mac account and sync them with iSync to your phone or Palm PDA. See pages 142-143.

iChat
Chat with AOL Instant Messenger (AIM) compatible clients over the Internet and share files. See pages 144-145.

Address Book
Keep track of contacts with fields for phone, address, Web site, e-mail address, and locate them via online maps. See pages 144-145.

Mail
A full-featured e-mail client that ties straight into your .Mac account and also lets you manage spam e-mail. See pages 146-147.

The pro choice

For creative professionals, free applications will only take you so far. Apple offers a wide range of industrial-strength solutions for: editing digital video with Final Cut Pro; film editing with Cinema Tools; creating DVDs with chapter markers and Web links using DVD Studio Pro; file and web sharing with the UNIX-strength Mac OS X 10.2 Server; movie compositing with Shake; Digital video authoring and playback with QuickTime 6 Pro; Web application development with WebObjects and remote control of Macs over Ethernet, AirPort or the Internet with Apple Remote Desktop.

Final Cut Pro
Create professional digital video productions complete with high-end effects and controls.

Cinema Tools
An add-on to Final Cut Pro allowing users to edit 16mm and 35mm film and HD projects.

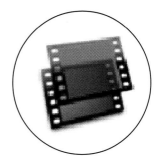

Shake
High-performance compositing software designed for large format film productions

DVD Studio Pro
A DVD authoring tool for full-featured DVD video discs including Dolby Digital 5.1 encoding.

QuickTime 6 Pro
Author MPEG-4 content and export as most common formats including a number of Web streaming presets. See pages 148-149.

QuickTime MPEG-2 Playback
Convert MPEG-2 video content into other formats, for the Web, CD-ROM, or DV tape. See pages 148-149.

Mac OS X Server 10.2
A platform for delivering scalable workgroup and network services with a solid UNIX foundation.

WebObjects
A tool to develop and deploy Java server applications as standards-based Web services.

Apple Remote Desktop
Remotely manage other Macs on a local network, AirPort wireless network or across the Internet.

Glossary

A

Active window
Current modal or document window (brought forward above other windows.) Active windows display distinctive details and are affected by users actions.

Administrator
The person with the privileges to administer users to the computer network. The administrator can create new users and organises privileges for each document or folder for each user.

Advanced memory management
The Mac OS X capability to automatically assign the correct amount of memory to an application. It puts an end toout-of-memory messages, as well as the need to manually adjust application memory.

AirPort
Apple's wireless networking technology using IEEE 802.11. Available in desktop, iMac, iBook and PowerBook G4s.

Alias
Alias allows files and folders to be multi-referenced without making multiple copies of these items.

Always-on Internet
A connection to the Internet that is always connected. Classed as DSL, ISDN or Cable Internet, the download speeds can vary between 8Kb to as fast as 500Kb per second.

Anti-aliasing
A technique used on a greyscale or colour bitmap display to make diagonal edges appear smoother. In the Classic environment, text smoothing is an option of the Appearance control panel.

Apple Desktop Bus (ADB)
This is the name for the superseded mechanism for connecting the mouse and keyboard to the Apple computer. It has since been replaced by USB.

Apple key
Also called the Command key, it is situated next to the space bar on most keyboards.
It has the Apple logo and cloverleaf or propeller pattern.

AppleTalk
Suite of network protocols standard on Macintosh computers. Can be integrated with other network systems, such as the Internet.

Application
Another name for programs such as Microsoft Word, Adobe Photoshop or FileMaker. In the mainframe environment, this refers to a process whereby many programs and databases are utilised for a final result.

Application Programming Interface (API)
The means by which application programs take advantage of operating system features.

Aqua
The new, more intuitive Mac OS X interface. Aqua includes expressive icons, vibrant colour, and fluid motion, as well as innovative features to help users navigate and organize their system.

B

Attachment
One or more files that can be attached to emails, so it can be viewed at the other end. Some ISPs limit the size allowable to send.

Bandwidth
The transmission capacity of the frequency interval used by a communications channel.

Beta
The status of a product that has already been extensively alpha and field tested. Available for public download but generally not guaranteed to be 'bug-free'.

Bit
A binary digit, the smallest information entity bitmap. A dot-by-dot description of an electronic image, with each dot represented by a binary digit (bit) that is 'on' (1) or 'off' (0).

Bitmap
Data structure representing positions and states of a corresponding set of pixels.

Boot
Booting, re-booting the computer refers to when the computer system is started. The computer runs through some internal checks and then loads its operating system from its main designated disk.

Browser
Application that allows users to see the contents of a Web server.

BSD (Berkeley System Distribution):
A version of UNIX developed by the Computer Systems Research Group of the University of California at Berkeley.

C

Byte
Eight bits makes one byte. It takes one byte to produce one character, such as the letter A, on the monitor.

Cache memory
Hardware device used to store the most frequently accessed data in memory. Used in conjunction with disk drives and meant to reduce access time by eliminating the rotational delay and seek time.

Carbon
A set of Mac OS X programming interfaces that allows software developers to update or 'tune up' applications to run in Mac OS X. Carbon applications take advantage of new Mac OS X features such as the advanced Darwin foundation, Quartz graphics, and the Aqua user interface.

CD-ROM
Compact Disc Read Only Memory. A version of the Compact Disc for storage of 'Read'Only Memory' digital data. User capacity is usually in excess of 600Mb.

Channel
In a QuickTime Player, a channel delivers interactive QuickTime TV content, which can include streaming video, streaming audio, and links to related information on the Web.

Classic
A software compatibility environment that allows you to run thousands of Mac OS 9 applications in Mac OS X. Mac OS 9.2 is the basis for the Classic environment, allowing previous versions of Macintosh software to work just as they do in Mac OS 9. They look like Mac OS 9 applications with the 'Platinum' user interface, and they do not make use of new Mac OS X features.

Clipboard
Also known as the pasteboard, the clipboard enables the transfer of data between applications and the Finders. It contains data that the user has cut or copied and is implemented using Core Foundation Pasteboard Services or the Cocoa NSPasteboard class.

Cocoa
The native programming language of Mac OS X. Cocoa is an application programming interface (API) that runs advanced, object-oriented applications. It is the fastest and most powerful way for developers to create new applications for Mac OS X. Like Carbon applications, Cocoa applications take advantage of all the advanced features of Mac OS X.

Compositing
In image editing, the process of combining several images or specific portions of images into one overall image.

Configuration
Group of settings for a particular networking component such as AppleTalk or TCP/IP.

ColorSync
Industry-standard architecture for reliably reproducing colour images on operating systems and devices such as scanners, video displays and printers.

Contextual menu
The convenient menu that

appears when you Control+Click on an item.

D

Darwin
The UNIX-based core operating system that is the foundation of Mac OS X, Darwin evolved from a joint effort by Apple engineers and programmers in the open source software community. UNIX and Linux software developers will appreciate the ease of porting existing UNIX applications to Mac OS X using Darwin.

Database
A collection of interrelated data items readable and searchable using keywords. It can either be a basic level structure or be relational, which stipulates that there may be many-to-one, one-to-many or many-to-many relationships to records in other linked files.

Disk
The hardware that holds data in the computer. Internal drives that you never actually see, but external hard disks can also connect via a network.

Disk image
This file represents a disk volume. The Disk Copy utility mounts any disk image after you double click on the file. A removable disk icon for the disk image appears on the desktop. Use the Finder to navigate to folders on the disk image just as you would navigate to find a file on a physical hard disk.

Directory
A folder, single level or root level of a disk. It displays a list of items

enclosed in that area. Possibly includes navigational guides to surrounding levels.

Domain
An area of the file system reserved for software, documents and resources. There are four domains: user, local, network and system.

DOS
The operating system for PCs which precedes more recent versions of Microsoft Windows.

Download
The moving of a file from one computer to another, either through an intranet, WLAN or the Internet.

Dock
The bar that appears at the bottom of the Mac OS X desktop screen. The Dock contains icons for launching applications. You also can minimise an open file and windows to an icon on the Dock, then click the icon on the Dock to reopen the window.

Drag
Holding the mouse button down and rolling the mouse, moving the cursor and an item, perhaps a folder or icon on the screen.

Driver
A file that provides extra functionality to your system such as a file needed to enable Mac OS X to use a particular printer or camera.

DSL
An addition to the standard telephone service that allows a constant internet service over a standard telephone line.

Dual-booting
Mac OS X supports dual booting, which means that

Mac OS X users can choose to start up their system using either Mac OS X or Mac OS 9.x.

DVD
Stands for Digital Versatile Disc, a form of optical disc that holds upwards of 4.7Gb of data. The DVD supports disks with capacities of from 4.7Gb to 17Gb and access rates of 600Kbps to 1.3Mbps. One of the best features of DVD drives is that they are backward-compatible with CD-ROMs. This means that DVD players can play old CD-ROMs, CD-I disks, and video CDs, as well as new DVD-ROMs.

E

Ethernet
This one of the most common LAN standards in networking. A newer version of Ethernet, called 100Base-T (or Fast Ethernet), supports data transfer rates of 100 Mbps. And the newest version, Gigabit Ethernet supports data rates of one gigabit (1,000 megabits) per second.

Encryption
A form of scrambling of files into un-readable form. This secures the contents for specific readers only. Decoding of the files can then be regulated.

Extensions
Small applications that run behind the scenes of the desktop, which can display and control timing, mail, fax reception, monitor calibration as well as many other house-keeping duties on the computer.

Extensions manager
An extra application that controls the activity and administration of the many

extensions that start up and run alongside the operating system.

External hard drive
A box connected by USB or FireWire to the main computer body. This hard drive may be used as a scratch disk or an extra area of storage for large files and applications.

Email Rule
A specification telling the email client how to deal with incoming traffic, such as instantly deleting a message from a source that sends junk mail.

F

Favorite
In the Finder or Microsoft Internet Explorer, this is an alias of a folder, file or page that you use frequently and can double click to open, wherever it may be.

File
The named document that you create in an application.

Firewall
Software (or computers running such software) that prevents unauthorised access to a network and therefore unauthorised spread of data.

Folder
Named after a physical folder, this is the place that you store files on a computer hard drive. It may have a name, and a colour, to classify the contents.

G

Gb
A gigabyte is exactly 1,000,000,000-bytes of data.

GUI
The Graphic User Interface, which includes folders, files, icons, pull-down menus and a point-and-click cursor system. As this is based on a system able to be seen, it is widely considered to be a more user friendly system that command-line interfaces.

H

Hacker
A hacker is considered to be a person with an intense interest in computers and also considered to be using this knowledge with malicious intent.

Hang
To have an application or the operating system stop responding to input for some reason. No movements or mouse-clicks will restore the desktop. In Mac OS X, only the offending application needs to be Force-quit to regain control.

Help Viewer
An application that helps you browse for help in Mac OS X.

HFS (Hierarchical File System)
Mac OS file-system format. Files are represented as a hierarchy of directories or folders, in turn containing files or folders.

Home folder
A folder set up to store files for your user name within a multi-user environment in Mac OS X.

HTML (Hypertext Markup Language)
Text file prepartion method to ensure that contents are displayed and link to other files on the World Wide Web.

Glossary

I

Icon view
A finder window, depicting each file and folder as an icon.

Insertion point
In a graphical application or text box, the point where the cursor sits flashing.

Internal hard disk
As the name suggests, it is the hard disk inside the computer. Named accordingin to your preference, this is the primary area where applications and files can be run from start-up.

Internet service provider (ISP)
Someone or a company who provides the necessary service for connection to the Internet.

iTunes
An audio application that enables Mac users to play audio CDs, create MP3 files, and build playlists.

K

Kernel
This is the pivotal component of the operating system. The kernel handles most of the interaction between the operating system and the hardware.
The Darwin core kernel is based on Mach 3.0 from Carnegie Mellon University and FreeBSD 3.2 (derived from the University of California at Berkeley's BSD 4.4 Lite), a core technology from two widely acclaimed operating system projects.

Keyboard repeat rate
The rate controls how rapidly the system duplicates the character.

L

Linux
An implementation of the UNIX kernel, originally written from scratch, with no proprietary code. The kernel as a whole is available under the GNU General Public License.

Login
Entering your name and password to gain access to Mac OS X after you start up the system.

M

Mach
Lowest level of the Mac OS X kernel. It provides basic services such as threads, tasks, ports, and interprocess communication (IPC), etc.

Magnification
A Dock feature in Mac OS X that increases icon size when the cursor is rolled over it.

Memory protection
System of memory management in Mac OS X where programs are prevented from being able to modify or corrupt the memory partition of another program. (Note: Mac OS 8 and 9 do not have memory protection).

Menu bar
The strip of commands that can be pulled down from the top of the screen with the mouse-click when an application is open.

Mount
When Disk Copy opens a disk image file, an icon is created for the application on the desktop.

Multitasking
The ability to carry out multiple programs concurrently.
Mac OS X uses pre-emptive multitasking while Mac OS 8 and 9 use cooperative multitasking.

N

Networking
Mac OS X offers UNIX-based networking with built-in support for PPP, AirPort, and Ethernet. Users benefit from quick and easy access to Internet service providers, as well as seamless local area network integration.

NeXT
A company called NeXT Software was founded by Steve Jobs in 1986. It created hardware that took advantage of object oriented technologies. NeXT Software was sold to Apple in 1997.

NeXTSTEP
NeXTSTEP is based on an operating system called Mach to which NeXT has added a UNIX interface. You can use the UNIX command-line if you like, but unlike your average UNIX system, NEXTSTEP is easier to use.

O

OpenGL
Contributing to the incredible graphics offered by Mac OS X, OpenGL is the world's most widely used 3D technology.

Optical disk
A platter-shaped disk coated with optical recording material on which information is read and written using a laser light, focused on a single line of material.

P

Pane
An alternate word for a window in a Macintosh desktop interface.

Password
A secret word or group of characters that you enter to login to Mac OS X and some web sites. Passwords limit access to authorised users only.

Pasteboard
Another name for the Clipboard.

PDA
Abbreviation for a Personal Digital Assistant, as introduced by the Palm and Handspring group of companies.

PDF (Portable Document Format)
File format for viewing documents independently of the original software, hardware, and operating system used to create them. A PDF file can contain any combination of text, graphics, and images.

Permission
Each user in the Mac OS X has their own list of folders and areas where they are permitted to enter. They have permission to use the contents of these folders.

Pixel
Basic logical unit of programmable color on a computer display or in a computer image. The size of a pixel depends on the resolution of the display screen.

Plug-in
External module of code and data separate from a host (i.e. an application, operating system or other plug-in) that can add features without needing access to the source code of the host.

Pointer
The little black arrow that is the point of interaction on the screen. Also named the cursor.

PostScript
Industry standard for printing and imaging, this language describes the appearance of a printed page and is an ouput format of Quartz.

PPP (Point-to-Point Protocol)
The Internet standard for transmitting network data, such as IP packets, over serial point-to-point links.

Pre-emptive multitasking
A Mac OS X function that prioritizes tasks according to their importance. You can do things such as check email, write a letter, or surf the web, and your Mac will continue to respond, even when executing processor-intensive tasks such as compressing a movie file.

Preferences
Files generated by every application as they are run. Each preference file holds API instructions and scripts that ensure relevant and constant application behaviour at each launch. System Preferences hold instructions for System start-up and housekeeping procedures.

Print Center
The Mac OS X application that enables you to install and control printers.

Privileges
Within Mac OS X, there are many areas that users are not able to enter unless they are also the administrator and owner of the machine. These are

the regulated privileges with the system.

Propeller key
Another name for the Apple Command key, first key to use in a combination command, like Command-Q for quit.

Protected memory
Mac OS X isolates each application in its own memory space, so if an application does crash, Mac OS X shuts it down without affecting anything else on your computer. You can continue working or playing on your Mac without interruption and without restarting your computer.

Public folder
This holds documents and files which are meant to be visible and useable by all users of the Mac OS X system on any computer in question. There are no privileges attached.

Q

Quartz
A powerful, high-performance new 2D graphics system developed by Apple. Quartz features on-the-fly rendering, anti-aliasing, and compositing of PDF for pristine, high-fidelity graphics. It even allows you to save as PDF in Mac OS X applications.

R

RAM
Random-access memory and one which a microprocessor can read or write to.

Removable disk
A removable drive which is attached with FireWire or USB if it is an External drive. Possibly ATA/100 if it is an internal drive.

Rendering
The conversion of a data-based description into a graphical image for display.

Resolution
Number of pixels contained on a display monitor.

S

Script
Series of statements that instruct an application or operating system to perform operations. Normally written in a scripting language such as AppleScript or Perl.

Server
Process that provides services to other clients in the same or other computers.

Sheet
Dialog associated with a specific window that appears to slide out from beneath the window title.

Shutdown
Under the Apple Menu. This can be used to close Mac OS X and power down your Macintosh.

Startup disk
The settings pane in the System Preferences application that lets the user set system and alert volumes, and choose the disk from which the Mac starts. This can also be used to select between the Mac OS X and older Mac environments.

Symmetric multiprocessing
A real boon for dual-processor Power Mac G4 systems. This feature allows Mac OS X to automatically assign both processors to handle operations and applications that are more

processor-intensive. With Mac OS X installed on a dual-processor system, certain operations run nearly twice as fast.

System Preferences
An application that, in part, replaces the Control Panels folder. It offers direct access to Mac OS X System Preferences, such as for date and time, monitor resolution and network configuration.

T

TCP/IP
Transmission Control Protocol/Internet protocol. A suite of protocols designed to allow Protocol/Internet communication between networks regardless of the technologies implemented in each network.

Terminal
A Mac OS X application used to access the UNIX command-line interface.

Toolbar
A row of icons or buttons that when clicked once, activate a specific command in a program.

U

Unicode
16-bit character set that assigns unique character codes to characters in a wide range of languages. (There are approximately 65 000 distinct Unicode characters that represent unique characters used in many languages.)

UNIX
The first non-proprietary operating system written in the C language, and the first open operating system that can be improved or enhanced by anyone. Darwin, the

foundation of Mac OS X, is based on UNIX.

URL
Uniform Resource Locator. This signifies a www. hypertext link, representing nearly every Internet link or service.

USB
Universal Serial Bus. A plug-and-play peripheral standard developed by Intel for keyboard, mouse, digital cameras, drives and printers. The high speed variation is USB 2.0 and its biggest competition is FireWire.

Utilities
Small applications that facilitate housekeeping tasks indirectly. Examples include system usage. File maintenance, disk copying etc.

V

Virtual memory
The method used to extend the memory available to your Mac by allocating part of the hard drive as a swap file. When built-in memory is not sufficient to meet operating system or program needs, Mac OS X uses the file to swap unneeded data. Beginning with Mac OS X, the memory needs of an application are established dynamically as needed.

Volume
A storage device or portion of that device that is formatted to contain folders and files of a particular file system.

W

Wireless Internet
Technologies that bring wireless connections to

the Internet by receiving satellite transmissions or fixed beams of signal.

Web page
A single document for display on the web.

Web site
A location on the Web that contains a selection of Web pages.

X

X
Signifies the numeral ten and is the system adopted by Apple for leveraging the Apple platform onto a UNIX base.

Y

Yahoo
One of the more successful web 'Search engine-turned-everything' companies. Having survived the dot.com crash, Yahoo has gone on to be one of the largest Web-based mail/chat/retail hubs.

Z

ZIP
A compression tool from PKWARE that works on PCs, Macs and UNIX computers. These compressed files are usually sent across the net as they can self-check for consistency while the file is being expanded. Aladdin Stuffit Expander (www.aladdinsys.com) can decode ZIP archives.

Zip drive
A removable storage device developed by Iomega Corporation, which can store up to 250Mb of data. The portable storage ability was a new feature.

On your marks ...

The X Factor

31 reasons to change

No wonder Apple calls it 'the world's most advanced operating system' with its crash proof, secure UNIX-based architecture, stunning Aqua interface and advanced features. Mac OS X is beautiful, fast, responsive, easy to use and takes care of multi-tasking and memory as quick as a flash and without you having to do a thing. If you aren't currently thinking of upgrading to Mac OS X or switching to the Mac operating system for the first time, you should be. And in this chapter we give you a little nudge into unknown territory and provide 31 reasons to help you consider this premium choice.

Open System with a huge number of UNIX/Linux applications

Mac OS X	Mac OS 9
This modern foundation is based on the advanced BSD (Berkeley System Distribution) UNIX system. This allows easy interoperability with UNIX systems and applications, allows developers to run many UNIX and Linux applications and includes an application called Terminal, which provides a command-line shell environment for experienced UNIX users. Mac OS X includes a Developer Tools CD with everything a developer needs to write applications for Mac OS X. Project Builder is the main development tool, providing a means to build Cocoa, Carbon, AppleScript , Java, and applications, in languages such as Objective-C, C, C++, Java, and AppleScript.	Mac OS 9 is seen as proprietary operating system that limits users' access to open source tools, applications, languages and protocols used in many environments.

Brilliant new imaging engine

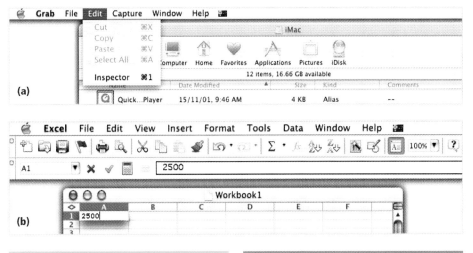

(a)

(b)

Mac OS X	Mac OS 9

Quartz displays text and graphics with crystal clarity, and it adds many new capabilities, including transparency, drop shadows, interleaved windows, and special effects that make the new Aqua user interface fun and easy to use. Because it is a powerful window server and layered compositing engine, it is responsible for everything you see on the screen. It double-buffers windows, eliminating flicker and flashing when you drag or resize them, has alpha channel support, and creates smooth edges for windows (even non-rectangular windows).

Mac OS 9 uses the 20 year old technology, QuickDraw to create screen displays. Originally designed for black-and-white displays, it has no built-in support for modern special features.

The finishing touch
(a) In the example above note that the pull-down menu is transparent. A very clever and thoughtful touch as it allows the window behind it to show through.
(b) Microsoft Excel X is a good example of cosmetic appeal to highlight important information.
See how the the active cell (complete with shadow) literally jumps off the screen, making it very easy to quickly find the cell.

The X Factor

31 reasons to change

Despite the fact that Mac OS X looks and feels as familiar as its predecessors, it's NOT actually the traditional Mac operating system most of us have become accustomed to. Under the hood lies a system with a difference. There's Darwin, an industrial-strength, UNIX-based core operating system that delivers exceptional stability and performance and the stunning new user interface, Aqua, built on innovative graphics technologies Quartz, OpenGL, and QuickTime. This combination brings graphics capabilities to Mac OS X beyond anything ever seen in a desktop operating system. And this is only for starters. See what else is now on offer.

3

Customizable tool bars

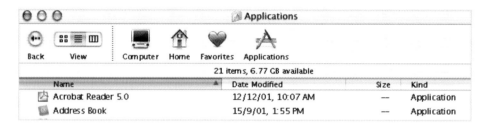

Mac OS X	Mac OS 9
Customize your tool bars! At the top part of each Finder window you will see the toolbar, made up of a number of icons (or buttons) most helpful to you. These icons can be customized (as can be seen from the View) or kept as they appear above. Useful toolbar icons include: the Home icon for personal items; the Favorites icon, a shortcut to all your favorite items; the Applications icon, complete with free Mac OS X applications as well as your own; iDisk, allowing Internet file storage; Burn, letting you burn CDs directly from the Finder; and Connect, allowing you to connect to Servers with the click of the mouse. (The View menu and the toolbar are discussed in more detail on pages 114, 115 and 84, 85 respectively.)	There are a wide variety of ways to add functionality to the OS 9 Finder through commercial and shareware applications. Each has its own configuration and way of displaying choices. No two work the same and many are confusing. Most users resort to making aliases of the applications they use often, but this is not practical as they are often left on the desktop and obstructed by overlapping windows.

Multiple users with secure file access

4

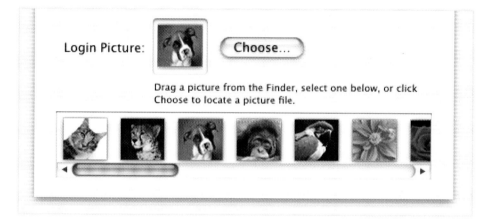

Login Picture: Choose...

Drag a picture from the Finder, select one below, or click Choose to locate a picture file.

Mac OS X

The Mac OS X UNIX-based foundation provides secure file access with built-in support for multiple users. Every user on the system has a secure login account and a Home directory for storing personal files, preferences, and system settings. When users log into their personal accounts on a Mac OS X computer, they get automatic access to their Macintosh, with their customized desktop, Finder, Dock, and applications, as well as all their personal files. Mac OS X also includes an option to present a login screen with a scrolling list of users. (see pages 252, 253 for more details).

Mac OS 9

Mac OS 9 has some support for multiple users, but it's very easy for one user to accidentally change another user's settings, or even delete documents.

DISABLE LOGIN

If you don't think it's necessary to have to login to your Mac, you can disable the login process. However, bear in mind that this will affect preferences such as desktop pattern, keyboard settings etc set by anyone else who shares your Mac.

TECH TIP

The X Factor

31 reasons to change

Sigh. 'No pain, no gain' is one of life's lessons and we have to wonder whether this philosophy applies to the acquisition of Mac OS X. We know that nifty new operating system has brought us many exciting and useful new features, but what have we lost along the way? Some that come quickly to mind include: • System Extensions. (Hey! This is a good thing – it means that you no longer have to figure out which extension is making your Mac freeze); • Control Panels – Mac OS X now has System Preferences – easier to figure out and better organized; • Memory Control Panel. Another plus! Now you never have to worry about managing memory again, Mac OS X takes all the responsibility; • Rebuilding the desktop. Although this was never too much of an effort, the symptoms that suggested it was time for desktop rebuilding were really annoying; • Preferences and fonts. They've been removed from the System Folder to ensure that no-one can fiddle with this all-important site. No fiddling, no system trouble. So far it all seems rather pain-free. Read on to find out more of what we've gained ...

Automatic network management

5

Mac OS X	Mac OS 9
If you're using AirPort and you connect an Ethernet cable, the network immediately switches over to use the Ethernet network. In addition, DHCP (dynamic host control protocol, which makes up a new IP address every time there is a connection to another computer) works seamlessly. No more resetting! You can log on to new AirPort networks, even closed ones, and Mac OS X enters the password for you.	Mac OS 9 requires Location Manager to switch over and use the Ethernet network. Besides having to switch settings manually, each of the related control panels (AppleTalk, Network, TCP/IP) need to be carefully configured for each Location Manager setting.

No more modal dialog boxes

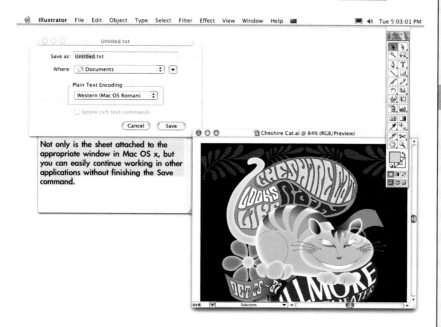

Not only is the sheet attached to the appropriate window in Mac OS x, but you can easily continue working in other applications without finishing the Save command.

Mac OS X

Mac OS X gives you the freedom to stop what you're doing and go on to something else. In this example, the user was in the middle of saving a document in TextEdit. Before doing this, he or she was distracted, headed straight to Adobe Illustrator and launched it. No warning messages involved at all. (Also note that the Save sheet is now attached to the appropriate window, making it all part of the same window which can be moved around the screen to your heart's content.)

Mac OS 9

Alerts, warnings and even the Save dialog box in OS 9 must be attended to before going on to something else. They prevent anything else from happening until the box at hand has been dismissed.

The X Factor

31 reasons to change

There's more than meets the eye with Mac OS X. Not only is its interface a sight to behold, but what lurks beneath is more than a little impressive. Focussing strongly on improved productivity, the new operating system has brought pre-emptive multi-tasking and multi-threading into their own. While pre-emptive multi-tasking enables the system to allocate processing power for each task individually, multi-threading ensures that a program can do more than one thing at a time. As you can see, the two go hand in hand to make your OS X experience efficient and fast all around. But wait, there's more ...

Intelligent user interface

7

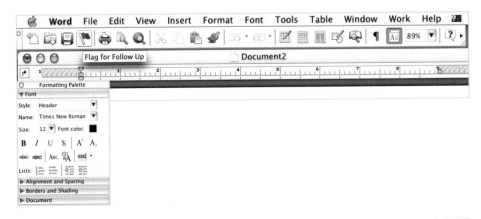

Mac OS X	Mac OS 9
Aqua's ocean-blue inspired look is designed to look like water with its many transparent, shiny and droplet-shaped elements. It just looks better. It also provides a consistent look and feel to Mac OS X-native applications (such as Microsoft Office). Aqua has a carefully crafted design that clearly communicates actions to users, such as the Genie effect.	Over a 20 year period Apple developed its user interface. Naturally this meant that many of its features would look different, depending on the Application that was open. It really was not pulled together quite so snugly.

Improved DVD viewing

Nonskip DVD (Digital Versatile Discs) viewing — background tasks will not interrupt playback.

Mac OS 9

In Mac OS 9, a movie could stutter or stall in playback if other system activities took over the computer. It's also possible for the audio and video to get out of sync.

The X Factor

31 reasons to change

Protected memory, pre-emptive multi-tasking, advanced memory management, and symmetric multi-processing are all features synonymous with Mac OS X, thanks to its UNIX-based core operating system known as Darwin. UNIX itself is complex to understand. In layman's terms, it is built upon three layers; • the hardware of the computer; • the kernel that performs the basic operations; and • the shell, on top of the kernel which runs a simple program that accepts input from a user and converts it to the appropriate commands to be sent to the kernel or to programs. Mac users fear not – you won't be quizzed on this technical subject. Apple has concealed the UNIX complexity from the end user. Which means that all you have to do is enjoy its wares ... and read more on the benefits of using OS X.

Access Windows servers

Mac OS X	Mac OS 9
Many users have diverse networks that mix computers running the Mac OS, UNIX, and Windows. Mac OS X delivers a number of technologies that make it simple to integrate the Mac into cross-platform networks. Users can natively connect to Windows and Mac OS X also includes connectivity to UNIX NFS servers, making it the perfect network client for universities, research labs, and open platform businesses.	In order to connect to Windows servers, Mac OS 9 users find it necessary to purchase, install and configure additional software to connect to Windows servers.

Network tools included for the troubleshooter

10

Mac OS X	Mac OS 9
Fully supported network management tools from Apple are included with Mac OS X. For example, the Network Utility application which allows you to check to see if a server is available (ie network connection is live). It's great for troubleshooting.	There are no built-in network tools in Mac OS 9. Users need to download shareware or purchase commercial applications to do even simple Internet troubleshooting (such as pinging your ISP's host to see if the network is down).

Summarization – it's magic!

11

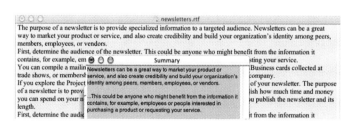

Mac OS X	Mac OS 9
Mac OS X will take a long document and automatically create a short summary of the content, based on some very sophisticated rules.	There is no way to automatically summarize a long document for quick review.

The X Factor

31 reasons to change

Mac OS X understands networking at a deep level, so you don't have to. Configuring Mac OS X to use a network is as simple as plugging in an Ethernet cable – the operating system does the rest, changing network settings on-the-fly, and all without a restart. This network dexterity is doubly impressive for laptop users, who can switch from AirPort to Ethernet (and back) by simply plugging in and unplugging an Ethernet cable. Mac OS X has the ability to detect the best connection and switch to the fastest one available automatically. Isn't that nifty? Nifty too, are these other new features of OS X. If you don't know much about them, you are just about to find out.

Undo mistakes (in the Finder too)

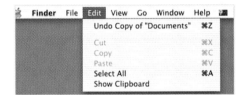

Mac OS X

Finder Undo can undo your last desktop action: dragging an icon into a different folder or to the Trash, renaming a folder, etc.

Mac OS 9

In Mac OS 9, when a mistake is made in a Finder operation (such as dragging a group of files into the wrong folder), the user needs to figure out how to correct the mistake—often a long and complex process.

Digital photography and the Web

Mac OS X

Apple provides the missing link to revolutionize the way we save, organize, share and enjoy digital images with iPhoto, the cool new software application that lets you:

- manipulate high-resolution images quickly;
- achieve consistent color from photo to Web to print;
- import your pictures from your digital camera, organize them, edit and improve them, and share them in a number of different ways;
- create your own custom coffee-table books – you can add titles and text to tell your story or describe your pictures. Then, if your Mac is connected to an inkjet printer, you can print your book pages and take them to a copy center for binding. You can even order a professionally-bound book;
- arranging them into digital albums and then changing them into a beautiful full-screen slide show, accompanied by your favorite music, with a touch of a button; and
- e-mailing them to friends, printing them on an inkjet printer or ordering Kodak prints over the Internet (US only).

Mac OS 9

Creating a Web page of photographs requires many steps and several different applications in OS 9.

The X Factor

31 reasons to change

Mac OS X has changed the way it handles filenames, embracing filename extensions – an option which provides better integration with Windows applications. Because this technology is designed using 'invisible' file type/creator codes to associate files with applications, Mac users can choose whether or not to view the file extension. This gives them the best of both worlds – they can enjoy the seamless and elegant file typing to which they've become accustomed, while benefiting from full file type compatibility with other platforms. See more about this on the pages displayed as well as another great feature you will be interested in. We hope you are still concentrating as there's more to come ...

Compatible with Windows filenames

Filename.exe

Mac OS X	Mac OS 9
Mac OS X uses Windows-style (three-letter) filename suffixes to identify the application needed to launch a document. Three-letter suffixes mean better integration with Windows applications. Users can set a preference that causes Mac OS X to hide the suffixes.	Mac OS 9 document filenames have the appropriate application embedded in the file itself, while Windows adds a three-letter suffix to the filename (.xls for Excel, for example). This means that sharing documents between Mac and Windows systems can be complicated, as neither operating system recognizes the way the other identifies the proper application to launch for viewing the document.

☐ Show warning before emptying the Trash
☑ Always show file extensions

The 'Always Show File Extensions' option is especially useful for compatibility with Windows systems. If you choose not to select it, the extensions will be invisible but lurking in the background. See also pages 98, 99.

Customization

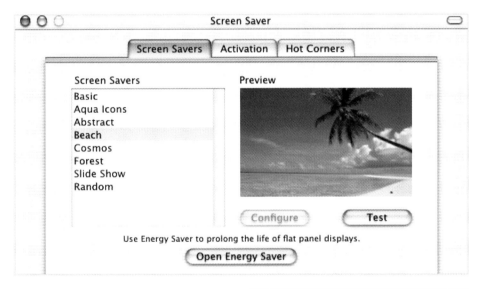

● ● ○	Screen Saver	⊂⊃

Screen Savers | Activation | Hot Corners

Screen Savers

Basic
Aqua Icons
Abstract
Beach
Cosmos
Forest
Slide Show
Random

Preview

(Configure) (Test)

Use Energy Saver to prolong the life of flat panel displays.

(**Open Energy Saver**)

Mac OS X

Macintosh users have always delighted in customizing their computers to reflect the way they work and to show their individuality. This can be done in Mac OS X by: • changing the color of Finder windows (and add pictures as backgrounds for each unique folder); • creating multiple views of files (including a new Column view that provides significant information in a very small amount of screen space); • adding virtually unlimited categories for grouping their files (through the comments field); and • allowing users to select their own pictures and have them animated as screen savers.

Mac OS 9

In Mac OS 9, users can customize their environments in many ways, but they often find that a variety of shareware or commercial applications are needed to add the customization features they need. Occasionally these shareware applications bring instability to the system.

The X Factor

31 reasons to change

A lot of Mac OS X's new features work behind the scenes, so even though you may notice improved power and more reliability, you won't actually be able to see why. It's a good thing too, as it allows you to get on to what you do best and the new operating system to take care of the rest. This sets it apart from previous operating systems and make the whole new OS experience really worthwhile.

Advanced memory management

Mac OS X still allows you to allocate more memory to applications in the Classic environment (as illustrated here), but manages memory very well on its own so there is no need to make any memory changes to its applications.

Mac OS X	Mac OS 9
Darwin's super-efficient memory manager automatically and precisely allocates the exact amount of memory needed by the application – no more, no less. This means that users no longer have to worry about how much memory an application needs to open large files.	In Mac OS 9, it's often necessary for a user to set preferred memory requirements for each application. As the user works on larger and more complex documents, it's common to have to quit the application and increase the amount of memory assigned to it.

Multi-tasking

Mac OS X

Pre-emptive multi-tasking works like an air traffic controller, watching over the computer's processor, prioritizing tasks, making sure activity levels are at maximum, and ensuring that every task receives the resources it needs. Darwin sets processor priorities depending on the importance of the task. When a new task comes along, the controller ensures that it receives an appropriate amount of processor time. Since applications can no longer 'occupy' the processor indefinitely, your system is far more responsive to the tasks you want to perform when you want to perform them, making for simultaneous multiple tasking and greater efficiency all round.

Mac OS 9

In Mac OS 9, the applications themselves determine when to allow other applications to use the CPU, so a complex task such as rendering a video transition or encoding video — tasks that can take several minutes or even hours — will fully occupy the processor until complete. (Even simple actions, such as holding down the mouse button, stop all running applications.)

The Dock

The Dock makes frequently used applications, files and directories (folders) easily available at all times. Folders within folders show up as hierarchical directories, making it very easy to navigate to frequently used files and application. (See pages 122-125).

Mac OS 9 only allows users to place folders under the Apple menu, in a complicated process. In addition, the folders are not visible on the desktop and can easily be forgotten.

CPU Monitor

The X Factor

31 reasons to change

Mac OS X allows you to do more in less time with Darwin, its rock-solid foundation, engineered for stability, reliability, and performance. Crash-resistant computing, memory management, simultaneous performance of multiple tasks and speed, speed and ... more speed are just some examples of productivity enhancements. More reasons for you to consider upgrading to a new Macintosh – that is, if you haven't already.

19

Built-in symmetric multi-processor support

Mac OS X	Mac OS 9
Two brains really are better than one – built-in support for dual-processor Power Mac G4 computers automatically takes advantage of both processors. Complex image transformations, video compression, or MP3 encoding operations can run up to twice as fast using Mac OS X on a dual-processor Power Mac G4. In fact, much of Mac OS X itself is multi-threaded, so applications that use system services such as sound, graphics, and networking accrue the benefits of both processors. This makes nearly every 'Built for Mac OS X' application perform better on dual-processor Power Mac systems.	Mac OS 9 has no built-in support for dual processors, so applications need to provide their own multi-processor support. This limits the benefit of multiple processors to just a few applications that were written to take advantage of the second processor – and even then, the performance boost is limited to specific functions

Stability

20

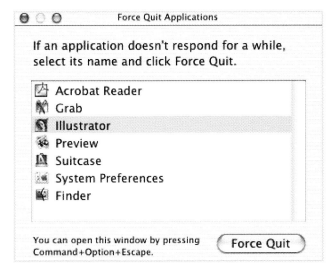

Mac OS X

Darwin ensures reliability and offers crash-resistant computing by protecting applications through a modern, robust, protected-memory architecture that allocates a unique address space for each application or process running on the computer. If an application attempts an illegal operation, such as accessing another application's memory space, the operating system simply shuts it down without affecting the rest of the system. You can continue working without interruption and without restarting your computer. These benefits also apply to applications that stop responding. Simply force any application to quit without fear of harming other applications or the system itself.

Mac OS 9

In Mac OS 9, when an application crashes, it can take down the whole system. Consequently, even though Mac OS 9 supports multi-tasking, users are hesitant to run other applications while important tasks are running in the background.

The X Factor

31 reasons to change

The Mac OS X user experience is truly a delight! Aqua, its elegant and powerful graphical user interface features gorgeous drop shadows to provide visual feedback, and translucent window borders and menus that don't obscure your view of what's important underneath – courtesy of the Quartz imaging model. This fascinating technology also comes with built-in support for the portable document format (PDF), bringing new meaning to 'what-you-see-is-what-you-get'. Now isn't this incentive enough for you to start your Mac OS X installation right now?

Preview pictures, movies and sounds in the Finder

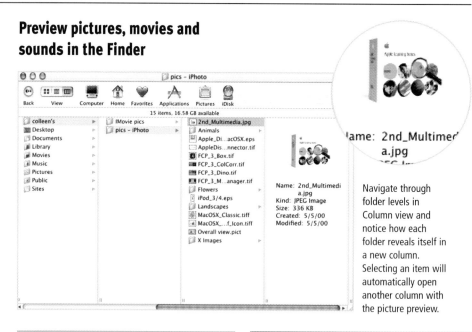

Navigate through folder levels in Column view and notice how each folder reveals itself in a new column. Selecting an item will automatically open another column with the picture preview.

Mac OS X	Mac OS 9
In Column view in the Finder, graphics, movies, and music files show a preview of their contents, allowing users to quickly find specific files. Using the arrow keys to move up and down a list of files quickly shows the previews.	Mac OS 9 has no way to preview movies, music, or graphics without opening them in an application. Users become frustrated trying to find needed files when they are not clearly named.

Brand-new screen imaging engine

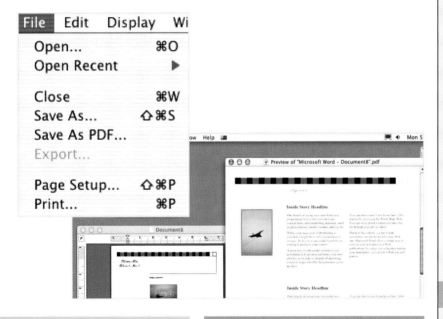

Mac OS X

Quartz is a powerful new 2D graphics system with built-in support for the Internet-standard Portable Document Format (PDF), making PDF a common file format for Mac OS X. You can therefore easily embed and share PDF between applications, and even 'Save to PDF' or 'Save to PostScript' from any Mac OS X application. Any PDF file saved in Mac OS X can be opened, viewed, and printed using PDF-compatible tools including Adobe Acrobat Reader 5—on all supported platforms.

Mac OS 9

Mac OS 9 uses QuickDraw to create screen images, so a translation step is needed to create PDF documents. In addition, with no built-in support for PDF, users need to buy additional software to create PDF documents.

The X Factor

31 reasons to change

The biggest change in the outward appearance of Mac OS X is the ways in which windows, menus and icons are drawn on screen by the Quartz imaging model. Depth projection, drop shadows, transparency, clever color use and fluidity all add to your operating system experience. Not to mention the fact that there is now greater Mac and Windows file compatibility than ever before.

23 See really long filenames

very_long_filename.doc

Mac OS X	Mac OS 9
Mac OS X will display filenames on multiple lines, supporting very long filenames. Windows files may have very long filenames—they are clearly displayed in Mac OS X.	Mac OS 9 can only display filenames up to 31 characters long. When presented with a long Windows filename, Mac OS 9 truncates the name and generates unique characters to assure it is not a duplicate. Users often don't know what the actual filename is.

WHAT? A PC KEYBOARD ON A MAC?
You will find a Function (Fn) key on most Mac laptops which, when held down with the Option, Command and Enter keys, take on the functions of a PC keyboard.

TECH TIP

Control your windows

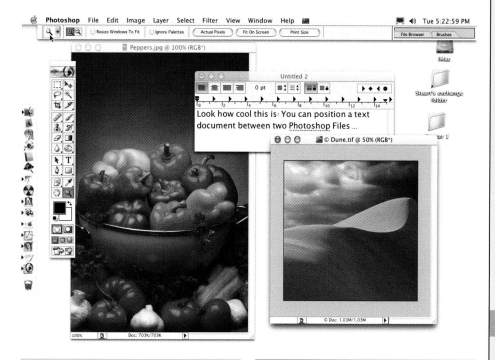

Mac OS X

An application's individual windows can be brought forward without bringing all of that application's windows forward. This means that a user can have several windows open, from multiple applications, and stack them on the screen in a logical order.

Mac OS 9

An application in Mac OS 9 brings all its windows to the front at once. When, for example, Excel becomes the active application, all of its windows are brought to the front, hiding all windows of other applications. This forces users to perform multiple steps to switch between applications, just to check the contents of a window.

The X Factor

31 reasons to change

Mac OS X makes the Macintosh the most open and interoperable computer system available. Built on industry standards, it delivers a secure, widely compatible operating system capable of interacting with common standard network platforms, standard file formats, cross-platform UNIX and Java applications, and standard hardware peripherals. Not only this but it also has the ability to automatically download software updates. Are you suitably impressed?

Online software updates

25

As you can see, updates can be set to run automatically or manually, and the user has the option to set how often he or she requires the system to check for updates.

Software Update

Software Update checks for new and updated versions of your software based on information about your computer and current software.

Update Software: ○ Manually
● Automatically

Check for updates: [Weekly ⬍]

Checking occurs only when you have a network connection.

Status: Software Update was last run at 11:04 AM on 27/2/02.

(Show Log...)   (Update Now)

Mac OS X	Mac OS 9
Mac OS X features the ability to download software updates automatically. This includes the latest security updates, which are automatically installed through the Software Update mechanism. And software updates are enabled by default, enabling a continuous improvement and extension of its capabilities.	While Mac OS 9 has a Software Update control panel, the design of the operating system requires updates to be rather large, sweeping changes. Incremental updates are held for distribution in a major release.

Easy network configuration

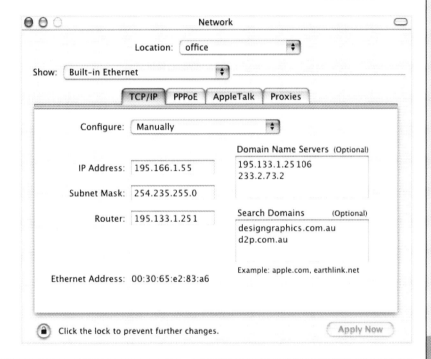

Mac OS X	Mac OS 9
In Mac OS X, the Network system preference allows a user to configure the physical network connection, TCP/IP configuration, PPoE dial-up configuration, and AppleTalk connection — in one clean, logical manner. Multiple configurations can be easily created from the single control panel, making it very easy for mobile users to connect at multiple locations.	Configuring a network connection in Mac OS 9 requires five different control panels: AppleTalk; Dial Assist; Internet; Modem; and TCP/IP. Multiple locations require custom configurations in each of those Control Panels, and a sixth Control Panel, Location Manager, to tie them all together. This is confusing, and users have difficulty configuring them correctly.

The X Factor

31 reasons to change

As the hub of the digital lifestyle, the Macintosh enables you to do more with your digital devices. Not only is its powerful PowerPC processor, and elegant graphical user interface getting rave reviews, but every Macintosh has standard USB and FireWire connections for connecting digital devices to your computer. In addition to this great hardware support, Apple includes powerful, easy-to-use tools for making your own movies, managing your music, and capturing photos from your digital camera. And with built-in support for burning music and data CDs, playing DVD movies, and even authoring your own DVDs, Mac OS X makes it easier than ever to share your creations with others … reason enough to get hooked … up?

27

iTunes

Apple's iTunes music software takes the confusion out of managing your personal music collection. It turns your Mac into a powerful digital jukebox, complete with easy-to-use tools to convert music from audio CDs, search and browse your entire music collection, and download songs to MP3 players. And you'll find a copy of iTunes in every Mac OS X-based computer. (See also page 138, 139 for an in-depth look at iTunes.)

iMovie

Mac OS X

With iMovie, users now have the ability to easily edit their movies, preserving the best moments and adding professional-quality effects and transitions. It's easy and fun to create movies you'll want to share over and over again with friends and family.

The X Factor
31 reasons to change

If you believe that Cocoa is a hot chocolate beverage and Apache an American Indian tribe, we've got news for you. As you would know if you had been paying attention so far, the Cocoa application environment, designed specifically for Mac OS X-only native applications, is the environment of choice for new applications, such as Mac OS X's Mail. Apache, on the other hand, is an open source Web server technology that runs more than 50 percent of the Web sites on the Internet, and is used in conjunction with Mac OS X's Web Sharing feature.

Intrigued, then read on ...

Mail

Mac OS X

Apple has built its own e-mail application called Mail, which supports all Internet-standard mail protocols, provides an easy-to-use interface for composing and reading e-mail, and includes the ability to create and view rich e-mail content with inline images and PDF, great fonts, and even sounds. It's ready to support your Mac.com or other Internet-based mail account and includes the advanced Sherlock search technology so you can easily find important information in your overflowing In Box.

Personal Web Sharing

Mac OS X

Now you can use Mac OS X's Personal Web Sharing to publish Web pages or share files on the Internet – or on your company's (or school's) local area network from a folder on your hard disk. You can display your documents on the Internet, or restrict access to a chosen few within a local area network.

Mac OS X's Personal Web Sharing makes it a snap. Once you're online, all you need to do is copy a file in HTML format to the Web Pages folder (in the Sites folder in your Home directory), and that's it. You're done — your page is ready for viewing.

The X Factor

31 reasons to change

The list of industry-leading applications for this major upgrade is long and varied, with each specifically designed to take advantage of core Mac OS X technologies, including the Aqua interface, Sheets and the Quartz graphics engine. Microsoft Office v. X suite is a good example of this. Its applications include a bold and classy new Aqua appearance that fits beautifully with the Mac OS X user interface. All the components of the Office v.X user interface – from dialog boxes to toolbar icons – have been Aquafied, offering a smoother and cleaner appearance.

29

Microsoft Office v.X

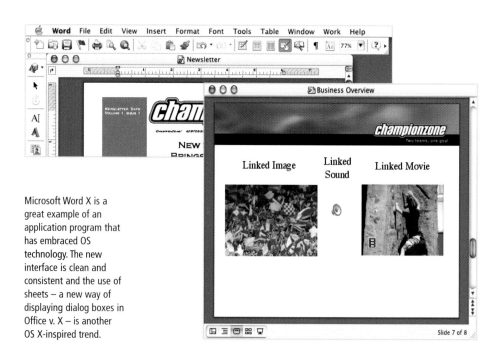

Microsoft Word X is a great example of an application program that has embraced OS technology. The new interface is clean and consistent and the use of sheets – a new way of displaying dialog boxes in Office v. X – is another OS X-inspired trend.

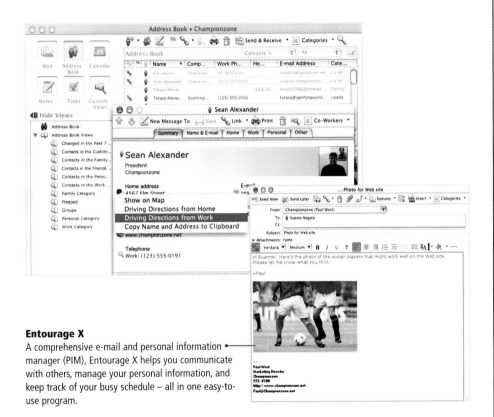

Entourage X

A comprehensive e-mail and personal information manager (PIM), Entourage X helps you communicate with others, manage your personal information, and keep track of your busy schedule – all in one easy-to-use program.

As the cornerstone of Office v. X, Entourage X highlights OS X ingenuity with its the new button interface to access each of the components.
It boasts a refined, easier-to-use interface, improved support for Internet standards, and several new features to help users manage
e-mail and personal information.

Surf 'board

If you work on one of the latest Mac models, you will find its Apple Pro Keyboard a delight to walk your fingers through. For those of you who need a crash course on what key goes where, this page is for you ...

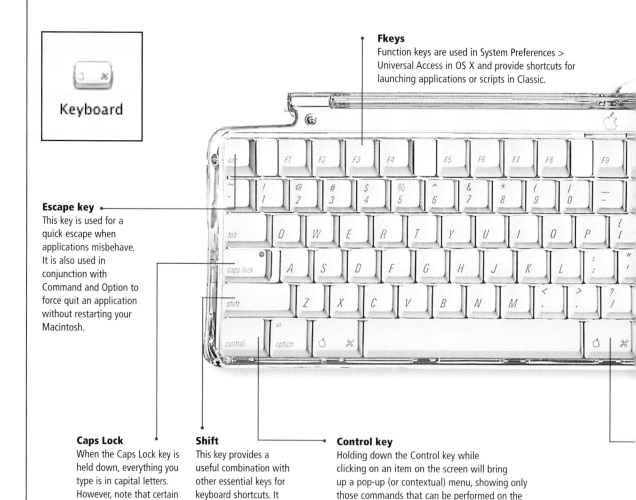

Keyboard

Fkeys
Function keys are used in System Preferences > Universal Access in OS X and provide shortcuts for launching applications or scripts in Classic.

Escape key
This key is used for a quick escape when applications misbehave. It is also used in conjunction with Command and Option to force quit an application without restarting your Macintosh.

Caps Lock
When the Caps Lock key is held down, everything you type is in capital letters. However, note that certain keyboard shortcuts will not work with the Caps Lock key down.

Shift
This key provides a useful combination with other essential keys for keyboard shortcuts. It also creates capital letters temporarily.

Control key
Holding down the Control key while clicking on an item on the screen will bring up a pop-up (or contextual) menu, showing only those commands that can be performed on the item you clicked on. The Control key is also commonly used for keyboard shortcuts. (Note that it is located on both sides of the keyboard.)

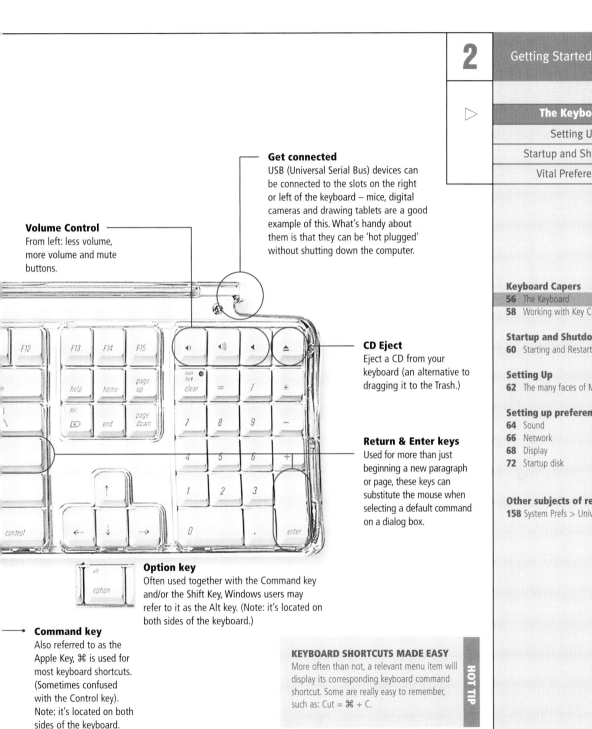

Get connected
USB (Universal Serial Bus) devices can
be connected to the slots on the right
or left of the keyboard – mice, digital
cameras and drawing tablets are a good
example of this. What's handy about
them is that they can be 'hot plugged'
without shutting down the computer.

Volume Control
From left: less volume,
more volume and mute
buttons.

CD Eject
Eject a CD from your
keyboard (an alternative to
dragging it to the Trash.)

Return & Enter keys
Used for more than just
beginning a new paragraph
or page, these keys can
substitute the mouse when
selecting a default command
on a dialog box.

Option key
Often used together with the Command key
and/or the Shift Key, Windows users may
refer to it as the Alt key. (Note: it's located on
both sides of the keyboard.)

Command key
Also referred to as the
Apple Key, ⌘ is used for
most keyboard shortcuts.
(Sometimes confused
with the Control key).
Note: it's located on both
sides of the keyboard.

KEYBOARD SHORTCUTS MADE EASY
More often than not, a relevant menu item will
display its corresponding keyboard command
shortcut. Some are really easy to remember,
such as: Cut = ⌘ + C.

HOT TIP

Unlock your font potential

Some cynics don't believe how Key Caps (Applications > Utilities),
a simple little window with a miniature onscreen keyboard, can
still be part of Mac OS X. But it is! This great invention that has
been around forever is here in all its glory, complete with a nifty
new layout and a concept that has stood the test of time.
Embrace it – it is usefulness defined!

Key Caps

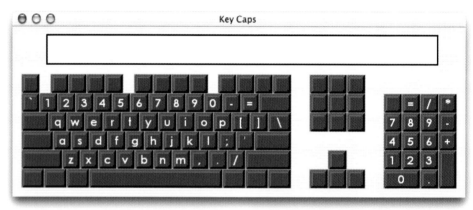

What's your combo?

If you press the Option key in Key Caps, you will see white borders around certain keys. The reason: they work with a combination of other keys only (mainly vowels). For example, if you require an accent on an 'e', select the Option key and quickly press 'e' and then 'e' again. You will then notice that the white bordered keys will all have changed and display the effect you are likely to get when pressing the Option key. (This is shown on all keys affected, not just 'e'.)

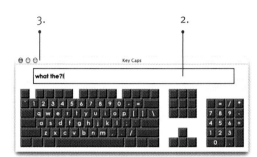

3.   2.   1.

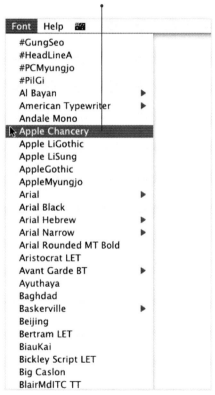

Walking keyboard

Did you know how simple it could be to make a bullet (•)? What about a checkbox (❑)? Instead of asking a mate, choose Key Caps (Applications > Utilities), then:
1. Go to the Font menu in the Key Caps application and select the Font you will be working with. Hold down the Apple, Option, Shift, Control keys (known as Modifier keys) to see how the characters change.
2. Once you have found what you are looking for, you can either memorize this, or use copy and paste into the application of your choice.

3. You want it ... how BIG?

Want to see the keyboard bigger? Simply select your green button (otherwise known as the zoom button) and hey presto, it enlarges.

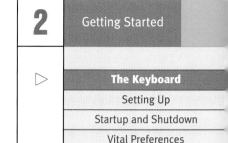

BUY YOUR FONTS ONLINE
Selecting 'Get Mac OS X Software' from the Apple menu will launch your Web browser and take you to 'Mac OS X Downloads', where you can purchase as many fonts as your heart desires.

TECH TIP

On your marks, get set ... Go!

You don't need to be a rocket scientist to learn how to start or restart your Mac. However, there are a few pointers that you just may find handy in Mac OS X such as a new easier way to use Force Quit, providing a little more security for your Mac and using keyboard shortcuts when you need to take emergency measures. So, pay attention ... although Mac OS X is very stable, you need to be prepared.

Security and more
Some users may be of the opinion that with all the security that OS X has in place, it's entirely impossible for unauthorized users to gain access to a system. But it's not. When a user logs out, the computer is not actually shut down. This means that if a user leaves his/her desk immediately after logging out, anyone can get on the system, click the Restart button and begin to operate the system once the Mac restarts and automatically logs the new user in. Hiding the Restart and Shut Down buttons will provide a little more security for a Mac and a little more peace of mind for the user.

May the 'Force' be with you
If something goes wrong but you can still use the mouse and make the Finder active, choose either:
(1) Force Quit from the Apple Menu. (Mac 'oldies' will recall that this command could previously be accessed only by shortcut key combinations).
(2) Restart to shut down and start up your computer in one quick move.
(3) If you are unable to use your mouse press the Reset button or turn off the power.
Note: you can also choose Force Quit from the Dock. (See page 125 for more details on this.)

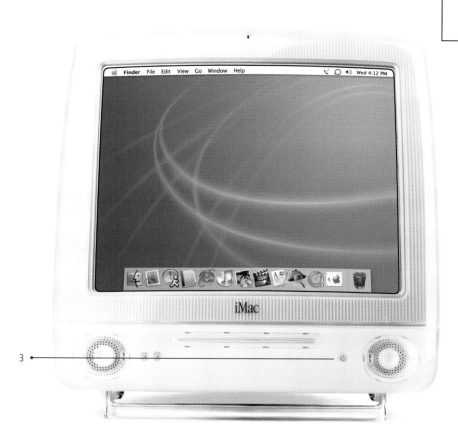

3 •———————————————————

Start all over again
If your Mac won't boot from a hard disk, or you have forgotten a password, you may need to start up the system from a Mac OS X CD-ROM. Here's how it's done:

• Insert CD-ROM;
• Restart, pressing and holding the C key;
• Click the Installer icon;
• Select Reset Password (if you have forgotten your old one) or Disk Utility (to undertake repairs).

KEYBOARD TO THE RESCUE
If your Mac freezes, press Command+Control and the Power button (or in some cases, Command+Option+Shift and the Power button) to force a restart. If the Finder freezes in OS X, chances are the underlying OS is still running. Try force quitting the Finder first.

HOT TIP

The many faces of Mac OS X

Congratulations – you are obviously the proud new owner of Mac's latest operating system. If you are one of the lucky ones, it has been preinstalled on your computer. If not, you are probably itching to install it and can't wait to be bowled over by its charm. But before you rush in, hold your horses ... you may want to read these pages first.

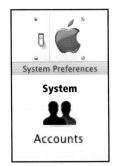

System Preferences

System

Accounts

First come, first served
When Mac OS X is initially installed, it will request a name and password for the first user account on your Macintosh (also known as the administrator). Administrators have the authority to: • install new programs into the Applications folder; • add fonts (to the Library folder) for everyone's use; • change certain System Preferences panels; • utilize NetInfo Manager and Disk Utility; • create new folders in areas that are out of bounds to everyone else; and • allocate user accounts.

1. One more place at the table
Plan to share your Mac? Set up accounts for other people by opening System Prefs > Accounts > Users.

2. Log-in limits
If you don't share your Mac or adopt an 'open door' policy with other users of your machine, you can disable the log-in requirement by unchecking this box.

3. The long and the short of it
Would you like your name to appear formal or informal, abbreviated or not? (Note: You can sign into the Mac with your name or a shortened version of it.)

4. Who have we here?
Selecting a password has become old hat to most of us – these days we do it all the time. Usually it is typed twice (second time under verify) and then you can give yourself a hint ... just in case you forget it sometime.

5. Picture perfect
Which pic associates with the user's name? Apple provides 20 to choose from along the bottom of the window, or you can choose your own.

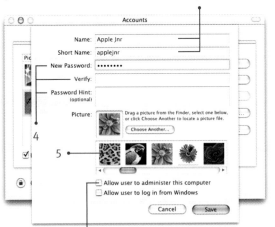

You are it
These options allow the existing administrator to allocate new user to now become the appointed administrator and/or log in from Windows.

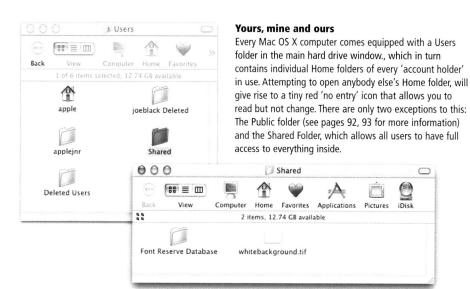

Yours, mine and ours

Every Mac OS X computer comes equipped with a Users folder in the main hard drive window., which in turn contains individual Home folders of every 'account holder' in use. Attempting to open anybody else's Home folder, will give rise to a tiny red 'no entry' icon that allows you to read but not change. There are only two exceptions to this: The Public folder (see pages 92, 93 for more information) and the Shared Folder, which allows all users to have full access to everything inside.

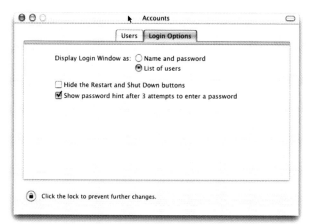

Just as you like it

Go to Login Options (System Preferences > Accounts) to set the following:

- display name and password and/or user list details in login window;
- Hide/Show Restart and Shut Down buttons; and
- 'Show password hint after three attempts to enter password', or don't show at all.

Setting up preferences - Sound

Customize the sound of your Mac with this unique set of
preferences, (Applications > System Preferences > Sound) where
you can select an alert sound and determine volume settings for
these and also general sounds.

System Preferences

Hardware

Sound

1. Sound icon
If you prefer not to open
this panel each time you
want to change the
volume, drop the sound
volume icon in the menu
bar instead.
You can also adjust
volume settings from
your Apple Pro Keyboard.

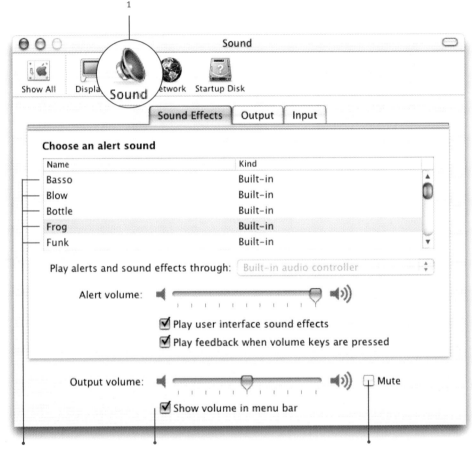

Alert sounds
Your choice! As you select
each of these, you will hear
its sound. The name
highlighted indicates the
new alert sound. Sounds can
be changed anytime.

Move over Beethoven!
Selecting this box will
allow you to move your
Sound Icon to the far
right of the menu bar for
easier access.

Sound of silence
This will mute all sounds on
your Macintosh (even your
alert sounds – so you, along
with anyone else in hearing
distance, won't know when
you are making a mistake!)

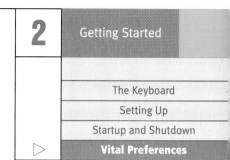
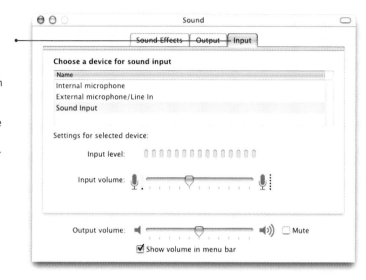

Extra, extra ... hear all about it!
Description of extra speakers on your system will be listed here for your convenience. (Choose the appropriate one to have your alert sounds played through).

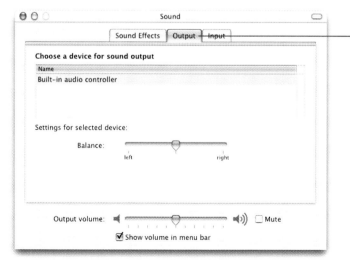

Sound blast
The Output pane is useful if you have installed extra speakers and want to have all your Mac sounds sent here instead of to the Mac's built-in audio controller.

Networking opportunity

Whether you want to connect your Mac to the Internet, your corporate network, or even the old PC that you put in the kid's room, the Network panel in System Preferences is where you plug in the required numbers. This panel also helps your Mac to automatically use whichever connection methods are available at any time: Ethernet, modem, Airport, or Bluetooth modem.

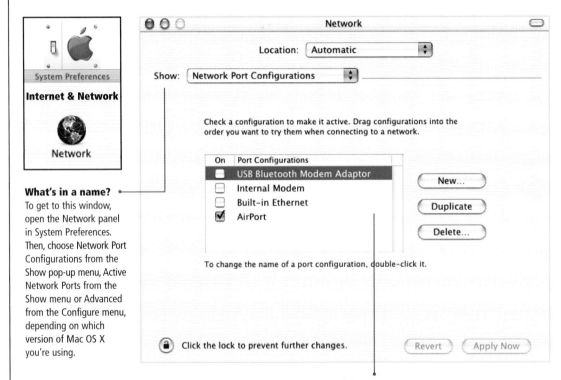

What's in a name?
To get to this window, open the Network panel in System Preferences. Then, choose Network Port Configurations from the Show pop-up menu, Active Network Ports from the Show menu or Advanced from the Configure menu, depending on which version of Mac OS X you're using.

Pick your ports
Because our Mac will not be using a modem, an Ethernet cable or a Bluetooth mobile phone to connect to the Internet, we have only put a tick in the AirPort checkbox. If you use Ethernet to connect to the Internet from your desk at work and a wireless AirPort network to connect from the meeting room, put ticks in both those boxes, sort the best connection method to the top, and configure both options. Then, your Mac will automatically select the best option that's available at any time.

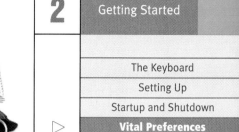

System
Preferences

AirPort options

Because we have selected AirPort in the Show menu, we can configure the TCP/IP and panes with the specific settings we require when we connect via AirPort. Each connection method can have its own settings.

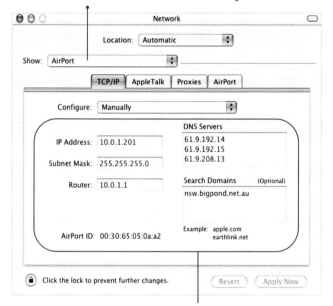

First things first

The option you pick here will affect the boxes that are available below. In fact, most parts of the Network panel are interdependent. If you find you just can't enter the setting you require in one part of the Network panel, it's probably because you've entered a contradictory setting somewhere else.

Endless numbers

The information entered here would come from your ISP or your company's network manager. So would the information under the Proxies tab. However, if you configured your Mac for Internet access when you first used Mac OS (see pages 262, 263) this data will be entered already.

OLD-FASHIONED ARCHITECTURES

Only enable AppleTalk if you must communicate with an old printer or Macintosh that does not know how to use contemporary standards like TCP/IP or USB. Using AppleTalk unnecessarily will reduce your network throughput.

TECH TIP

Setting up preferences – displays

Adjust your monitor exactly the way you like it with Mac OS X's display settings, which assist with: • controlling the size of screen picture and resolution; • color depth settings and calibration adjustment; • lighting adjustment; • flicker minimization and • size and positioning changes. It's easy, go to Applications > System Preferences > Displays.

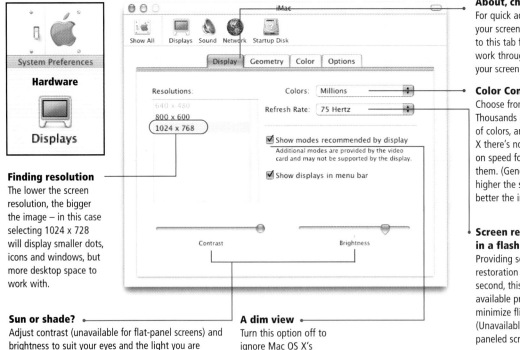

About, change!
For quick adjustment to your screen controls, go to this tab first. It will work through most of your screen requirements.

Color Control
Choose from 256, Thousands and Millions of colors, and in Mac OS X there's no compromise on speed for any of them. (Generally, the higher the setting the better the image.)

Screen restoration in a flash
Providing screen restoration by the second, this option is available primarily to minimize flicker. (Unavailable for the flat-paneled screen).

Finding resolution
The lower the screen resolution, the bigger the image – in this case selecting 1024 x 728 will display smaller dots, icons and windows, but more desktop space to work with.

Sun or shade?
Adjust contrast (unavailable for flat-panel screens) and brightness to suit your eyes and the light you are working in. (Note: most Apple monitors and keyboards have their own brightness controls too.)

A dim view
Turn this option off to ignore Mac OS X's recommended resolution settings (those considered off limits are dimmed. See resolution setting sizes, far left.)

Ablaze with color •———
When the 'Color' tab is selected,
you can choose to select: (a) a
preconfigured profile for your monitor, or

• (b) the Display Calibrator Assistant to
calibrate your display yourself. (It's really
easy, but you should know more about
ColorSync when you dabble with this.)
Turn to pages 90, 91 and pages 162, 163
to read more about ColorSync.

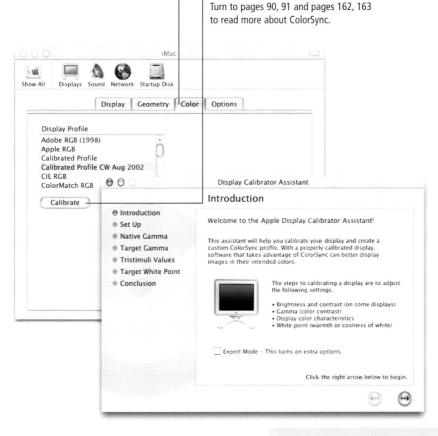

COLORSYNC AND YOUR MONITOR
ColorSync's monitor calibration system
compensates for debilitation of the
monitor's age, phosphor set, ambient light,
white point or monitor type in order to
better display images in their intended
colors.

SYNOPSIS

Setting up preferences – displays (2)

If you've ever looked at yourself in a distorted mirror, you'll relate to Apple's new Geometry feature. It's cute and funky and best of all, if you mess up, you can change it back to what it was before! (Psst ... while you're in play mode, have a look at the all-new Screen Effects and Energy Saver – useful and easy to use.)

System Preferences

Hardware

Displays

1. Funky formula
No, your maths lesson doesn't start here – the only geometric equation you will be doing with this tab is experimenting with buttons and arrows to perfect (or imperfect) the image on your screen. (Note: These settings apply to CRT monitors only.)

2. Motion control
Satellite control buttons for each settings option allow you to experiment with the image of your screen until you get the desired effect. (Don't worry if you don't, you can always revert to normal!)

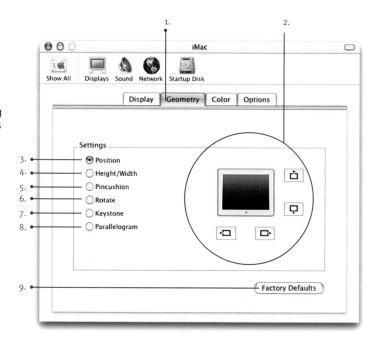

3. Positions, please
Up, down, left or right – this setting allows you to choose and select your screen positioning preference.

4. Wide or tall?
Contract or expand your screen (handle with caution if you 'scrunch' too much).

5. Sewing circle
Special effects gone wild! Convex or concave? It's your choice.

6. Dizzy spell?
Rotate your screen to the right or left – a 'dizzying' effect.

7. Top o' the morning
Your image will appear wider or narrower at the top than at the bottom with this option selected.

8. S-t-r-e-t-c-h
Stretch your screen left, stretch your screen right ... this skew effect – what a delight!

9. What a relief!
Although the desired effect is cool, it may not be exactly .. er ... practical, shall we say? No problem – this button reverts to the original settings, so you can experiment with your settings over and over again.

Sleeping beauty
To save energy, put your computer to sleep by choosing this option (Applications > System Preferences > Energy Save > Sleep), which turns off the display and stops the hard disk from running.

Clicking the sleep tab of the Energy Saver window will allow you to:
• set up your computer to sleep automatically; and
• set the overall time or even a separate time for your display and your hard drive.

Good health and long life
Regardless of what the image of your screen ultimately looks like, you will need to protect your display. Hence the screen saver (Applications > System Preferences > Screen Effects) which starts automatically after several minutes whenever your computer is idle. With it you can: • select or use your own pictures for a screen; • select the time until the screen saver starts; and • use 'hot corners'. (See pages 156, 157 for more details.)

Startup disks galore!

Startup Disk makes it easy for you to choose the disk you want your computer to start up from (or even which CD you want to boot an operating system from). Choose the system that you want, click on it, press Restart and 'Bob's your uncle' – each time you boot up your computer it will launch the operating system of your choice.

1

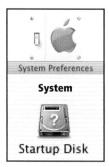

System Preferences

System

Startup Disk

1. What a choice!
Selecting this icon (Applications > System Preferences > Startup Disk) gives you a choice of disks to start up or restart your system with.

2

3

Startup Disk

Show All   Displays   Sound   Network   Startup Disk

Select the system you want to use to start up your computer

Mac OS Z1-9.2.1
on iMac

Mac OS X, 10.2
on iMac

Network Startup

You have selected Mac OS X, 10.2 on the volume "iMac".

Click the lock to prevent further changes.

Restart...

2. Which is which?
In case you weren't paying attention, Mac OS X provides a description of your current operating system. (Also highlighted, for ease of reference). By selecting System 9 as your Startup Disk, you are physically changing the operating system (almost like going back in time, without any presence of OS X at all). In order to revert back to Mac OS X you will have to change your Startup Disk in OS 9. (Confused? We tell you more on pages 176, 177.)

A fresh start
Just as you would restart your system after any software installation, you would select the 'Restart' button once you have changed operating systems.

3. Enough of this!
If you're happy enough with the way your operating system runs, you can prevent further changes by selecting the lock.

Mac OS Z1-9.2.1
on iMac

Time travel from within

Don't get confused: selecting System 9 as your
Startup Disk is completely different from selecting
System Preferences > Classic. For one, the Startup Disk
and Classic are individual options under System
Preferences. For another, Classic is OS 9 running
as a process inside OS X.

TWO SYSTEMS ON THE SAME HD? TUT, TUT!
Welcome to the future. It's no longer a problem – in
fact its almost a pre-requisite. Some of the programs
you use may be written for Classic while others may
be written for OS X, so it's important to have access
to both operating systems with the greatest of ease.

HOT TIP

What's happening?

Whenever you need assistance with your system or applications, the Help menu will come to your rescue. Quick to locate (it's one of the Finder menus) and simple to use, this service is also extended to other applications, theoretically giving you help from just about anywhere you will be working on your Macintosh. Apple has done it again!

Help Center

Back to basics
Lost your way and want to return to a screen you wanted at least three screens before? Simply select the back button until you find what you are looking for. (If you have chosen to customize your toolbar by adding the forward button, it will do the same thing reversed). Note: Select 'Customize Toolbar' in the Help Viewer's View menu and make your changes from the drop-down sheet.

Support and more
Selecting the Help menu will launch the Help Viewer, an application used to display information from various Help files on your Hard Drive.

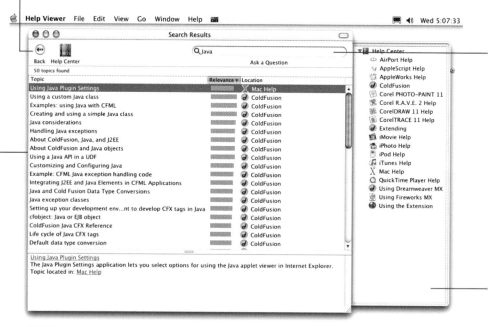

How do you do?
By default, the MacHelp window will appear, providing information to new users, featuring OS X improvements, news and support details. It also provides examples of how to pose questions.

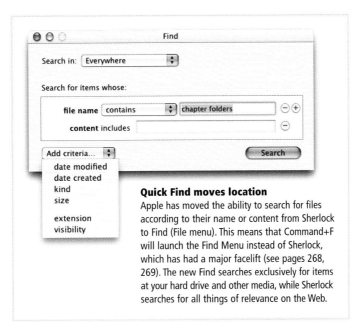

—• **Life saver**
Once you have posed
your question or made
an enquiry, a list of
relevant topics will
appear for quick and
easy selection.
The degree of relevance
and source of help is
documented alongside
the topic and the lower
panel of the Help Viewer
window will display
a summary and link of
selected topic.

Quick Find moves location
Apple has moved the ability to search for files
according to their name or content from Sherlock
to Find (File menu). This means that Command+F
will launch the Find Menu instead of Sherlock,
which has had a major facelift (see pages 268,
269). The new Find searches exclusively for items
at your hard drive and other media, while Sherlock
searches for all things of relevance on the Web.

—• **Information nucleus**
This panel, which
contains a list of source
information locations,
appears beneath the
window and can be
hidden at any time by
selecting its edge and
dragging to the left.
(To bring it back, select
edge and drag to the right)

 iPhoto Help

AppleScript Help

Application assistance
You can get relevant
assistance from many Mac
OS X applications installed
such as iPhoto Help, iPod
Help and AppleScript Help. A
list of these are displayed on
the panel alongside your
Help Viewer.
(See Information Nucleus, left)

 iPod Help

Show and tell

Lost? Need to know what the computer you are working on is all about? Go to the Apple Menu and choose 'About this Mac'. It will help you: • to check which version of the operating system you are using; • see how much RAM (random access memory) you have available; and • see the kind of processor you are running.

Processor power
You probably know this already, but we'll tell you anyway – Mac OS X runs on the PowerPC processor, designed by the Apple, IBM and Motorola alliance and based on the IBM Power chip. The kernel, Darwin, is able to handle computers with multiple processors, as you can see here.

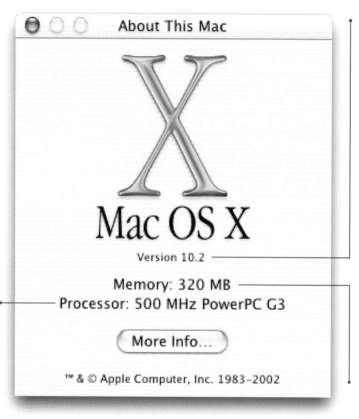

Version in view
All applications these days have a version number which coincides with the date of its release – Mac OS is no exception. But what does it all mean, and how does the sequence of numbers affect us? The formula is something like this:
• the leap to an entirely new number often means a complete program revision;
• a one decimal modification (for example 10.1 means improved functionality and new features); and
• a two decimal modification, such as 10.1.2 indicates very minor fixes which usually do not require interface changes.

Apple bytes
How do you know how much memory is installed in your Mac? It's easy – select 'About this Mac' from the Apple menu and hey presto! your answer magically appears!

Apple menu
Of all the menus on the menu bar, this is the only one which remains constant regardless of the application you are using or where you are on your computer – meaning that you can depend on everything in this menu to be exactly as you left it. It also means you can use it any time. (See also pages 102, 103.)

EMBEDDED INFORMATION...
Click on 'About this Mac's version number and the OS X build number appears. Click again and ... hey presto ... it's your OS X serial number!

TECH TIP

Hide and seek

Filing systems have always been part of our daily working life and not surprisingly, are a part of our digital world too.
The quick and clever filing concept of folders and icons that the Macintosh operating system is famous for, has been redeveloped in OS X and has advanced to an improved, streamlined and very clever system indeed.

Cyber storage
Everything on your Mac is represented by an icon – whether it's a document, program, folder and disk. These colorful images can be moved, copied or double-clicked to open. Folders, too, are easily identifiable. Some have special icons to match their special functions., others belong to an actual application and have designs with visual clues of what they do. But they all have one thing in common – they're there to make your entire Macintosh experience easier.

Connection Barometer
The Computer window (Go > Computer) has also changed in a big way. It houses the icons for all the disks connected to your machine, as well as the Network icon, which shows up even if you aren't actually on a network. It can also be accessed by clicking the Computer icon on the Finder toolbar. (See also pages 118, 119.)

Why bother?
Opening your hard drive icon (upper right of the screen) reveals a few folders that you can't do anything with. So, why are they there? Mac OS X has more security than ever before and many folders that are out of bounds to regular users, are the ones that keep the system running properly. They should not be fiddled with unless you know what you are doing, and have risen to the ranks of root user or administrator. (See pages 248, 249 more in-depth information on this.)

OS X organizer

Mac OS X makes it easy to find your way around its main folder. In short: • the Library folder contains fonts, Internet plug-ins and other items available to all users of your computer; • the Applications folder contains applications (of course you knew that!); • the System folder contains the Mac OS X system and cannot be changed; and • the Users folder contains the names of all the people using your computer.
(Read all about this on pages 88, 89.)

Mac manoeuvres

• Dragging a file or folder from one folder to another on the same disk, moves it.

• Dragging a file or folder to another drive (or other media) automatically copies it.

• Holding down the Option key while dragging a file anywhere on the same disk copies it.

InDesign 2.0 alias

Alias Antics

An alias is a 'signpost' to a document or application. And, because it's really only a ghost image, it occupies very little space on your hard drive. Of course, if you are a Mac 'oldie' you know this already, but if you're not, notice how easy it is to create an alias. Go to File > Make Alias, or press Command+Option and drag the original icon to the spot you'd like the alias to live in. (See also page 202, 203.)

A walk in the park

Icons, windows, menus, folders and sub-folders are all part of the extraordinary Macintosh environment that is so simple to familiarize yourself with. On this page we introduce you to the items that you are likely to bump into first …

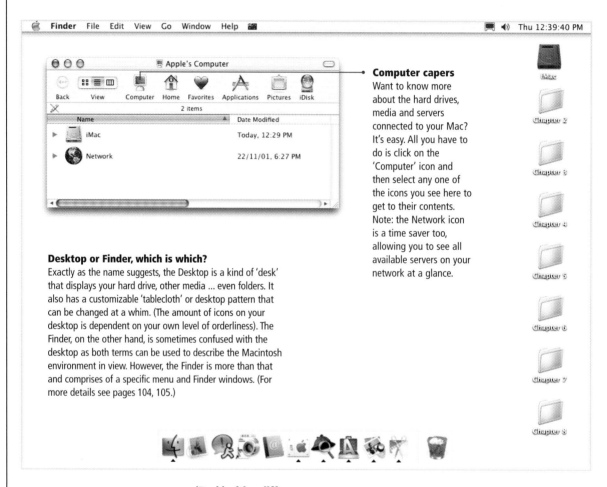

Computer capers
Want to know more about the hard drives, media and servers connected to your Mac? It's easy. All you have to do is click on the 'Computer' icon and then select any one of the icons you see here to get to their contents. Note: the Network icon is a time saver too, allowing you to see all available servers on your network at a glance.

Desktop or Finder, which is which?
Exactly as the name suggests, the Desktop is a kind of 'desk' that displays your hard drive, other media … even folders. It also has a customizable 'tablecloth' or desktop pattern that can be changed at a whim. (The amount of icons on your desktop is dependent on your own level of orderliness). The Finder, on the other hand, is sometimes confused with the desktop as both terms can be used to describe the Macintosh environment in view. However, the Finder is more than that and comprises of a specific menu and Finder windows. (For more details see pages 104, 105.)

'Dock' with a difference
A wonderful new navigation shortcut tool, the Dock is explained in full detail later in this chapter. Frequently used icons are immediately available, so it is a much needed asset to Apple's new operating system.

The Dock

File menus

New OS X structure

Favorite Favorites

This is a fabulous feature! Your own list of favorites can be easily updated – 'Add to Favorites' (Command+T) automatically creates an alias of the object you have clicked on and drops it into the Favorites folder. You can also remove any aliases from the Favorites folder that are no longer the flavor of the month! Note: Favorites is not to be confused with the Dock.

Ain't Apple grand!

Apple provides you with applications for learning and enjoyment – specially stored in this Applications folder, and more information on these can be found on

the pages to follow. Note: the icon you see here is actually an alias of the Applications folder, displayed in the window that opens when you double-click on the hard drive.

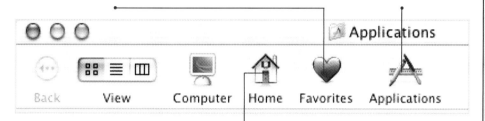

No place like Home

This button will take you to your very own Home folder (older brother of the Desktop folder), complete with features vital to your creative wellbeing.
It's appropriately named too, as it is the place to

go back to if you're lost. Another cool feature is that every user who shares a Macintosh will own a tailor-made Home folder – for their own viewing purposes only. (No-one can change your Home unless they login with your user name and

password or are granted access privileges to folders in your Home.) Your Home also contains a Public folder, which other users can access if you turn on File Sharing. (It's a folder that bears the name typed in when you first installed OS X.)

> **YUP, THE FINDER HAS CHANGED!**
> It's cool — you can use a single window in the Finder instead of multiple windows. (If you really miss those precious multiple windows, hold down the Command key when you double-click a folder and *voilá*, a separate window appears.)
>
> HOT TIP

Move over Big Brother

If you're curious about the workings of your Mac's central processing unit, then the CPU monitor (Applications > Utilities) is made just for you. Standard, Floating and Expanded Windows provide a varied perspective of your CPU. For more depth and detail it can be used with Process Viewer, an application that summarizes processes the CPU is working on.

CPU Monitor

Why use it?
The CPU Monitor application is great for those that want to know how hard the CPU works during digital video editing and rendering. If you feel that it's not really relevant to you or a bit out of your depth, don't worry about it.

What's up?
Choose 'Open Process Viewer' from the CPU monitor menu to see which processes are currently running on your computer. Process Viewer is often used in conjunction with 'Top' (Select 'Open Top' from the Processes menu) in the Terminal.

QUICK VIEW
For ease of use and observation, display your CPU Monitor application icon in the Dock or in a floating window on the desktop.

HOT TIP

| tor | Processes | Window |

Display Standard Window
Toggle Floating Window
Display Expanded Window

Clear Expanded Window

Open Process Viewer ...
Open Top ...

A touch of UNIX

If you have been operating your Mac as the UNIX machine it is, you'll feel quite comfortable selecting 'Open Top' from the CPU Monitor's 'Processes' menu. It launches the Terminal application (discussed in more detail on pages 284-289) – great for those in the know, but definitely not for the beginner or average user!

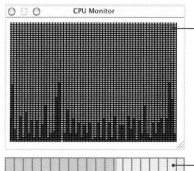

CPU Monitor

OS X does windows

Mac OS X provides three different views for workload observation. Choose from Standard, Floating or Expanded Windows or select all three!

```
O O O                    Terminal — ttyp1
Processes:  51 total, 3 running, 48 sleeping... 128 threads           12:44:34
Load Avg:  0.63, 0.60, 0.47    CPU usage:  10.7% user, 8.0% sys, 81.2% idle
SharedLibs: num =    7, resident = 2.19M code, 160K data, 560K LinkEdit
MemRegions: num = 3294, resident = 46.5M + 11.5M private, 68.3M shared
PhysMem: 37.4M wired, 137M active, 45.3M inactive,  220M used,  100M free
VM: 1.39G + 3.62M   8794(0) pageins, 622(0) pageouts

PID COMMAND      %CPU   TIME    #TH #PRTS #MREGS RPRVT  RSHRD  RSIZE  VSIZE
725 screencapt   0.0%  0:00.08  1    23    24   128K   736K   748K   22.5M
716 top          7.1%  0:05.60  1    14    18   240K   336K   532K   13.6M
715 tcsh         0.0%  0:00.07  1    10    15   340K   588K   780K   5.73M
714 login        0.0%  0:01.02  1    12    33   240K   388K   568K   13.7M
713 Terminal     0.8%  0:02.02  3    61   105   1.26M  6.44M  5.52M  43.4M
709 CPU Monito   2.6%  0:08.41  1    64    93   1.10M- 4.88M  3.59M  40.3M
696 Sherlock     0.0%  0:31.59 10   120   190   8.77M  5.63M  12.0M  51.4M
675 readconfig   0.0%  0:00.16  2    18    19   244K   336K   1.03M  13.6M
658 TMServer     0.0%  0:00.25  1    38    39   240K   1.06M  1.02M  22.7M
655 NetCfgTool   0.0%  0:00.15  1    16    17   208K   320K   964K   13.6M
440 writeconfi   0.0%  0:02.10  1    21    26   1.50M  692K   2.45M  15.4M
435 Grab         0.8%  1:13.76  4   135   163   5.99M  25.1M  22.7M  72.5M
424 System Pre   2.5%  3:37.00  6   189   363   5.34M  13.7M  14.5M  57.3M
```

Just the way you like it ...

Windows opened in OS X provide a pleasing view with Aqua enhanced graphics and subtle aids to make navigation, choice of presentation and file finding as quick as a blink. On your OS X journey you will come across Finder windows (via folders or disks), Document windows (via applications) and even a 'Customize Toolbar' window to personalize functionality. Here's some quick examples.

Three different views
Take your pick: (from left) Icon view, List view, and the 'all new' Column view, which displays folders in multiple levels.

3 colored buttons
Red closes the window; yellow minimizes the window and moves it to the Dock (with the assistance of the Shift key you can slow it down) and green zooms in and out to the last manually-dragged size.

Past and future
These handy little transparent buttons bear the symbol of both a back arrow and front arrow to help you toggle back and forward via your current window.

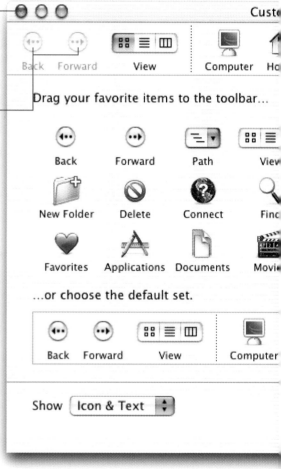

Drag your favorite items to the toolbar...

Back · Forward · Path · View

New Folder · Delete · Connect · Find

Favorites · Applications · Documents · Movie

...or choose the default set.

Back · Forward · View · Computer

Show [Icon & Text]

Pop-up menu
If you click the name of the folder you are currently viewing while holding down the Command key, a hidden pop-up menu will miraculously appear. This will provide you with the route of the current folder's origin.

Title bar
This handy bar provides the name of the folder you are currently viewing and also allows you to move the window around when it's dragged.

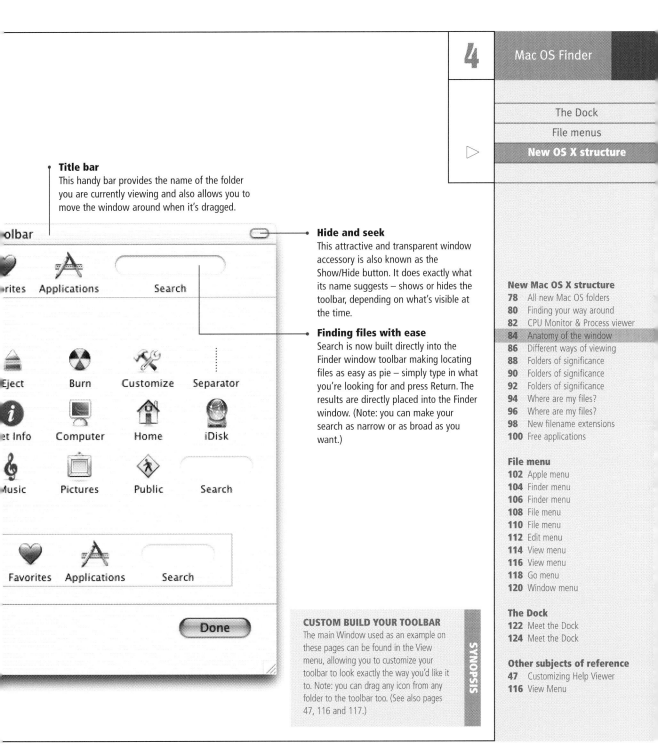

Hide and seek
This attractive and transparent window accessory is also known as the Show/Hide button. It does exactly what its name suggests – shows or hides the toolbar, depending on what's visible at the time.

Finding files with ease
Search is now built directly into the Finder window toolbar making locating files as easy as pie – simply type in what you're looking for and press Return. The results are directly placed into the Finder window. (Note: you can make your search as narrow or as broad as you want.)

CUSTOM BUILD YOUR TOOLBAR
The main Window used as an example on these pages can be found in the View menu, allowing you to customize your toolbar to look exactly the way you'd like it to. Note: you can drag any icon from any folder to the toolbar too. (See also pages 47, 116 and 117.)

SYNOPSIS

So many views, so little time!

The Mac OS X developers have thought of everything – not only does the new system still cater for those that prefer viewing their files in List or Icon mode, but there is now an all-new Column mode too. It's neat, handy and something we should have had long ago. We believe you're going to like it ... a lot.

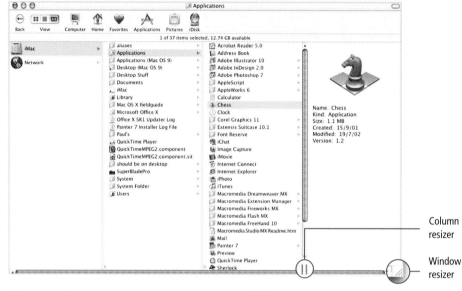

Column resizer

Window resizer

One thing leads to another

Selecting one column in Column view will display its contents. That in turn, will allow you to view its particular offerings and so on and so on ...

Eventually you will know that you have reached the 'end of the road' when the last column displays an icon of its contents. And you can trace it all back by way of the highlighted trail. Drag the scroll bars to navigate easily through each column.

Columns galore

To display a window in Column view, click this button (the Column view) or go to the 'View' menu bar in the Finder and select 'as Columns'.

Column view

Just one click

You can have as many columns in your screen as your heart desires. The sizer in the bottom right corner extends your window horizontally, while this will resize the columns proportionally. (Note: holding down Option and dragging the column resizer will rescale the respective column.)

Lists and more

The popular List view can be accessed here, or from the Finder's menu bar (choose View > as List).

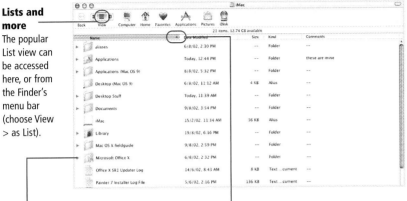

Disclosure triangles
These nifty little objects allow you to view the contents of a folder without opening any other windows. Copying, deleting and moving files is much easier here too, as it eliminates the need for window-opening actions. (No more wear and tear on the wrists!)

Expanding triangles
View contents in List view from top to bottom or bottom to top, depending which way the expanding triangle points.

List view

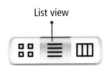

Icon view
All Mac users love the icons view, although its not exactly practical. Fortunately Mac OS X caters for everyone, so icon evangelists can choose and change their

preferred viewing options to suit (binoculars were never like this! Access Icon view as illustrated above, or go to the Finder Menu > View > as Icon.

Arranging icons
This icon tells you how your icons are arranged, as per presets in your View Options box (View menu). You can adjust by: • arrangement; • icon size; • snap to grid; or • background color. (See also pages 114-117 for further info.)

Icon view

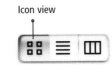

Significant others

Your Mac OS X disk is cleverly and comprehensively organized. Certain folders are there for entertainment value and ease of use, while others must be fully understood to be properly utilized. On these pages we introduce you to the Users folder (it contains the home folders of all the people using your computer) and the Library folder, responsible for storing folders that hold information the Mac needs to run your 'Home'.

Users

Mac of many faces

It's important to understand the convenience of the User concept. If you are the only person who ever uses the computer you are still considered one of the 'users' and you have a password (it's the one you choose when you excitedly turned on your Mac for the first time). If you are in a position where you share your computer – regardless of the frequency, you will note that each person who logs in to the system has a Home folder individually named inside the Users folder. In this case it's a good idea to familiarize yourself as much of this multi-user environment as possible.

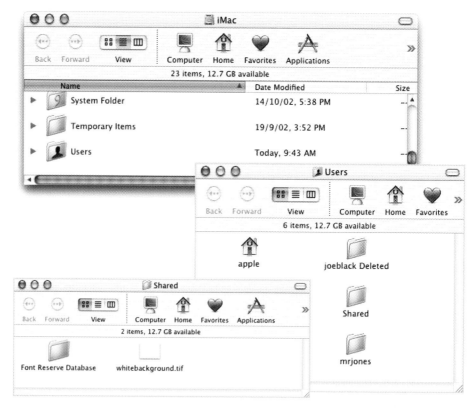

Discover how you can have unique access to certain folders, files and documents and customize your computer without anyone else being able to change your individual settings. (see Chapter 1, page 39 for more information). The more you experiment, the more streamlined your system will become.

(see Chapter 1, page 39 for more information).

COMPLETE NEW OS STRUCTURE
Your main hard drive window can be compared to previous versions of the Mac's System Folder in that many of its folders provide storage for the operating system itself and can only be utilized for administration purposes, nothing more.

SYNOPSIS

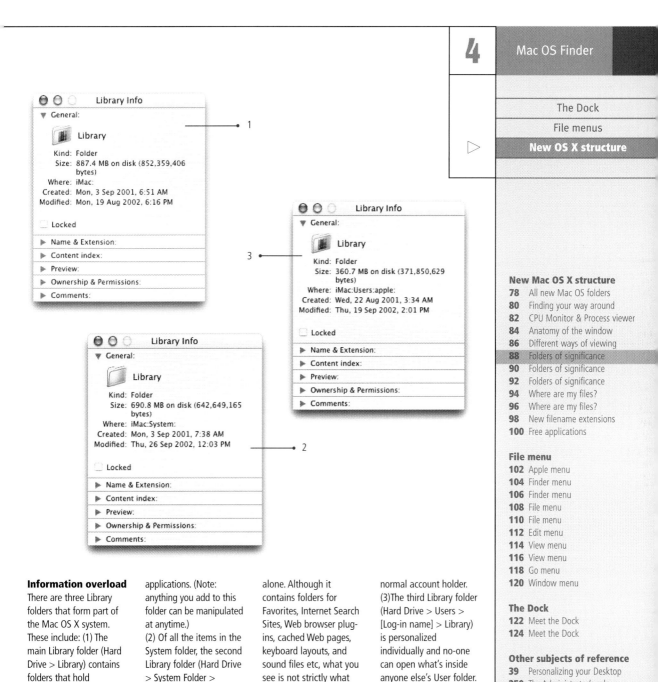

Information overload
There are three Library folders that form part of the Mac OS X system. These include: (1) The main Library folder (Hard Drive > Library) contains folders that hold information the Mac needs to run your Home, such as fonts and applications. (Note: anything you add to this folder can be manipulated at anytime.)
(2) Of all the items in the System folder, the second Library folder (Hard Drive > System Folder > Library) is the only one that can be manipulated by the administrator alone. Although it contains folders for Favorites, Internet Search Sites, Web browser plug-ins, cached Web pages, keyboard layouts, and sound files etc, what you see is not strictly what you will get as the administrator has entirely different view to that of a normal account holder. (3)The third Library folder (Hard Drive > Users > [Log-in name] > Library) is personalized individually and no-one can open what's inside anyone else's User folder. (See pages 250, 251 regarding the administrator's role.)

Significant others (2)

The Utilities folder is easy to find – it's one of the folders that live in your Applications folder (located on your main hard drive window). Each utility that lives there performs a specific (and vital) function. And because there are so many of these friendly little beasts, here's a synopsis of each.

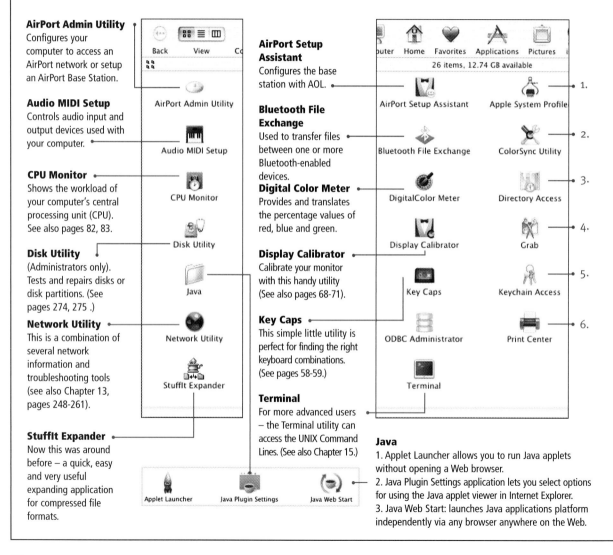

AirPort Admin Utility
Configures your computer to access an AirPort network or setup an AirPort Base Station.

Audio MIDI Setup
Controls audio input and output devices used with your computer.

CPU Monitor
Shows the workload of your computer's central processing unit (CPU). See also pages 82, 83.

Disk Utility
(Administrators only). Tests and repairs disks or disk partitions. (See pages 274, 275 .)

Network Utility
This is a combination of several network information and troubleshooting tools (see also Chapter 13, pages 248-261).

StuffIt Expander
Now this was around before – a quick, easy and very useful expanding application for compressed file formats.

AirPort Setup Assistant
Configures the base station with AOL.

Bluetooth File Exchange
Used to transfer files between one or more Bluetooth-enabled devices.

Digital Color Meter
Provides and translates the percentage values of red, blue and green.

Display Calibrator
Calibrate your monitor with this handy utility (See also pages 68-71).

Key Caps
This simple little utility is perfect for finding the right keyboard combinations. (See pages 58-59.)

Terminal
For more advanced users – the Terminal utility can access the UNIX Command Lines. (See also Chapter 15.)

Java
1. Applet Launcher allows you to run Java applets without opening a Web browser.
2. Java Plugin Settings application lets you select options for using the Java applet viewer in Internet Explorer.
3. Java Web Start: launches Java applications platform independently via any browser anywhere on the Web.

Chinese Text Converter   IM Plugin Converter

Asia Text Extras

Console

Disk Copy

Installer

NetInfo Manager

Process Viewer

1. Apple System Profiler
Answers almost any question about your Mac. (See also pages 280-281.)

2. ColorSync Utility
Works hand in hand with ColorSync preferences to specify color profiles for devices. (See pages 162, 163.)

3. Directory Access
Used to select NetInfo domains or other directories, set up search policies, and define LDAP data and attribute mappings.

4. Grab
Mac 'oldies' know that screen snapshots can be taken by pressing Apple+Shift+3. This still works in OS X but you can utilize Grab as an alternative.

5. Keychain Access
This utility helps keep track of passwords, automatically authenticating them to servers or Web sites. It's also used for secure storage of credit card numbers, PINs, etc.

6. Print Center
Look what's taken over the previous versions' Chooser – the Print Center. It manages everything and anything to do with printing. (See pages 256, 257.)

Asia Text Extras
Thanks to Unicode support, OS X comes with high quality Asian fonts, among others. Users will notice improved input due to the utilities in this folder.

Console
A Unix tool, the Console application displays technical messages from the Mac OS X system software.

Disk Copy
You'll need Disk Copy to open or create a disk image, which, in theory, looks and acts like a real disk but is actually a file.

Installer
Installing new software is now a breeze with the Installer. It's automatic, useful and disappears as quickly as it starts up!

NetInfo Manager
Everything that goes on behind the scenes of Mac OS X is managed by this well-structured database. (See also page 279.)

Process Viewer
A useful tool for administrators and programmers, this utility displays which system processes are running more.

Significant others (3)

By now you will have realized that Mac OS X is a true multi-user operating system with an exceptionally advanced security system. Although certain folders (such as the System folder) are out of bounds, there are others which can be accessed by the privileged few and others that can be accessed by anyone (such as the Public folder). The trick is to be aware of which folders you are using when filing various items. So pay attention!

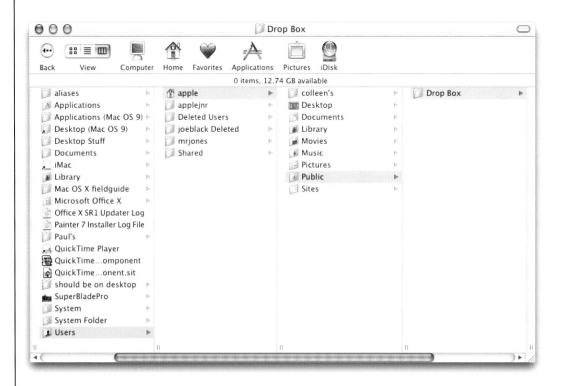

Dirty laundry
Whatever you drop into the Home > Public folder will be accessible to anyone using your computer, unlike the rest of the Home folders which are out of bounds to those that don't have the privileges to view them. The Public folder can be opened on your computer (Users folder — open folder named for the person) as well as on someone else's computer. It's easy: connect to their computer as a guest (Go Menu > Connect To Server) and mount the appropriate user's hard drive.
(Have no fear, nothing can actually be removed from the Public folder – data will only be automatically copied to another user when in transit.)

▷

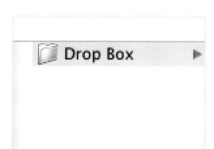

Give and take
Each user's Public folder has a Drop Box, a folder similar to the mail box outside your place of residence. Although anyone can drop anything into anyone's Drop Box, the user can only open his or her own Drop Box to view or copy the contents. Note: if you have something that you need all other users to access, or there is no problem if others see what you are sending to a particular user, utilize the Shared or Public folder.

System folder ... or not?
Mac OS X does not have the kind of System Folder you were accustomed to in previous systems. Instead, it has a folder named 'System' which is out of of bounds and has a larger number of files than before, all arranged very differently. (You will also notice that the new operating system has also done away with the System file and Finder file, previously found in Mac OS 9.)
Note: don't be confused. If you are looking for Control Panels to change settings, they can be found in System Preferences from the Apple menu.
(See also pages 102, 103).

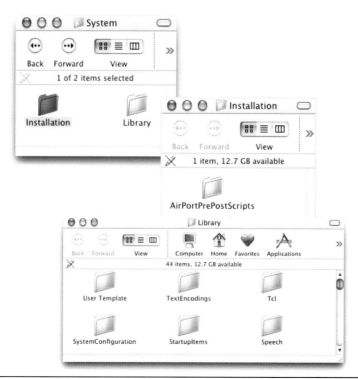

Enquiring, mind! (1)

Macintosh 'oldies' are quite familiar with the 'Get Info' command in previous versions of Mac OS. In Mac OS X it changed to Show Info for a brief spell and then reverted back to Get Info in OS X 10.2. Still located in the File menu with the same shortcut keys, it offers impressive new features and greater variety. No doubt it will prove to be a very handy and well-used feature for Mac users – whether they are new to the system or not.

What's this?
The information that you glean from Mac OS X's 'Get Info' command really depends on the item you've selected. In this example, the user has the ability to get information in six different ways.

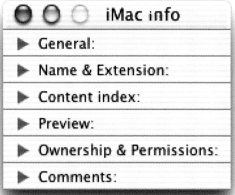

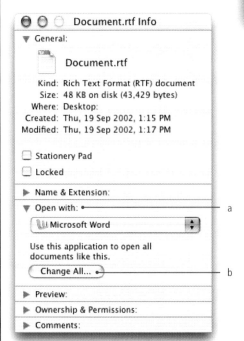

Easy open
It's often infuriating to receive files that have been created in an application that you may not have heard of or don't use enough to actually purchase.

Assigning such a file to an application that you do have is therefore quite a bonus. It's easy – simply click on the file you can't access, select File > Get Info, then choose 'Open with' (a) from the drop down-menu. Assign one application to open all files with the particular file format you have selected and confirm with 'Change All' (b).

Be warned
Once you have done this you will get a warning message ensuring that you are aware of the consequences of these changes.

Classic memory

Most Mac 'oldies' love the ease of which you can allocate more memory to applications in Classic. (Provided of course that you have enough RAM to spare.) Mac OS X still allows you to do this in the Classic environment (see (c)), but manages memory very well on its own so there's no need for users to make any memory changes to applications.

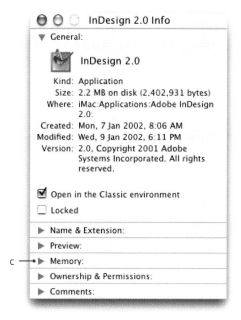

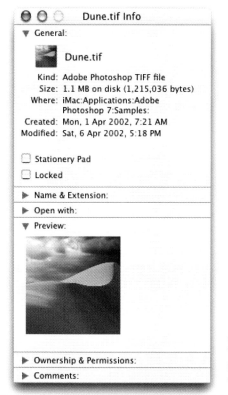

c —→

Quick look

Text documents, PDFs, images and movies can be previewed in the Get Info window, and individually depicted.

Enquiring, mind! (2)

Mac OS X will show you the information you need to see depending on: what kind of file format you are looking at; whether it has originated in a Carbon or Classic environment; what kind of file extension it has; and the status of the user's role in viewing and changing files. To find out exactly what we mean, select a variety of different files and go to File > Get Info (Command+I). You're bound to have an array of different dialog boxes at your disposal. This is what some of them are for.

Plain 'n simple

General information is available for any item you choose. This includes details such as the kind of item you are enquiring about, the size of the item, where it can be found as well as when it was created and modified. Additional details which may pop up (depending on what items you have selected), include: • Select New Original (when opening an Alias); • Name & Extension; • Preview; • Ownership & Permissions; and • Comment. (These are all discussed in further detail within this chapter.)

Hide or show?

Would you like to see the filename extension or not? This little box has a big part to play in your viewing abilities. Note: it works in conjunction with the 'Always Show File Extensions' checkbox in Finder Preferences (see pages 98, 99).

TECH TIP

QUICK FIND - FILES AND FOLDERS.
To see the hierarchy of your folders while in window view, hold down the Command key and click on the window title.

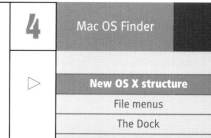

Classic opening

Carbon applications (those that are able to work in both Mac OS 9 and OS X), can be opened in the Classic environment with a simple click of this button (a).

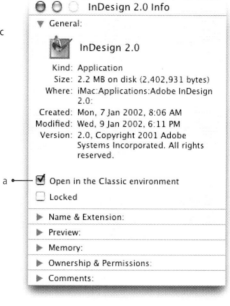

Privileged few

If you would like to find out individual privileges for an item, you can do so with the 'Get Info' command (Command+I). It will tell you who can do what with the item, and if you have the privileges to change the sharing privileges, this can be done here too.

Extending or pretending?

In a bid to encourage Mac and Windows file compatibility, Mac OS X has changed the way it handles filenames. It has embraced an option which has been available to PC Files since DOS first said hello to the world. What is it? The filename extension, of course.

Filename extensions made simple

'What exactly is a filename extension?', you may ask. In short, it consists of a period (.) followed by three letters which identify the file. What can be particularly confusing to a user is Mac OS X's ability to add its own extension to a file. For example; if you have already saved a document complete with filename extension, Mac OS X will automatically add a filename extension to it resulting in a double extension!

Fortunately, Mac OS X lets you choose whether or not you want to see filename extensions – both globally or individually. You can also preset an extension to a particular application, so OS X knows what to do with as soon as it sights the extension.

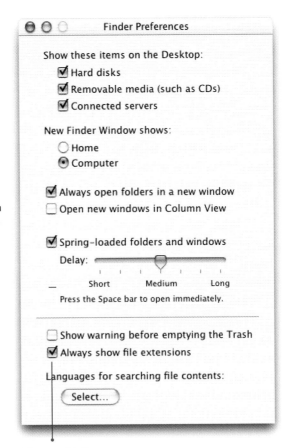

Show and tell

The ' Always show file extensions' option is found in Apple > Finder Preferences. If you choose not to select it, file extensions won't appear at all. (Note: this is a global setting and will affect ALL your file names!)

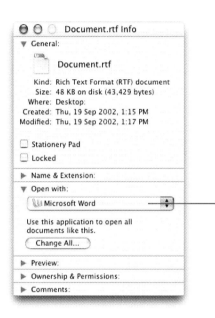

Sense of belonging

With Mac OS X you have the freedom to assign an application to open certain file formats. For example, whenever you receive a file with the .doc extension, you can assign it to a document such as Microsoft Word. This means that whenever a .doc file is visible, it will immediately be transformed into a Microsoft Word document, complete with matching icon. Pressing the 'Change All' button will ensure that every file with that extension will be opened by the application you choose. (Note: the 'Change All' button will only be visible when you have designated a particular application to an extension.)

Now you see it, now you don't

Should you wish to choose different extension options for individual files, select the files one at a time and choose File > Get Info > Name & Extension from the File menu. Then decide whether you want the particular extension to be hidden or not.

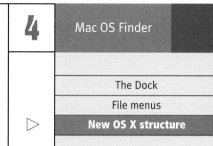

Fancy, free and full of fun

Mac OS X comes with a lot of freebies, including a range of software that can be immediately accessed. Stored in the Applications folder, these programs can be reached in a variety of ways, such as by: pressing Command+Option+A; choosing Go from the Finder menu and then selecting Applications; or by clicking the Applications button (on the toolbar in any Finder window). On these pages we whet your appetite.

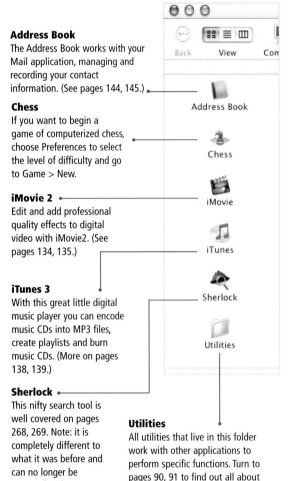

AppleScript
A great invention, use AppleScript third-party scripts or Mac OS X to automate repetitive tasks. (More in Chapter 17.)

Clock
You may have noticed that you have a clock in the menu bar (it's on the right hand side of your screen), elaborately controlled by System Preferences > Date and Time (see 166, 167). The clock seen here is mainly used to enable changes to time displayed.

Address Book
The Address Book works with your Mail application, managing and recording your contact information. (See pages 144, 145.)

Chess
If you want to begin a game of computerized chess, choose Preferences to select the level of difficulty and go to Game > New.

iMovie 2
Edit and add professional quality effects to digital video with iMovie2. (See pages 134, 135.)

iTunes 3
With this great little digital music player you can encode music CDs into MP3 files, create playlists and burn music CDs. (More on pages 138, 139.)

Sherlock
This nifty search tool is well covered on pages 268, 269. Note: it is completely different to what it was before and can no longer be accessed with Command+F.

Internet Connect
This program dials your ISP or connects to AirPort or Ethernet. (See Chapter 13 for more details.)

Mail
In addition to Internet Explorer you will get this email program free of charge. What a bargain! (See also pages 146, 147 for greater detail).

Utilities
All utilities that live in this folder work with other applications to perform specific functions. Turn to pages 90, 91 to find out all about them.

Stickies
Aha, one of Apple's best kept secrets. Or is it? If you aren't using these, you should be. These electronic post-it notes are perfect reminders for almost anything.

Calculator
This little desk accessory has been around since Mac first said hello to the world. Use it with the mouse or numeric keypad keys, it's simple to use and handy for almost anything!

iChat
This instant messaging application uses Rendezvous networking technology and has built-in compatibility to AOL Instant Messenger. Read all about it on pages 144, 145.

Internet Explorer (IE)
Microsoft's Web browser for the Mac, it ships free with Mac OSX. It can also be accessed from the Dock.

Preview
This option views, open and prints not only portable document files (PDFs) but most graphics files too.

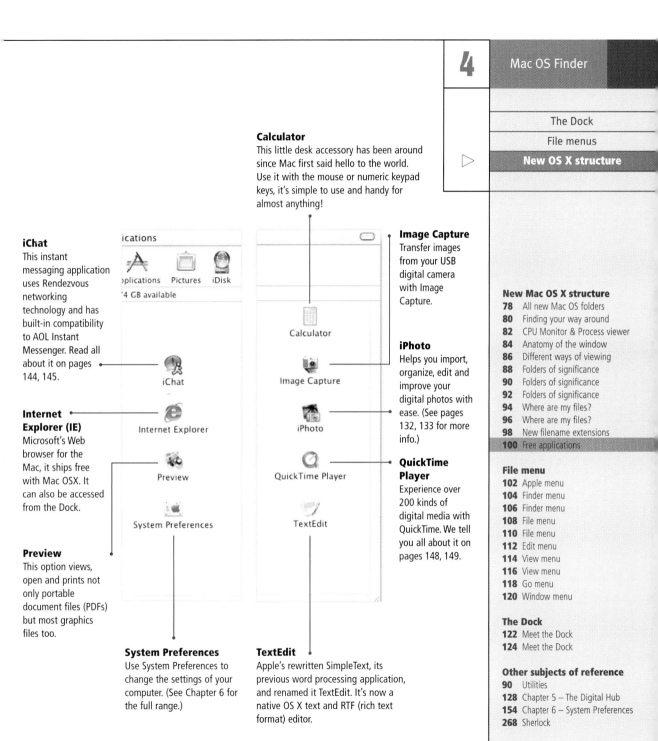

Image Capture
Transfer images from your USB digital camera with Image Capture.

iPhoto
Helps you import, organize, edit and improve your digital photos with ease. (See pages 132, 133 for more info.)

QuickTime Player
Experience over 200 kinds of digital media with QuickTime. We tell you all about it on pages 148, 149.

System Preferences
Use System Preferences to change the settings of your computer. (See Chapter 6 for the full range.)

TextEdit
Apple's rewritten SimpleText, its previous word processing application, and renamed it TextEdit. It's now a native OS X text and RTF (rich text format) editor.

All-new Apple menu

The new Apple menu is very different to those included in previous versions of Mac OS. For one, the Apple icon is blue instead of rainbow colored and for another, it's no longer customizable, so what you see is pretty much it. Don't worry, though, the good ol' Dock gives you the freedom that you may think you've lost. (Read all about it further on in this chapter).

Help at hand
When selected, 'About This Mac' shows what version of Mac OS X is running and indicates how much memory it has (see also pages 76, 77).

What's your preference?
Opens System Preferences window (the full range can be found in Chapter 6).

Zzzzzzzz
Choose this to put your Mac into its low-powered sleep mode. (If you don't know what this means, you haven't read page 70. Go Back!)

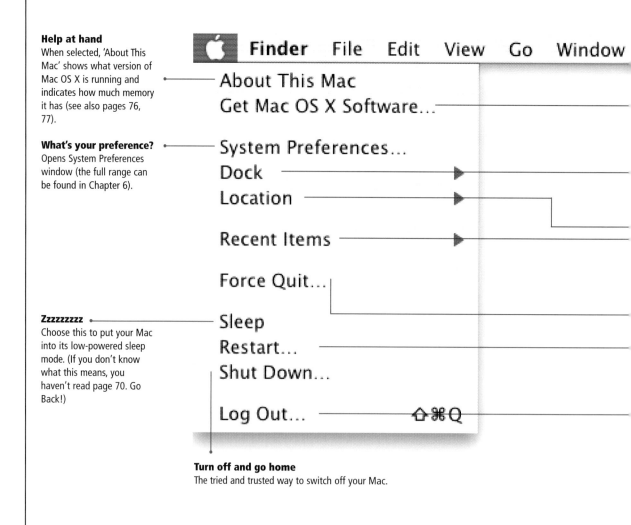

Finder File Edit View Go Window

About This Mac
Get Mac OS X Software...

System Preferences...
Dock
Location

Recent Items

Force Quit...

Sleep
Restart...
Shut Down...

Log Out...   ⇧⌘Q

Turn off and go home
The tried and trusted way to switch off your Mac.

Web connection
Launches Web browser and takes you to 'Mac OS X Downloads'.

Customizing items
Experiment with the Dock to your heart's content (see also pages 122, 123.)

Configuration capers
Switch network configurations in a flash (more details on pages 66, 67.)

Memory surge
Recently used items can be recalled. Pick the one you need if it's there. (Note: these items are customizable.)

Enough of this!
This command could only be accessed with shortcut keys in previous Mac OS versions. Now, you can choose this option – it brings up the Force Quit Applications dialog box allowing you to choose the application you want to quit. (Explained in more detail on pages 60, 61.)

Starting over
Instead of shutting down your Mac and then restarting it, this command allows you to do both steps in one.

Now, that's considerate
This command logs out the user who is currently logged in, after quitting all running user applications. This allows users to be switched without restarting or shutting down.

Finding the Finder

As the name suggests, the Finder gathers information for you and helps you to do the same. A useful tool, it also allows you to control the way you want your desktop to look and act. The Finder menu controls the way your Finder looks and acts, and as you will see on these pages, it's simple to use.

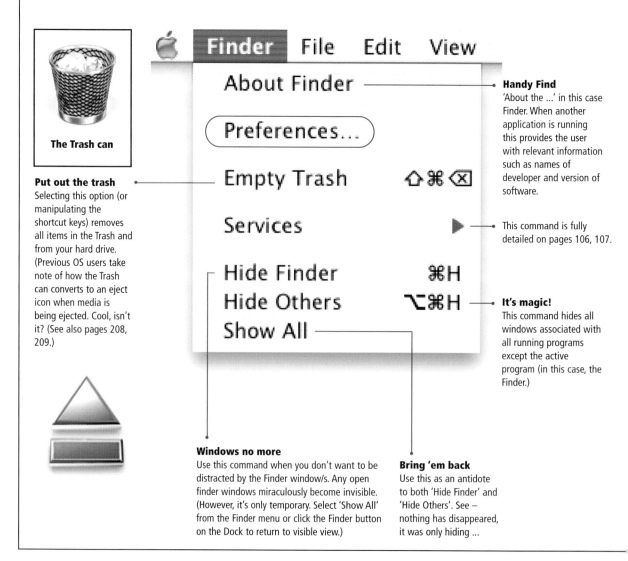

The Trash can

Put out the trash
Selecting this option (or manipulating the shortcut keys) removes all items in the Trash and from your hard drive. (Previous OS users take note of how the Trash can converts to an eject icon when media is being ejected. Cool, isn't it? (See also pages 208, 209.)

Handy Find
'About the ...' in this case Finder. When another application is running this provides the user with relevant information such as names of developer and version of software.

This command is fully detailed on pages 106, 107.

It's magic!
This command hides all windows associated with all running programs except the active program (in this case, the Finder.)

Windows no more
Use this command when you don't want to be distracted by the Finder window/s. Any open finder windows miraculously become invisible. (However, it's only temporary. Select 'Show All' from the Finder menu or click the Finder button on the Dock to return to visible view.)

Bring 'em back
Use this as an antidote to both 'Hide Finder' and 'Hide Others'. See – nothing has disappeared, it was only hiding ...

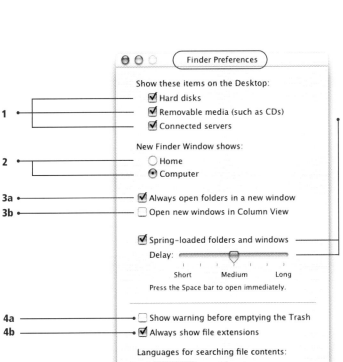

Finder Preferences

Show these items on the Desktop:
- ☑ Hard disks
- ☑ Removable media (such as CDs)
- ☑ Connected servers

New Finder Window shows:
- ○ Home
- ◉ Computer

- ☑ Always open folders in a new window
- ☐ Open new windows in Column View

- ☑ Spring-loaded folders and windows
  Delay: ——————————
  Short   Medium   Long
  Press the Space bar to open immediately.

- ☐ Show warning before emptying the Trash
- ☑ Always show file extensions

Languages for searching file contents:
(Select...)

1
2
3a
3b
4a
4b

Spring has sprung
Spring-loaded folders is a great new feature introduced into all three Finder views. When you hold an item over a folder instead of dropping it in immediately, a window will zoom open beneath your cursor to reveal the contents within and the moment you move out of the window it will disappear. The settings here (left) allow you to choose whether you want this option active and how long you prefer to wait for your folders to open as you drag.

Your choice entirely
Get the desktop to look exactly the way you want it to (well, almost) by:
1. Selecting the Disks, Removable media and Connected Servers checkboxes if you require hard drives, CDs, DVDs and other types of disks to appear on the desktop. (If you prefer to see nothing but a pristine desktop, deselect these boxes. You can still work with them when they aren't visible. Simply go to the Finder window and click the computer button to see them.)

2. When you click on the Finder icon in the Dock and there are windows currently open, you can specify which one you want to come forward by selecting from the pop-up list attached to it. (See also pages 122-124.)
3. (a) Users that want the familiarity of previous Mac operating systems will probably prefer to see a new window for each folder opened. (The old comfort zone speaks first).
(b) Ensure that each window

opened appears in Column view by selecting this option.
4. (a) If you are confident about what you throw out, uncheck this box. The Trash will be emptied without warning when you choose 'Empty Trash'.
(b) Are you the type who likes to see extensions to identify what kind of file you are dealing with?
If so, ensure that this box is checked. If not, keep it unchecked and test your general knowledge.

Finding the Finder (2)

If you have always wished for the kind of operating system that allows you to utilize common features from one application to another, wish no more – every Mac OS X Cocoa program now has 'Services' (Go to Finder and its right beneath 'Empty Trash'). With this command you can mix and match spelling checkers, drawing tools and calculation methods between Cocoa applications. In addition, some third party applications now only exist as Services.

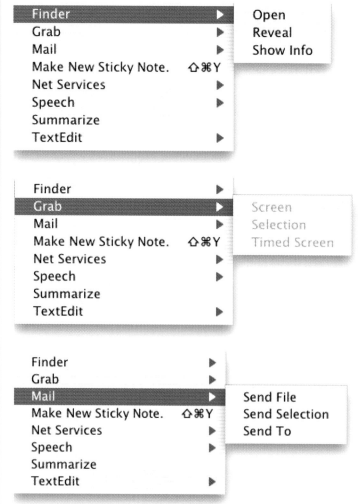

Finder within
Gaining access to the Finder is often a complete pain when you have a number of different applications open. In the latest version of OS X, Services has included the option for users to go to the Finder from within their current application by merely selecting it from a menu. Beats having to travel back and forth between applications and the Finder, doesn't it?

Grab it quick
For those of you who make images (screen shots) of what is visible on your monitor for training purposes or troubleshooting, Grab is a program for you. With it you can 'snap' the entire screen, a selection of it, or make a timed screen capture and *voilá,* it displays the image in a new window. You can then print it, close it without saving, or save as a TIFF file. (See also pages 90, 91 for more info). For Mac 'oldies', you can still create screengrabs using Command+Shift+3. Having Grab in your Services menu, just means that you can call it up from within the program you are currently working on, instead of toggling around OS X.
Note: a great new feature of Mac OS X 10.2 is the return of Command+Shift+4 to capture a window. Hit the Space Bar and as you roll over a window it will highlight in blue. Click to capture.

Please Mr Postman
When browsing the Internet, you often come across text you want to pass on to someone else. The good news is that you no longer have to go to the trouble of selecting the text, copying it, launching your e-mail program, pasting the text and sending it. You can now have your selected text pasted into a new outgoing e-mail message in Mac OS X Mail. How? Select the text you want and go to Services > Mail. It's that simple.

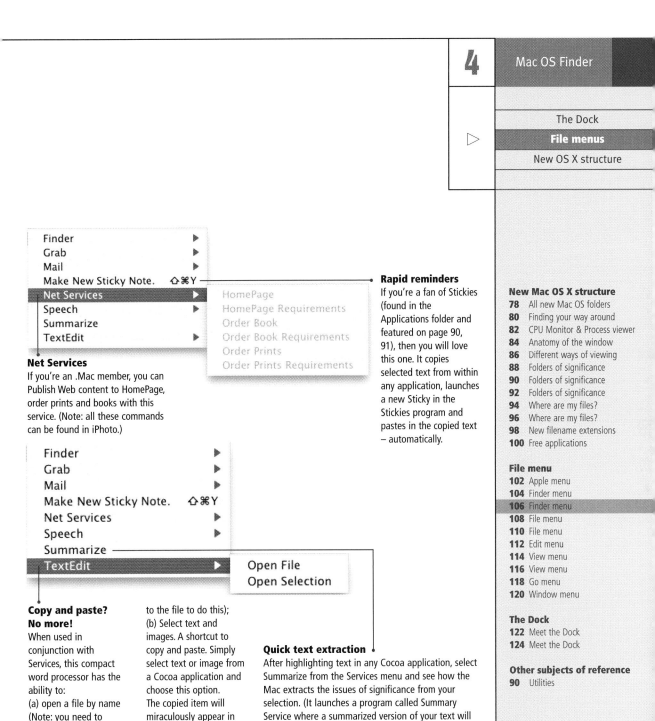

Net Services
If you're an .Mac member, you can Publish Web content to HomePage, order prints and books with this service. (Note: all these commands can be found in iPhoto.)

Rapid reminders
If you're a fan of Stickies (found in the Applications folder and featured on page 90, 91), then you will love this one. It copies selected text from within any application, launches a new Sticky in the Stickies program and pastes in the copied text – automatically.

Copy and paste? No more!
When used in conjunction with Services, this compact word processor has the ability to:
(a) open a file by name (Note: you need to indicate a full UNIX path to the file to do this);
(b) Select text and images. A shortcut to copy and paste. Simply select text or image from a Cocoa application and choose this option. The copied item will miraculously appear in TextEdit.

Quick text extraction
After highlighting text in any Cocoa application, select Summarize from the Services menu and see how the Mac extracts the issues of significance from your selection. (It launches a program called Summary Service where a summarized version of your text will greet you.)

Quick and easy file management (1)

File management is an essential part of every Mac OS user's
workday existence, so it would be advantageous to get to know
the File menu inside out – keyboard shortcuts included.

Find the Finder
Have all the Finder windows
disappeared? Never fear –
you can easily open a new
one by selecting this menu
option. (Note: this particular
shortcut key was used to
create a New Folder in
previous Mac operating
systems). Another way to
select the Finder is to go to
its icon in the Dock (see
more about the Dock later in
this chapter).

Putting a lid on it
Closing one window is easy – you can
choose this option (or the shortcut keys)
or simply select the red button to the left
of the window.
To close more than one window at a time,
hold down the Option key and select the
red button to the left of the uppermost
window, or press Option+Command+W.
Marvellous, isn't it?

Where is it?
The Find command has always been
available for Mac users. Prior to Mac OS X
10.2, it launched Sherlock. Now it brings up
the all new Find dialog.
(See pages 268, 269.)

File	Edit	View	Go	Window	ト

New Finder Window	⌘N
New Folder	⇧⌘N
Open	⌘O
Open With	▶
Close Window	⌘W
Get Info	⌘I
Duplicate	⌘D
Make Alias	⌘L
Show Original	⌘R
Add to Favorites	⌘T
Move to Trash	⌘⌫
Eject	⌘E
Burn Disc…	
Find…	⌘F

Folder fun

The New Folder command is the same as it has always been, and it does exactly as the name suggests – it makes folders. Only difference is that the shortcut key that we have all become accustomed to, has changed to Command+Shift+N. Take note of this – should you press the wrong keyboard combination out of habit you will get a new window and not a new folder!

Open sesame!

Opening a folder or document is easy. Simply double-click or if preferred, select the icon to be opened and go to File > Open.

(The Open command is also useful if you have more than one icon selected. Try it, and you will see that it opens selected icons almost simultaneously).

Info at a glance

Just about anyone who wants to find out anything about a file or folder will be keen to use this command. It's easy and versatile and you can find out things such as: • What application (and version of it) created the file; • How much space the item takes up (Note: only the item, not the disk drive!); • Location and where it was created; • Where it is found; • Creation and modification details; • Format options (for disks only).

You can also choose to lock the folder or file for safety and make any file a stationery pad. (When opened, the file will present itself as new, and the original will remain untouched — much like a template.) Any comments that you would like to add about the file or folder can also be included in this box. Note: information provided in the Info window depends on the kind of item selected. We expand on this on pages 94-97.

(Word of caution: Classic's Get Info command changed to Show Info in earlier versions of OSX and then reverted back to Get Info in OS X 10. 2. Confused? We are too!)

InDesign 2.0 Info

▼ General:

InDesign 2.0

Kind: Application
Size: 2.2 MB on disk (2,402,931 bytes)
Where: iMac:Applications:Adobe InDesign 2.0:
Created: Mon, 7 Jan 2002, 8:06 AM
Modified: Wed, 9 Jan 2002, 6:11 PM
Version: 2.0, Copyright 2001 Adobe Systems Incorporated. All rights reserved.

☑ Open in the Classic environment
☐ Locked

▶ Name & Extension:
▶ Preview:
▶ Memory:
▶ Ownership & Permissions:
▶ Comments:

Quick and easy file management (2)

Convenience is the key to managing your documents effectively.
Many of the commands under the File menu help make tasks such
as duplication and alias creation as easy as pie. Additionally,
notice new methods of ejecting media and making aliases.

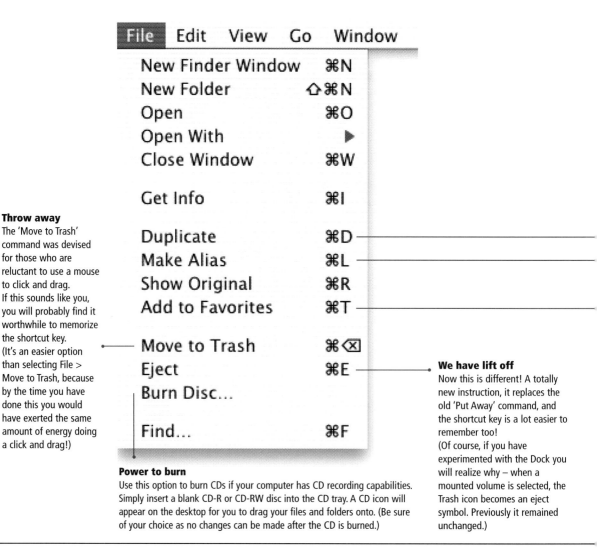

Throw away
The 'Move to Trash'
command was devised
for those who are
reluctant to use a mouse
to click and drag.
If this sounds like you,
you will probably find it
worthwhile to memorize
the shortcut key.
(It's an easier option
than selecting File >
Move to Trash, because
by the time you have
done this you would
have exerted the same
amount of energy doing
a click and drag!)

We have lift off
Now this is different! A totally
new instruction, it replaces the
old 'Put Away' command, and
the shortcut key is a lot easier to
remember too!
(Of course, if you have
experimented with the Dock you
will realize why – when a
mounted volume is selected, the
Trash icon becomes an eject
symbol. Previously it remained
unchanged.)

Power to burn
Use this option to burn CDs if your computer has CD recording capabilities.
Simply insert a blank CD-R or CD-RW disc into the CD tray. A CD icon will
appear on the desktop for you to drag your files and folders onto. (Be sure
of your choice as no changes can be made after the CD is burned.)

Double trouble

'Duplicate' is a nifty feature and one that should not be confused with the 'Copy' command (located in the Edit menu). Highlight or choose one or more icon/s and select the 'Duplicate' command.

Note: duplicated items are not copied to the clipboard, but rather immediately actioned (this is perfect for the more impatient user).

Where to from here?

An alias is a 'signpost' to a document or folder – in fact, any icon at all. It is simple to make: highlight the icon/s of your choice, select Make Alias, and hey presto! It's done. (Note: if you prefer to use the shortcut key – it's changed from the previous operating system, and no longer Command+M.) (See pages 202, 203 for more details on the Alias.)

Will the original please stand up?

It's all very well having an alias, but what happens when the original item (from which the alias was made) is corrupted or deleted? Or, what happens if you upgrade an application but forget to upgrade the alias with it? 'Show Original' is a quick way of diagnosing whether there is, in fact, an original.

Favorites

Easy access

Almost anything can be added to the Favorites folder by way of this command. It's dead easy – simply select documents, folders and/or servers and choose 'Add to Favorites'. The system makes an alias and sends it to Favorites (located in the Finder window toolbar). To view, click the Favorites button (it's shaped like a heart).

A BROKEN ALIAS?

Sometimes the Mac loses track of the original to which the alias points. When clicked on, a 'broken' alias will provide you with the options to delete it, fix it or ignore it. (See pages 202, 203 for more details on the Alias.)

HOT TIP

The Edit menu – same as ever?

If you want to edit or change data, the Mac OS X Edit menu is the place to go. It's reliable and almost as familiar as it used to be, with just a few subtle exceptions. Head this way and we will show you what they are ...

Edit	View	Go	Window	Help	📟

Undo Move of "Photoshop attachments.pdf"	⌘Z
Cut	⌘X
Copy "Chapter 4"	⌘C
Paste item	⌘V
Select All	⌘A
Show Clipboard	

Clipboard contents: picture

So that's where it's stored!
The minute you Cut or Copy an item it is immediately positioned on the clipboard. As soon as you Cut or Copy something new, that item supercedes the original. Once you select the Paste command, the clipboard releases a copy of the item and positions it where required.

TECH TIP

MULTIPLE CHOICE MADE EASY
To highlight more than one icon, hold down Shift and click select. However, in List view, Shift-click only highlights consecutive selections. For random selections, or to deselect in List view, hold down the Command key and click select.

Quick choice
The Select All command is both useful and time saving. It can be adapted to almost anything you do. For example: in Finder mode it can be used to select all your media on the desktop and then open them simultaneously. When a window is opened, Select All enables you to choose all your icons at once. When you are in Column mode on a window, Select All chooses only the items in the column where an item has been selected.

Slip, slop slap

No matter what computer you've used, the 'Cut, Copy and Paste' principle applies. This is how it works:
• **Cut** represents exactly what the name suggests. You cut something out either to paste it elsewhere, or get rid of it altogether (notice how the shortcut key X resembles a pair of scissors). It's almost the same electronically, except the item cut gets relocated to the clipboard for onward travel – almost like a 'removal van'. • **Copy,** on the other hand is quite different. The 'removal van' is not required in this case. Instead, the Mac operating system uses a kind of 'camera' to memorize the item to the clipboard, leaving the original one untouched. • **Paste** transports the last item Mac OS X has memorized or removed from the clipboard to the new specified position. (Remember, the item you paste must be your most recent cut or copied item.)

Oops!

The Undo option has always been relied on by Mac users. Now, Mac OS X takes Undo a step further – not only does it undo actions in text mode but it acts on icons too. For example, if you duplicate or move any item to the Trash, you can change your mind and undo it. As always, it only undoes one previous action. If you attempt to repeat an Undo, it will redo the action. (A great help to those who have an aversion to decision-making.)

SCISSORS AND GLUE

In Mac OS X Cut, Copy and Paste does not only apply to text. You can use it on graphics, pictures palettes within applications – even on the desktop itself. Have some fun and do some quick experiments.

TECH TIP

A different point of view (1)

Icon presentation is an all-important facet of the new Macintosh operating system. Apple has gone to great lengths to provide users with as many options as possible to tailor windows to individual requirements. As with most things in Mac OS X, the options you choose are easily altered. (Very important to those who believe that its their prerogative to change their minds – again and again and again ...)

Take your pick
Experienced users will probably find that they gravitate to the View menu for old time's sake. A quicker and more convenient way of changing the way folders are presented on the toolbar, but it's a matter of choice, really. (See also, pages 86, 87.)

For the tidy among us ...
As the name suggests, 'Clean Up Selection' tidies up your icons. (You will notice that this option is not available when your files are viewed by List or Column mode).
'Arrange by name' goes hand-in-hand with 'View as icons' and 'Clean Up Selection'. So, apart from having a very tidy looking window, you can view icons in alphabetical order too!

View	Go	Window	Help

✓ as Icons　　　　⌘1
as List　　　　　 ⌘2
as Columns　　　⌘3

Clean Up Selection
Arrange　　　　　　▶

Hide Toolbar　　　⌘B — 2.
Customize Toolbar...
Hide Status Bar ——————— 1.

Show View Options ⌘J

Modification station
To modify desktop view, click randomly on the desktop, open View Options and set the icon arrangements and size you require for your desktop. (See pages 116, 117 for full details.)

MAGIC CARPET RIDE
Here's a quick way of finding items in a window. While in View mode, type the first couple of letters of the item you are looking for. Sit back and watch how the window automatically scrolls up or down and selects the relevant item (Note: if you don't type enough letters in your search, you may find that the item selected is not the one you want. It will be in the alphabetical vicinity, so simply press the tab key until you get to the right one.)

HOT TIP

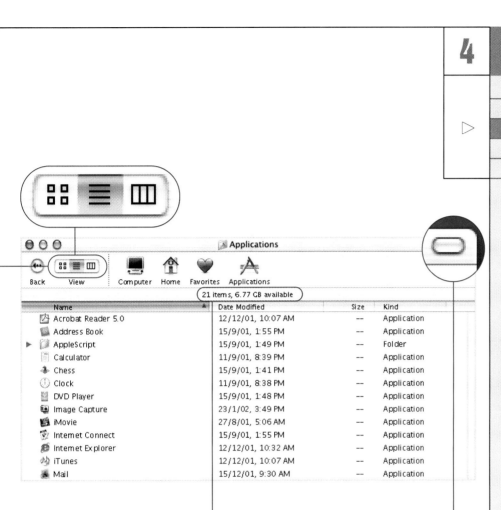

1. Fact file

The status bar is helpful for a number of reasons – for example, it provides information on how many items are contained within each window and calculates the amount of disk space these items occupy. If you don't need to see this regularly (or at all) select 'Hide Status Bar' and it will vanish ... at least until you show it again.

2. Now you see it, now you don't

If the toolbar is something you don't think you will ever become accustomed to, or something that you feel wastes too much space, simply hide it. However, should you change your mind – fear not, it will be there, waiting in the wings. Simply select 'Show Toolbar' and see it return! (Note: an alternative is to click on the Hide/Show toolbar button.)

A different point of view (2)

Being able to change things to your liking is a great philosophy of Apple's. With new features such as customizing your tool bar and changing your view options, the user's individuality is greatly encouraged. The more control you have over what you want to do and how you want things to look, the better your work (or play) performance. We show you how to optimize this. Read on.

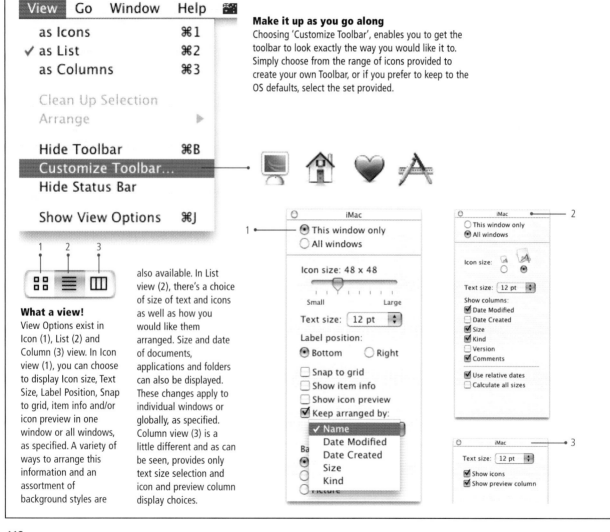

Make it up as you go along
Choosing 'Customize Toolbar', enables you to get the toolbar to look exactly the way you would like it to. Simply choose from the range of icons provided to create your own Toolbar, or if you prefer to keep to the OS defaults, select the set provided.

What a view!
View Options exist in Icon (1), List (2) and Column (3) view. In Icon view (1), you can choose to display Icon size, Text Size, Label Position, Snap to grid, item info and/or icon preview in one window or all windows, as specified. A variety of ways to arrange this information and an assortment of background styles are

also available. In List view (2), there's a choice of size of text and icons as well as how you would like them arranged. Size and date of documents, applications and folders can also be displayed. These changes apply to individual windows or globally, as specified. Column view (3) is a little different and as can be seen, provides only text size selection and icon and preview column display choices.

Personal Favorites
To list regularly used Favorites in your toolbar, go to View > Customize Favorites and either select icons of your choice, or choose the default set provided (cornered off) and drag to the toolbar.
Note: if you choose more icons than you are able to view, a tiny double arrow (>>) will appear at the end of the Toolbar, listing all the extra icons chosen that could not fit in the toolbar.

But wait, there's more ..
How would you like your Favorites to be displayed? Text only, icons only, or text and icons? Decisions, decisions!

PUFF OF SMOKE?
Deleting icons from your toolbar is similar to deleting icons from the Dock – with one exception. When you drag icons from the Dock they turn into a puff of smoke. When you drag icons from the toolbar to the desktop they simply .. er .. disappear.

TECH TIP

Going places

The Finder's Go menu is a novelty to the new Mac operating system and a useful alternative to clicking icons of the same description in your toolbar. As well as this, it offers quick 'flights' to destinations of your choice and the ability to connect to a server without going elsewhere. Take a look.

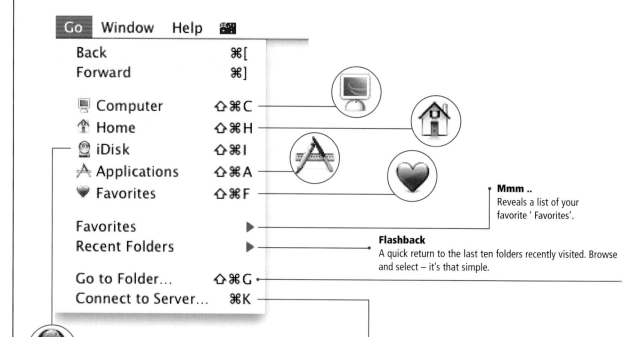

Mmm ..
Reveals a list of your favorite ' Favorites'.

Flashback
A quick return to the last ten folders recently visited. Browse and select – it's that simple.

iDisk ... what's this?
Meet the iTools online collection: iDisk, iCards, Email and Homepage, available on the Internet for Macintosh users only. iDisk comprises 20Mb of personal storage space on Apple's Internet servers as well as a FTP (File Transfer Protocol) site for sharing big files with other users. Selecting this option under the Go menu will enable you to launch your iDisk, provided that you have set your iTools member name and password in System Preferences first. Note: this is exclusive to .Mac members. (See also pages 212, 213.)

Share and share alike
If you are confident enough to begin accessing shared files, try the following steps, once you have selected 'Connect to Server':
• select the network you want to access; • select the machine to which you want to connect to;
• if the machine you require isn't found, type its IP (Internet Protocol) address in the Address Field; Click Connect;
• type in username or password or Guest and click Connect again; and
• choose the volume you want to mount and click ok. (Note: for more in-depth information on this, see chapter 12.)

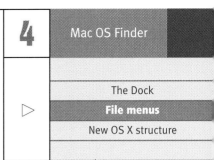

More than a click away

To select items filed under Computer, Home, Favorites or Applications, you have the option to choose from the Go menu instead of clicking on these icons in the Finder window toolbar (above).

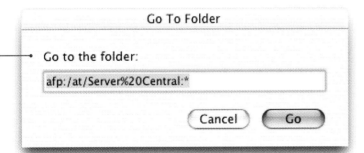

'Do not pass go'

No, we aren't playing Monopoly, we're simply pointing out how easy it is to move around Mac OS X. The 'Go to Folder' command gives you options that you never had in previous versions of the Mac operating system. The pop-up dialog box attached to this command allows you to type the name of the folder you want to go to and then select 'Go' to move on. As an alternative, you can indicate a pathname rather than a folder name. When doing so note that: (a) names are case-sensitive;(b) should begin and end with the slash (/); and (c) can indicate as many levels of the directory as possible. For example: /iMac/Applications/Apple Script/.

Window of opportunities

The Mac OS X Window menu has been revamped. While some items may be familiar to long-time Macintosh users, others are completely different. And while you are getting to know as much as possible about your windows, there's a whole range of 'magical' effects to make the experience worthwhile.

Window   Help

Zoom Window
Minimize Window   ⌘M

Bring All to Front

✓ iMac

As big as ...
This option allows for the window to resize to the width of the screen. (Note: if you prefer to change the window to adjust to the size of it contents, choose the maximize button (green) from Finder window.)

Quick check
For those of you who believe finding windows is a complete pain, this one is for you. All open windows will be listed in this window and to select one you only have to click.

A closer view
You may have to play with this option for some time before it finally sinks in. It works most effectively if you have a number of finder windows open which become obstructed when you launch an application. By clicking 'Bring All to Front', you will bring all finder windows in front of your application. We think it's really nifty.

Aladdin's lamp
This option is an alternative to the minimize (amber) button found in any window – it moves the window to the Dock, and if specified, the effect is that of the 'genie' in the bottle. Apart from being a convenient option, it can also provide hours of fun for the young at heart. (See more about the Dock and the Genie effect on pages 122-125.)

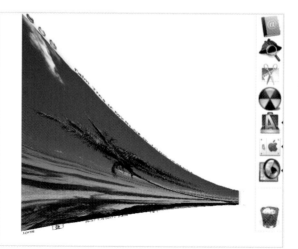

Quick Shrink
Double-click on a window's title bar and watch it minimize (an alternative to both the amber button and the 'Minimize Window' command.) (Note: holding down the Shift key will minimize your window in slow motion.)

The Dock

▷ **File menus**

New OS X structure

Image courtesy of **Canon PhotoEssentials** from the **Architecture & Stone** collection.
Visit: www.photoessentials.com

Dancing in the Dock (1)

Meet the Dock – a unique strip of icons (located at the bottom or side of the desktop), it combines the functions of what Mac 'oldies' were accustomed to in the previous operating system's Application menu, Apple menu, Launcher and Control Strip. At first you may find it difficult to get used to, but after a while you'll take to it as a duck takes to water. And the beauty is that you, the user, can control the way it looks and acts exactly as it suits you.

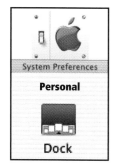

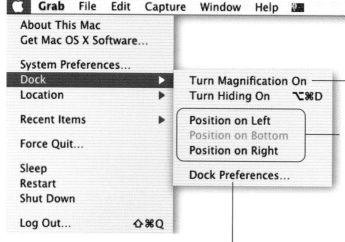

Where to now?
Position your Dock in a different spot or hide it altogether. (To resuscitate it, select 'Turn Hiding Off' from the Dock menu, 'Hide and Show' from the Dock dialog box, or simply choose the shortcut keys.

As you prefer
Dock Preferences can be selected from the Dock pull-down menu (under the Apple menu) or from Applications > System Preferences. Some abilities are duplicated from the Dock menu, but there are others (such as how you'd like to minimize windows) exclusively found in these preferences.

Through the looking glass
A fun effect which makes it easy to see what's available on your Dock as you drag through items with your mouse, it's controlled by:
(a) sliding the magnification bar (Dock > Dock Preferences) to the left or right; and
(b) Selecting Magnification On/Off from the Dock menu.

In the groove
(a) Change the size of your dock with this easy-to-use slider (or click on the Dock and drag its dividing line).

(b) Do you want the application opening on the Dock to do the 'Shake, Rattle & Roll'? Then ensure that this option is selected.

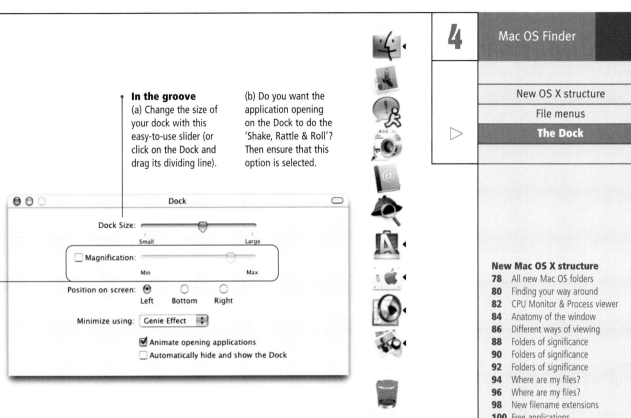

Shrinking Violet
By now you have probably noticed how cool a window slides into the Dock when it's minimized. It will either produce a 'Scale' or 'Genie' effect, depending on what you select in your Dock Preferences dialog box. (And it has different effects depending on where your Dock lies.)

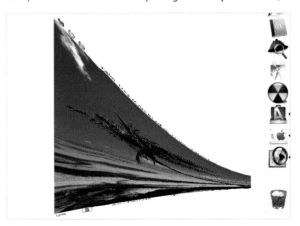

Dancing in the Dock (2)

Oh, what fun it is to work with the Dock. You can move icons of your favorite applications, utilities, documents, folders and disks in and out of it with ease (and animation), find out all the information it has to offer with a mere click of the mouse and immediately see running applications and active documents. Come with us for a closer look ...

Adobe Illustrator 10

1

Easy come, ...
Moving icons into the Dock is simple. Click on the icon of your choice, drag it to the dock and watch how the other objects scuttle away, making room for it. (Note: the icon you have in your Dock is only an alias of the real thing and therefore can come to no harm.)
There's a neat filing system too – applications and utilities go left, documents, folders and disks go right of the white divider line (1).

... Easy go
Removing icons from the Dock is great entertainment value. Select it, drag it away and ... poof .. it vanishes into a puff of smoke.

What's on?
The first thing that a Mac 'oldie' will notice when introduced to OS X is that the old Application menu no longer exists. Horror of horrors – this could mean that there is no longer any indication of which applications are open! But nothing could be further from the truth.
See those tiny black triangles beneath certain icons on the dock? Well, they display which applications, documents and utilities are currently running.

▷

Back to my roots

Need to find the location of a document lodged in your Dock? Click and hold the icon you require and a pop-up menu will appear. Choose 'Show in Finder' and it will reveal all. (Note: the Finder icon contains a pop-up box which specifies the name/s of window/s currently open. In the case where there are more than one, you can bring a window forward by clicking on its name in the pop-up box.)

Applications only

(a) When working with an Application's pop-up menu on the Dock (Control-click or hold down your mouse on icon on the Dock), note that selecting Option and Command gives you the choice to 'Force Quit' that particular application or see all its active documents.

(b) If you have a few documents open from various Applications, hold down Option and click on the Application you want to work on and all others will vanish!

New concept

The digital hub

When Steve Jobs first coined the term digital hub, Apple was well on the way to making the Mac the center of the emerging digital lifestyle. Today Apple's hub strategy looks complete with solutions for digital video, digital photography, digital music, DVD, mobile phones, and PDAs. What's more, all of these solutions are free with your Mac purchase. So the Mac advantage is a simple one: the company that makes the hardware, makes the software, and has a solution for each aspect of your digital lifestyle.

Digital music
iTunes acts like a digital jukebox allowing you to manage, label, categorize and rate your MP3 music collection. Integrating with Apple's iPod, you can take your MP3s wherever you go.

PDAs
Using iSync you can synchronize your contacts and schedules with your Palm OS-compatible PDA.

Gadget wrangling
Central to Apple's digital hub idea is the ability to manage your digital gadgets. In addition to digital video cameras, digital still cameras, and MP3 players, Mac OS X also lets you synchronize contacts and schedules with your Palm-compatible PDA, or Bluetooth-enabled mobile phone using the new iSync application. Using a .Mac account, you can also share your details between home and office.

Mobile phones
Synchronize contacts and schedules with your Bluetooth-compatible mobile phone.

Digital video
Affordable digital video cameras, Apple's FireWire interface and the free iMovie application kick-started the desktop video editing revolution. With iMovie, anyone with a Mac can edit their digital movies, add effects, titles, transitions and even prepare their movies for DVD delivery.

Digital photography
Apple's iPhoto solution allows you to organize, edit and share your digital memories. With iPhoto you can order prints of digital photos online or even order a bound photo album containing digital photos on high-quality paper and a linen cover.

DVD movies
Create your own DVD movies that can be played on most consumer DVD players.

The death of the computer?
In recent years, powerful digital devices have led some to believe that the death of the computer is upon us. The other side of this coin is that with small screen sizes, slower processors and interfaces that can be inconsistent, these digital devices don't provide the experience you're used to on a Mac.

Apple contends that the digital lifestyle is easier and more consistent through its digital hub of a Mac with Mac OS X running applications such as iPhoto, iDVD, iMovie, iTunes, and iSync. This hardware/software combination extends the usefulness of everything from digital video and still cameras, to MP3 players, PDAs, and mobile phones.

Things you get for free

Not too long ago the most you could hope for when buying a new OS were a few utilities. In contrast, Mac OS X provides iPhoto, iDVD, iMovie, iTunes, iChat, iCal, iSync, Mail, Address Book and QuickTime. As soon as you plug in your new Mac, you're able to download and organize your digital photos, edit your digital video, create interactive DVDs, manage your MP3 collection, manage contacts and time, synchronize calendars and contacts with PDAs or mobile phones, chat online, manage e-mail and control 'spam'. Cost: $0.

Applications

iPhoto	iMovie	iDVD	iTunes	iCal
www.apple.com/ iphoto/	www.apple.com/ imovie/	www.apple.com/ idvd/	www.apple.com/ itunes/	www.apple.com/ iCal/
Connect digital still cameras via USB or FireWire.	Connect digital video cameras via FireWire	Create interactive DVDs featuring digital video.	Manage your MP3 music collection.	Schedule/share calendars on web or your devices.
Shipped with Mac OS X 10.2: Version 1.1.1	**Shipped with Mac OS X 10.2:** Version 2.1.2	**Shipped with Mac OS X 10.2:** Version 2.1	**Shipped with Mac OS X 10.2:** Version 3.0	**Shipped with Mac OS X 10.2:** N/A
Latest version via Software Update: 1.1.1	**Latest version via Software Update:** 2.1.2	**Latest version via Software Update:** 2.1	**Latest version via Software Update:** 3.0.1	**Latest version via Apple web site:** 1.0
Ships free with: • G4 Tower • G4 Power Book • iMac • iBook	Ships free with: • G4 Tower • G4 Power Book • iMac • iBook	Ships free with: • All SuperDrive-equipped systems.	Ships free with: • G4 Tower • G4 Power Book • iMac • iBook	Ships free online: www.apple.com/ ical/

Pro users
www.apple.com/powermac/
But wait, there's more. With the Power Mac G4, professional customers also get: Sherlock 3; DVD Player; Disc Burner; Microsoft Internet Explorer; Acrobat Reader; Art Director's Toolkit; FAXstf; FileMaker Pro Trial; Graphic Converter; OmniGraffle; OmniOutliner; PixelNhance; Preview; and Snapz Pro.

iSync	iChat	Mail	Address Book	QuickTime
www.apple.com/isync/	www.apple.com/iChat/	www.apple.com/mail/	www.apple.com/macosx/	www.apple.com/quicktime/
Synchronize PDAs, or Bluetooth mobile phones.	Chat client compatible with AOL's AIM.	Email client with anti-spam and .Mac integration.	Email client with anti-spam and .Mac integration.	Movie player with MPEG-4 support.
Shipped with Mac OS X 10.2: N/A	**Shipped with Mac OS X 10.2:** Version 1.0	**Shipped with Mac OS X 10.2:** Version 1.2	**Shipped with Mac OS X 10.2:** Version 1.0	**Shipped with Mac OS X 10.2:** Version 6.0.1
Latest version via Apple web site: 1.0	**Latest version via Software Update:** 1.0	**Latest version via Software Update:** 1.2	**Latest version via Software Update:** 1.0	**Latest version via Software Update:** 6.02
Ships free online:	Ships free with:	Ships free with:	Ships free with:	Ships free with:
www.apple.com/isync/	• G4 Tower • G4 Power Book • iMac • iBook	• G4 Tower • G4 Power Book • iMac • iBook	• G4 Tower • G4 Power Book • iMac • iBook	• G4 Tower • G4 Power Book • iMac • iBook

Consumers
www.apple.com/imac/
With every iMac and iBook purchase, Apple customers also get:
Sherlock 3; Acrobat Reader 5; DVD Player; AppleWorks 6; AOL; Quicken 2002 Deluxe; World Book Mac OS X Edition; Microsoft Internet Explorer; Otto Matic; and Mac OS X Chess.

iPhoto

The problem with digital photography before the arrival of iPhoto was a lack of consistency in the transfer and managing of digital photos between the various camera manufacturers. The release of iPhoto took the reasonably tricky task of downloading, managing and sharing digital photos and simplified it to the point where anybody can start their own digital photo library.

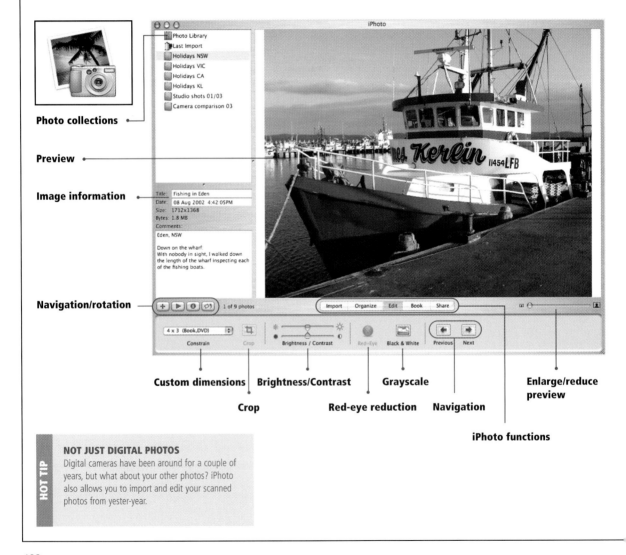

Photo collections

Preview

Image information

Navigation/rotation

Custom dimensions

Crop

Brightness/Contrast

Red-eye reduction

Grayscale

Navigation

Enlarge/reduce preview

iPhoto functions

Categorize your photos

iPhoto allows you to categorize individual photos or groups according to keywords and labels. You can even create your own labels and apply them to groups of images at once. Once your photos are categorized, you can quickly find them with the search function which looks through your photo collections looking for keyword or label matches.

Image editing

Though you'd never mistake iPhoto for Adobe's Photoshop, you can perform simple image editing with iPhoto. Presets constrain images to formats such as DVD and images can be improved with brightness/contrast adjustments and red-eye reduction. You also have the choice of making images grayscale.

Image sharing

iPhoto offers a wide range of output possibilities including: printing to your inkjet printer; creating a slideshow; e-mailing your photos via Mail; ordering prints or bound albums online (US only); output for the web; and creating desktop pictures or screensavers.

iMovie

Though iMovie was not the first digital video editing app, it was certainly the first instantly usable solution. In concert with the Apple-developed FireWire interface and the explosion of affordable DV cameras, iMovie was the first to bring video editing to the consumer. In its second version, iMovie allows users to capture and edit their digital video through a simple interface which supports titling, effects, transitions and sound effects.

Lights, camera, action!
iMovie is a ridiculously easy way to create polished movies from your digital video footage.

Import/Edit **Preview** **Shuttle controls**   **Movie clips**

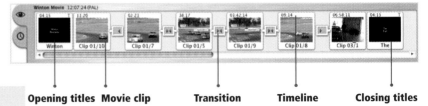

Opening titles **Movie clip**   **Transition**   **Timeline**   **Closing titles**

Transitions

Watch any movie or TV show and you'll see transitions between scenes. The transitions are there to ease you into a new environment rather than jarring your eyes with an immediate switch between footage. iMovie gives you a handful of transitions which you can customize with a time slider and direction pad. Preview transitions under the Transitions tab, and when you're happy, drag it between the clips on the timeline.

Titles

You're in the movie business for the fame right? So, don't forget to give yourself due credit in the movie credits. You can select your own fonts and sizes along with speeds and pauses of effects. While you're at it, you can also choose from a wide range of text effects for the opening titles such as bouncing, drifting and flying. If you're making your own music videos, there's also an option for music video titles just like you see on MTV.

Effects

Everybody knows that today's movies are all about the effects. You don't have to risk a box office flop thanks to iMovie's stable of effects such as Sepia Tone, Soft Focus and Water Ripple. Thanks to the extensible nature of iMovie, you can also download additional effects from a number of companies such as: Gee Three (www.geethree.com); Virtix (www.virtix.com); CSB Digital (www.csb-digital.com); and eZedia (www.ezedia.ca).

Making an iMovie

Digital video camera
Start with a DV camera with iLink (FireWire) connection, and with a single click import your video.

Edit footage with iMovie
Organize and edit clips by dragging them into the timeline, then add transitions and effects.

Export for iDVD
Export your movie to one of many mediums including DVD via the iDVD export option.

iDVD

The DVD age has well and truly arrived and with digital video under control using iMovie, it was an obvious next step for Apple to target DVD creation. Supplied free with SuperDrive (DVD-burner)-equipped Power Mac G4s, 1GHz PowerBook G4s or iMacs, iDVD helps take your digital video creations from iMovie and deliver them as Hollywood-style DVDs with motion menus, soundtracks, and slideshows.

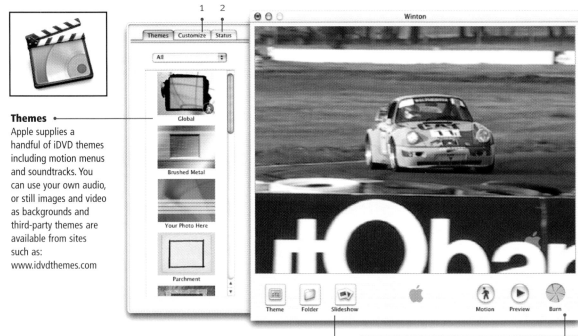

Themes
Apple supplies a handful of iDVD themes including motion menus and soundtracks. You can use your own audio, or still images and video as backgrounds and third-party themes are available from sites such as: www.idvdthemes.com

Slideshow
The slideshow is a great feature allowing you to show off your photos with background music and you can include navigation arrows for viewers to skip between photos with their DVD remote.

Preview and burn
While creating your DVD you can turn off motion menus to give your nerves a rest. Also, rather than risk an imperfect production, be sure to test menus and controls before burning your DVD.

HOT TIP

I CAN'T CUT THAT
iDVD 2 gives you about 90 minutes worth of video per DVD, so keep an eye on movie lengths during the editing stage to avoid tough 'cutting room' decisions after you've already edited the video.

1. Customize
The Customize tab gives you controls over: Background and Motion Duration; Audio; Titles Color, Font and Size; Button shape, Position, Font, Color and Size. You can also create short movies in iMovie to use as motion buttons.

2. Status
The MPEG-2 encoding required for DVDs takes a reasonable time to process, so the Status tab gives you an idea of how well the background processing is progressing.

Digital video camera
Start with a DV camera with iLink (FireWire) connection, and with a single click import your video.

Edit footage with iMovie
Organize and edit clips by dragging them into the timeline, then add transitions and effects.

Make your DVD with iDVD
Create animated menus, buttons, slideshows, choose the audio and encode the video in iDVD.

Burn a DVD for playback
Preview the DVD with the menu control, then burn the DVD for playback on most DVD players.

iTunes

For anybody who has been converting their CDs to MP3 for more than a year, the need to manage an MP3 collection is a constant challenge. iTunes allows you to put your music into a virtual jukebox and provides you with some great playlist features to make sure your favorite tunes don't get lost behind the couch. It can also automatically create playlists based on details such as the year the song was recorded, or even your most frequently played songs.

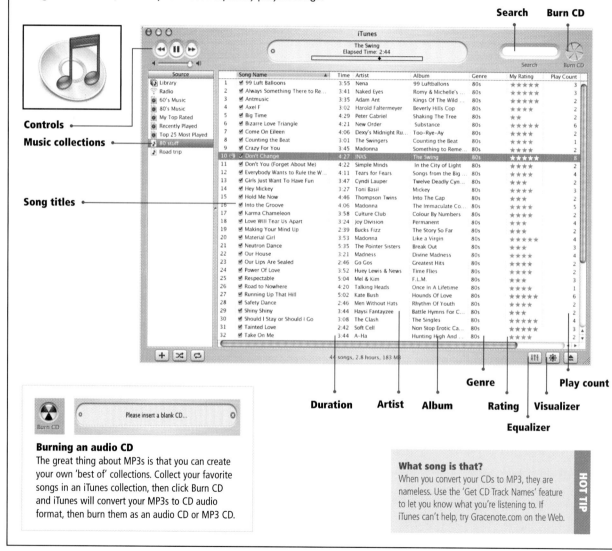

Search

Burn CD

Controls

Music collections

Song titles

Duration **Artist** **Album** **Rating** **Visualizer** **Genre** **Play count**

Equalizer

Burning an audio CD
The great thing about MP3s is that you can create your own 'best of' collections. Collect your favorite songs in an iTunes collection, then click Burn CD and iTunes will convert your MP3s to CD audio format, then burn them as an audio CD or MP3 CD.

What song is that?
When you convert your CDs to MP3, they are nameless. Use the 'Get CD Track Names' feature to let you know what you're listening to. If iTunes can't help, try Gracenote.com on the Web.

Radio

If you've got a reasonable Internet connection, you can listen to an increasing number online radio stations categorized by decade, genre or spoken word. A Bit Rate column will give you an indication of the bandwidth requirements and your likely success at an uninterrupted listen.

Equalizer

A welcome addition to iTunes 2.0 was the Equalizer allowing you to choose from a number of presets depending on the type of audio you're listening to. Among the 22 presets are: Acoustic; Rock; Spoken Word; Small Speaker; Electronic; Jazz; Latin; Piano; Hip Hop; Dance; Classical; Vocal Booster; Pop; Bass Booster; Treble Booster; Bass Reducer; Lounge; Vocal Booster; and more.

Encoding

'Ripping' your CDs involves compressing the CD quality audio into MP3 format (at 1/10th the size). MP3 audio quality is dependent on the encoding bit rate which iTunes allows you to specify up to 320Kbps.

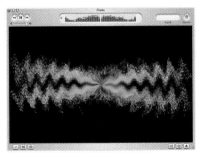

Visualizer

For a more visually pleasing experience, iTunes' Visualizer will create random swirling patterns based on the audio being played. You can choose to play the Visualizer at full screen for a 'Rave party' effect as you jump up and down to your favorite tune.

Sound Check

A Sound Check option in iTunes 3.0 analyzes your MP3 library and optimizes volume levels for consistent playback.

iSync

One of the new kids on the block released after Mac OS X 10.2, iSync adds to Apple's digital hub foundation by allowing you to connect and synchronize contact and scheduling data between your Mac and your mobile phone, Palm-compatible PDA, iPod and .Mac account. This means that the information on your iMac will be wirelessly synchronized with your Bluetooth-compatible Sony Ericsson phone and vice versa without your lifting a finger.

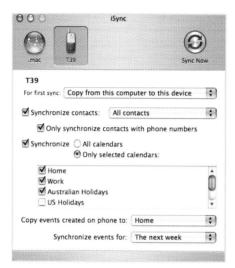

What can you sync with iSync?

- Compatible Palm OS devices:
  Any Palm OS devices capable of syncing with HotSync 3.0 or later and Palm Desktop 4.0 or later for Mac OS X.
- Compatible mobile phones:
  Sony Ericsson T68i
  Ericsson T68
  Ericsson T39
  Ericsson R520
- Other compatible devices:
  Any Apple iPod (using version 1.2 or later of iPod software).

.Mac

iSync allows you to synchronize your work and home Macs by storing Address Book and iCal data on your .Mac account. By storing the latest information on your .Mac account, you always have access to the most recently updated information regardless of which one of your Macs you may be using.

iPod

With the latest iPod software (version 1.2 or later), you can use iSync to transfer your Mac OS X Address Book contacts and iCal calendar info from your computer to your iPod. To synchronize your iPod you choose Add Device in iSync's Devices menu, double-click the iPod in the Add Device window to add it to the devices you want synced.

Got Bluetooth?

Before you can start syncing to your mobile phone, you'll need to invest in a Bluetooth adapter. At this stage, there's not a lot of choice in adapters. Apple sells D-Link's Bluetooth USB Adapter at its store (www.applestore.com or www.apple.com.au/store/). You'll need to download Apple's Bluetooth software (Technology Preview 2.1), and plug in the D-Link DWB-120M Bluetooth USB Adapter to any available USB port. Launch the Bluetooth software to find wireless Bluetooth-enabled devices within range of your computer to pair with. And once you select the Bluetooth device on the list and click the Pair button, you're connected.

Palm OS device

iSync can synchronize your Address Book contacts, iCal calendars and To Do information on your Mac with your Palm's contacts and calendar. Palm synchronization requires iCal and HotSync 3.0 (or later) for Mac OS X. Like adding an iPod, you need to choose Add Device in iSync's Devices menu, then double-click the Palm device in the Add Device window to add it to the devices you want synced.

Mobile phone (Bluetooth-enabled)

iSync allows you to wirelessly sync a number of GPRS Bluetooth-enabled phones such as the Sony Ericsson T68i to your Mac to synchronize events and appointments, names, phone numbers and e-mail addresses. Using a Bluetooth adapter, your Mac can transfer data wirelessly over several feet so you don't have to manually enter details into your phone.

iCal

iSync multiplies the usefulness of iCal by allowing you to travel with your most up-to-date appointment information. Even more useful is that any details you enter into your mobile phone or PDA while away from your Mac will be synchronized when you return to the office or home.

Address Book

Like iCal, the Address Book becomes indispensable when used in concert with iSync. Now wherever you enter contact information, those details can be synchronized with your mobile phone, PDA and Mac giving you the most up-to-date information without the hassle of typing it in three times.

> **TOO MUCH?**
> Apple's iCal is a great tool and you can certainly get carried away subscribing to every available calendar. When using iSync, toggle off some calendars so you don't overload your poor old phone.
>
> **HOT TIP**

iCal

The point of the digital hub is seamless integration and improved organization. Your digital video and photos, MP3s and DVDs might be organized, but how about you? iCal allows you to get on top of your schedule by: showing potential time conflicts; setting timely e-mail or audio reminders; using daily, weekly and monthly views; providing a linked To Do list; and adding a Web publishing option for your calendars.

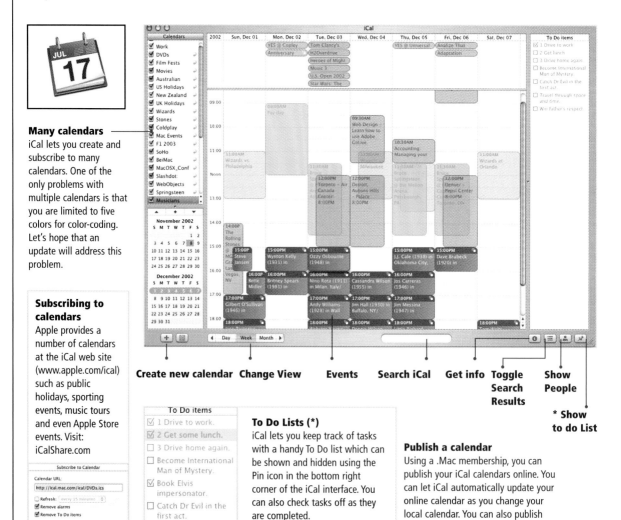

Many calendars
iCal lets you create and subscribe to many calendars. One of the only problems with multiple calendars is that you are limited to five colors for color-coding. Let's hope that an update will address this problem.

Subscribing to calendars
Apple provides a number of calendars at the iCal web site (www.apple.com/ical) such as public holidays, sporting events, music tours and even Apple Store events. Visit: iCalShare.com

Create new calendar · Change View · Events · Search iCal · Get info · Toggle Search Results · Show People · * Show to do List

To Do Lists (*)
iCal lets you keep track of tasks with a handy To Do list which can be shown and hidden using the Pin icon in the bottom right corner of the iCal interface. You can also check tasks off as they are completed.

Publish a calendar
Using a .Mac membership, you can publish your iCal calendars online. You can let iCal automatically update your online calendar as you change your local calendar. You can also publish iCal calendars on any WebDAV server.

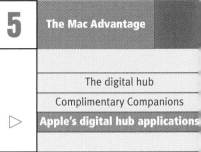

Make it recurring

For an event which recurs such as birthdays, anniversaries or religious holidays, you can select the exact date or the day of the month such as the first Sunday of the month. You can also specify how long you want this event to recur for.

Set some reminders

If you need to be reminded occasionally, iCal has some insurance against forgetting the unforgettable. You can choose to be reminded by an onscreen dialog, an alert sound or an e-mail. You can also individually specify when you'll be reminded by each alert, so you can give yourself a few timely reminders.

Invite your contacts

Taking advantage of the Address Book, you can invite your contacts to an event by dragging them onto the event from the 'Show the People' window in iCal. When your list of invitees is complete, simply click on the 'Send Invitations' button to get the invites sent.

RECORD AN EVENT

You can use the Event Info window to enter the details of your event. In the main window you can enter the title of the event, its duration, the calendar it is attached to and the event's status such as Tentative, Cancelled or Confirmed.

LAST WORD

Talk is cheap

Faster than e-mail, more discrete than a phone call, and cheaper than dialling long-distance, 'instant messaging' has taken the world by storm. With Mac OS X 10.2, having a conversation via keyboard couldn't be easier, thanks to its free, built-in instant-messaging tool, iChat.

Who are you?
Before you can chat, you'll need a .Mac or AOL/AIM 'screen name', such as your .Mac username (if you've subscribed to Apple's optional .Mac service). If you already have a screen name, enter it and your password into the Accounts panel of iChat's Preferences. If you do not, register with AOL (www.aim.com) or Apple (www.mac.com).

Magic messaging
You can instantly find and chat with any Mac OS X 10.2 user on your local network, thanks to nifty behind-the-scenes technology called Rendezvous (or Zero Configuration Networking – Zeroconf for short). Just ensure that you and your buddies have put a tick in the 'Enable Local Network Messaging' checkbox in the Accounts panel of iChat's preferences. Then, they'll appear in your Rendezvous window – accessible from iChat's Windows menu whenever you're online. (You might have to select 'Log Into Rendezvous' from iChat's iChat menu first).

Instant menu
To add this handy menu to your menu bar, put a tick in the 'Show Status In Menu Bar' checkbox in the Accounts panel in iChat's Preferences. From this menu, you can easily logon, logoff, and open your buddies list, from which you can initiate a chat session with any friends or colleagues who are online.

A thousand voices
iChat makes it easy to create a 'chat room' for a group of your friends — or a quick business meeting. Just select 'Go To Chat' from the File menu, give your chatroom a unique name, and then click the Go button. Other iChat users can use the same command to access your chatroom. To save a transcript of your meeting, put a tick in the 'Automatically Save Chat Transcripts' checkbox in the Messages panel of iChat's Preferences. The Show Folder button allows you to see and change where iChat stores these transcripts.

Chat away

To chat with someone on your local network, double-click their name in iChat's Rendezvous window. To chat with someone in your buddies list, double-click their name in the Buddies window. To add someone to your buddies list, select 'Add A Buddy' from iChat's Buddies menu. If you've already added this person to your Mac OS X Address Book, just click on their name and then the 'Select Buddy' button. To bypass the Mac OS X Address Book, click the 'New Person' button, then enter your buddy's IM service type (.Mac or AIM/AOL) and screen name.

Worth a thousand words

If you've added a picture of yourself to your Mac OS X Address Book, you should see it linked to your voice bubbles in iChat. (If you have not, just drag a photo of yourself to the silhouette in your Buddies or Rendezvous window.) When you chat with another iChat user, you should see their picture, too. Smilies (or 'emoticons') are another great way of humanizing what you type with pictures – just select Insert Smiley from iChat's Edit menu, or tap out one of the traditional symbol, like ;-) for a wink. (Hint: View this symbol sideways.)

😊 Smile
😉 Wink
☹️ Frown
😕 Undecided
😮 Gasp
😄 Laugh
😗 Kiss
😛 Sticking out tongue
😳 Embarrassed
🤐 Foot in mouth
😎 Cool
😠 Angry
😇 Innocent
😢 Cry
🤐 Lips are sealed
🤑 Money-mouth

Mail

Fast, fabulous, e-mail – trustworthy, easy and fun. Sending messages via e-mail is still the most popular use of the Internet. To find out what all the fuss is about, fire up Mac OS X's built-in e-mail program, called Mail.

Little black book
We typed 'Inv' and Mail entered the rest of this name and address, because it found Invented Person and her e-mail address in Mac OS X's Address Book, where we had recorded it earlier. If someone sends you an e-mail, you can quickly add them to Address Book by selecting 'Add Sender To Address Book' from Mail's Message window. Otherwise, select Address Book from Mail's Window menu to import addresses or add them manually.

Color and movement
Click the Font and Color buttons to decorate your e-mail message, but be warned: some e-mail programs could have difficulty displaying any message you've decorated in this way. To strip all decoration from your message, select Make Plain Text from Mail's Format menu. To create all future messages as plain text, select Plain Text from the Format pop-up menu in the Composing panel of Mail's Preferences.

Miss manners
Always add a meaningful subject line to your e-mail message. This is good etiquette, because it will help your pen pals to find your message after they file it among dozens.

Picture perfect
To add a picture to your message, just drag it into your message window. Their own e-mail program will determine whether your pen pals see the picture in the body of the message or as an attachment. To make it easier for other e-mail programs to display your pictures and to make them smaller for e-mailing), use Preview (in Mac OS X's Applications folder to save them as well-compressed JPEGs.

Dude, where's my mail?

If you have problems reading all your mail while connected to the Internet and are sometimes warned that your mailbox is full, then your e-mail account may be using a technology called IMAP behind the scenes. (Apple's .Mac e-mail service defaults to using IMAP, for example.)

- Short-term solution: transfer your mail from the IMAP server to your own Mac. To do this, select a mailbox linked to the IMAP account, then select 'Synchronize Account' from Mail's Mailbox menu. Wait while Mail copies the messages, then select 'Take Mailbox Offline' from the Mailbox menu.
- Long-term solution: force Mail to transfer every message from the server to your Mac immediately. To do this, select the IMAP account in the Accounts panel of Mail's Preferences and then click the Edit button. Tick the 'Remove Copy' checkbox under then Advanced tab, and select 'Right Away' from the pop-up menu.

Spam, spam or spam

Junk e-mail – often called 'spam', after a famous Monty Python skit – can take all the fun out of e-mail, until you discover the Junk Mail filter included with Mail 1.2 and later. The filter is in training mode when you start using Mail. Teach it to recognize spam by clicking the Junk button within each piece of spam it misses, and the Not Junk button within every message it falsely accuses. Once Mail has learnt the difference between spam and desirable e-mail, select Automatic from the Junk Mail submenu under Mail's Mail menu. Then, Mail will automatically move all spam to the Junk mailbox. To have Mail simply delete all spam, select Custom from the Junk Mail submenu, then select Delete Message under Perform The Following Actions.

QuickTime Player

QuickTime has been around for over ten years which makes it the elder statesman of digital media playback. Evolving from multimedia CD-ROMs to Internet delivery of digital video, QuickTime has added a wide range of codecs to keep it at the forefront of streaming media playback. QuickTime 6 became the basis of the MPEG-4 standard, positioning it well in the current evolution of digital video compression, and with licensing issues worked out, it's set to prosper with over 25 million downloads already.

QuickTime Player
The QuickTime Player is the front-end of Apple's multimedia technology which allows you to watch movies from your hard drive, movies embedded in Web pages such as movie trailers, or even live streaming video over the Web. It provides basic controls for watching movies with Play, Pause, Fast Forward, Rewind, Start and End buttons. Users are also able to drag the timeline slider to a particular point in the movie and adjust the volume as needed.

Adjust volume   Movie   Shuttle controls   Playhead   QuickTime: What's On

Harry Potter and the Chamber of Secrets
Image courtesy of Warner Bros.
Visit: www.harrypotter.com

QuickTime show
For examples of QuickTime media:
MPEG-4 — www.apple.com/ quicktime/gallery/mpeg4.html
AAC Audio — www.apple.com/ quicktime/gallery/aac.html

HOT TIP

QuickTime at the movies

One of the more popular uses for QuickTime is to view the latest movie trailers. Apple's QuickTime site (www.apple.com/quicktime/), keeps track of the latest movie trailers from all of the major studios and even some of the smaller ones. Simply click on the movie poster or movie title under each studio to view the trailer. Note: download time will vary according to your Internet connection.

QuickTime at play

Gamers are catered for with the Game Trailers Web page (www.apple.com/games/trailers/) which features a good range of trailers for Mac games.
The QuickTime site will also appeal to music lovers with a wide range of musical genres (www.apple.com/quicktime/whatson/).
Watch music videos, live concerts and interviews with your favorite artists all within the QuickTime Player.

Why go to QuickTime Pro?

Apple offers QuickTime Pro at US$29.99 which adds media authoring features and extra playback options such as full screen viewing. At the top of the list of features for QuickTime Pro are the import and export options. With the current version you are able to author MPEG-4 content and export as AVI, BMP, DV Stream,

| QuickTime Player | QuickTime Pro | Streaming Server | Broadcaster |

FLC, Hinted Movie, AIFF, Toast Video CD, QuickTime Media Link, Image Sequence, Picture, System 7 Sound, QuickTime Movie, and uLaw.
QuickTime Pro also allows you to cut, copy and paste video and audio giving you basic editing capabilities.
On the playback front, you have

the luxury of viewing video in full screen mode. You can also control brightness, color, treble and bass and then save those settings with your movie.
Finally, you can prepare movies for streaming with a huge range of presets to compress streaming audio and video for Web delivery.

OS X
anatomy

Under the hood

Combining the power of UNIX with the simplicity and elegance of the Macintosh has resulted in a super-modern operating system engineered to take the Macintosh platform through the next decade. On these pages we introduce you to new and open standard technologies that make Mac OS X what it is today – the most stable, compatible and interoperable desktop operating system available.

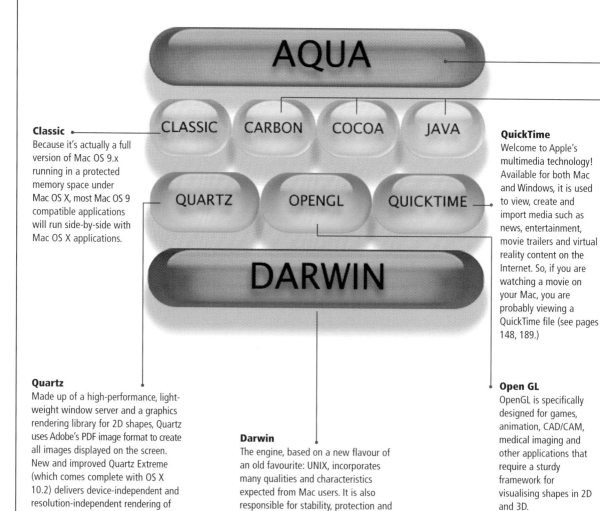

Classic
Because it's actually a full version of Mac OS 9.x running in a protected memory space under Mac OS X, most Mac OS 9 compatible applications will run side-by-side with Mac OS X applications.

QuickTime
Welcome to Apple's multimedia technology! Available for both Mac and Windows, it is used to view, create and import media such as news, entertainment, movie trailers and virtual reality content on the Internet. So, if you are watching a movie on your Mac, you are probably viewing a QuickTime file (see pages 148, 189.)

Quartz
Made up of a high-performance, light-weight window server and a graphics rendering library for 2D shapes, Quartz uses Adobe's PDF image format to create all images displayed on the screen. New and improved Quartz Extreme (which comes complete with OS X 10.2) delivers device-independent and resolution-independent rendering of anti-aliased text, bitmap images and vector graphics.

Darwin
The engine, based on a new flavour of an old favourite: UNIX, incorporates many qualities and characteristics expected from Mac users. It is also responsible for stability, protection and industrial strength of Mac OS X.

Open GL
OpenGL is specifically designed for games, animation, CAD/CAM, medical imaging and other applications that require a sturdy framework for visualising shapes in 2D and 3D.

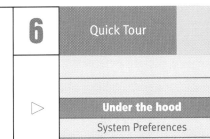

Interface.

Developer Frameworks.

Displays & Sound.

Core OS.

Aqua
Aqua's ocean-blue inspired look is designed to look like water with its many transparent, shiny and droplet-shaped elements. In addition to bringing simplicity and elegance to the Macintosh, it simplifies many common computing tasks with innovative, time-saving organizational features such as the Dock, the new Finder and system menus.

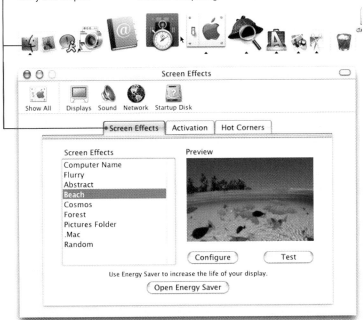

Carbon
To make software development for Mac OS X easier, Apple created Carbon, a collection of system elements that work in both OS 9 and OS X.

Cocoa
Descended from the NeXTSTEP programming interface, Cocoa, the development environment for Mac OS X, takes advantage of all Mac OS X's features.

Java
Development and execution of Java programs are allowed on Mac OS X, including 100 percent Pure Java applications and applets.

▷ Under the hood

System Preferences

Up close and personal

The level of importance of various Mac OS X preferences is directly proportional to the ease at which they are found. Located in the Apple menu, Dock and Applications folder (first window you come across when your hard drive is selected), the range covers everything. However, handle with caution and be aware that unless you are an administrator you won't have the authority to change as many preferences as you may like to. Let's begin with a few of the set marked 'Personal'.

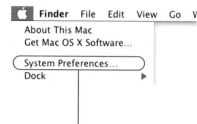

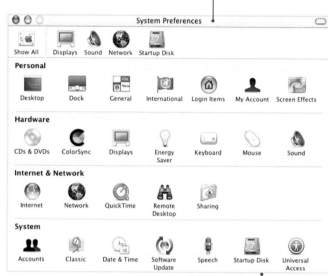

Color your world
Changing your desktop pattern has never been easier. Either select defaults from Apple Background Images, Nature, Abstract, Solid Colors or load a folder of your own.
The Pictures folder drop-down menu exhibits the range of your own loaded selection.

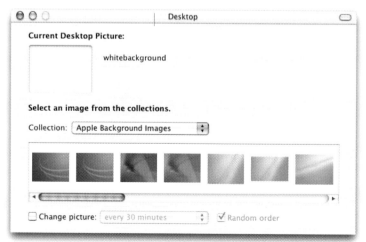

Just as the 'Dock'tor ordered

Dock Preferences give you the choice of changing the position of the Dock, hiding it away, changing its size, and providing special effects for its icons. Read all about this marvellous new feature on (see pages 122-125).

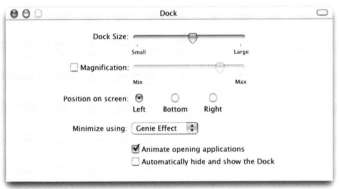

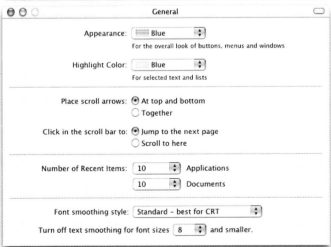

System Preferences

Generally speaking

Minor changes can be made here which don't impact too drastically on your windows, menus, buttons, scroll bars and fonts. These preferences simply allow you to bring a bit of your own style and discernment to the workplace.

General

Under the hood

System Preferences

A slice of Apple pie

Never before has it been so easy to customize your creative workplace ... thanks to Mac OS X. Utilize your 'Personal' Login preferences to full potential. For example, you can split up your jobs into various user accounts, each with their own set of fonts and applications sets. Then, ease your daily stress load by changing your screen saver – although it's not really necessary with today's CRT displays, it is sheer (and vital) pleasure!

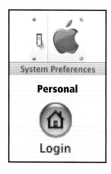

Efficient application
Mac 'oldies' will recall the previous systems StartUp Items folder. This has been replaced by the Login System Preference which cleverly allows applications to automatically start or documents to open when a specific user logs into an account.

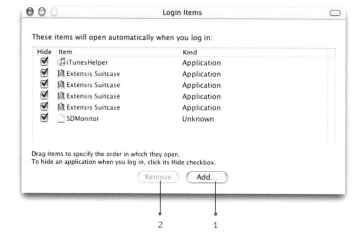

Login setup
Login is simple to set up:
1. Once you are in the Login Items pane (System Preferences > Login) click the 'Add' button.
2. A sheet will appear revealing all items on your System. Select the application you want to start automatically when you login and click on 'Add.'
3. To get rid of any of application you no longer want the system to start up with, at any time, simply select from the Login Items list and click on 'Remove'.

Save-a-screen
With Screen Effects you can: • Select the module of your choice from the Screen Savers list; • Reset various parameters (where

possible) by selecting the Configure button; • Protect flat-panel display and enable screen-dimming by selecting the Open Energy Saver button.

System Preferences

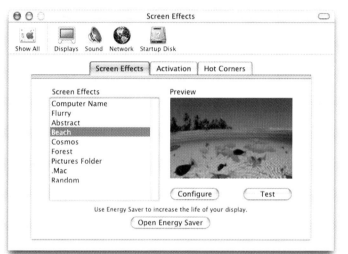

Musical corners
To select a corner to which you can move the mouse to manually start the screen saver, select the Hot Corners button.

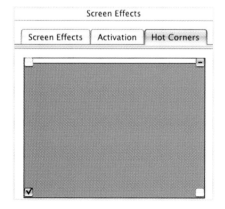

Of passwords and timeframes
Click the Activation tab and set a timeframe for screensaver activation. If you don't require

password-protection, select this option. If you do, you will have to enter your user account password to enter or exit the screensaver.

User friendly access

Individualize the way you work with Universal Access. Going beyond the requirements of the U.S. Federal Government's Section 508 Accessibility statute, the system provides smooth, elegant features to those with difficulties using computers. The pages before you reveal how to allocate one key to do the work of many, navigate integral system controls via the keyboard and prevent unnecessary key repetition.

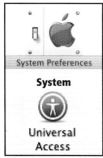

Access control
Universal access features for Seeing, Hearing, Keyboard and Mouse panes can be turned on or off courtesy of these check boxes. They control shortcuts, assistance devices and text-to-speech.

Catch those Zzzz's ...
If you think there is something wrong with your keys (they may be repeating for apparently no reason at all), select this option from (1) or via the mouse pane. (Universal Access > Mouse > Open Keyboard Preferences > Full Keyboard Access.)

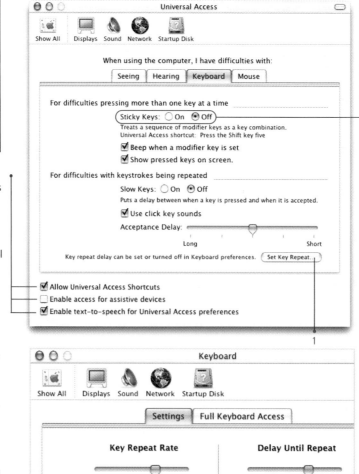

Stick 'em up!
Selecting a series of combination keys can be a problem, which is why many Mac 'oldies' will be delighted to discover that the popular 'Sticky Keys' (from days gone by) has not been discontinued. It works on the 'sound and sight' principle and is a great help for setting the pace of any keyboard combination.
 Activate it by:
(a) pressing 'On' in Sticky Keys (or tap the Shift key five times);
(b) indicating whether or not you would like:
• the system to beep when modifier key is set;
•pressed keys to appear on the screen;
(c) tap a keyboard combination, one at a time and at a comfortable pace.

Under the hood

System Preferences

Note: These panes are fully
detailed in Keyboard preferences
on pages 164, 165.

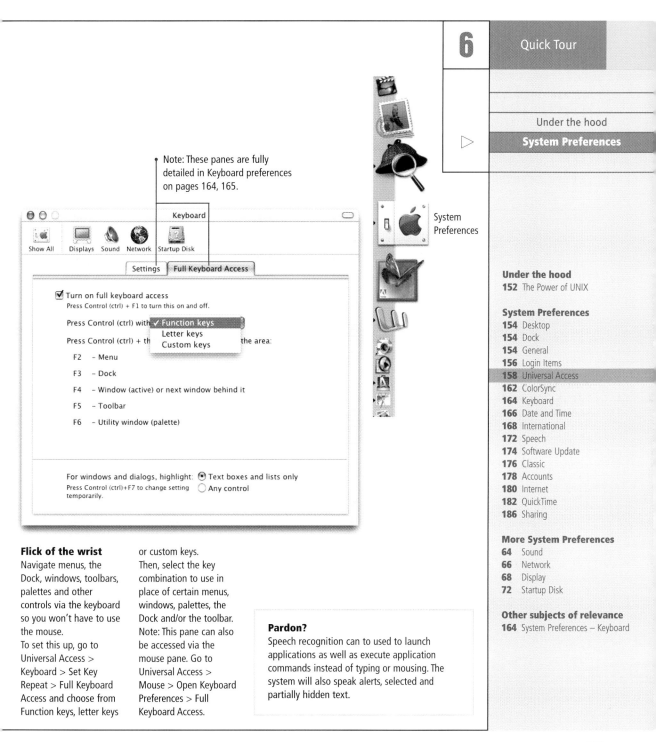

System
Preferences

Flick of the wrist
Navigate menus, the
Dock, windows, toolbars,
palettes and other
controls via the keyboard
so you won't have to use
the mouse.
To set this up, go to
Universal Access >
Keyboard > Set Key
Repeat > Full Keyboard
Access and choose from
Function keys, letter keys

or custom keys.
Then, select the key
combination to use in
place of certain menus,
windows, palettes, the
Dock and/or the toolbar.
Note: This pane can also
be accessed via the
mouse pane. Go to
Universal Access >
Mouse > Open Keyboard
Preferences > Full
Keyboard Access.

Pardon?
Speech recognition can to used to launch
applications as well as execute application
commands instead of typing or mousing. The
system will also speak alerts, selected and
partially hidden text.

User friendly access (2)

Users with keyboard difficulties aren't the only ones to benefit from Universal Access technology. Users with impaired vision will be impressed with Mac OS X's range of options to magnify what's on screen. Users with hearing difficulties, can set up their Macs to flash the screen instead of beeping an alert. Users experiencing difficulty with the mouse can use the numeric keypad to move the cursor around the screen. It's control, convenience and help all the way ...

Access control
Universal Access features for seeing, Hearing (1), Keyboard and Mouse (2) panes can be turned on or off courtesy of these check boxes.
They control shortcuts, assistance devices and text-to-speech.

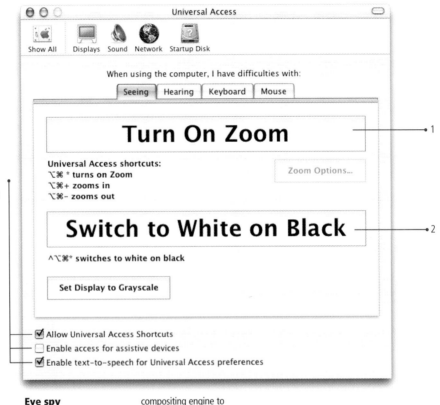

Eye spy
Mac OS X provides a range of options to help those with impaired vision see what's on the screen.
(1) The 'Zoom' display option uses the Quartz rendering and compositing engine to magnify the screen contents and make graphics and type smooth.
(2) The White on Black option gives display higher contrast, allowing text to be read more easily.

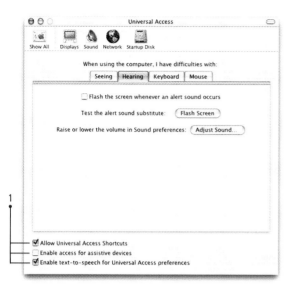

System
Preferences

Flash that screen!

Users who have difficulty hearing may not require a beep alert. A flashing screen is an optional alternative for this, and can be tested before final selection has been made. Note: this pane takes you to Sound preferences for those who prefer a beep alert but may require to adjust the volume.

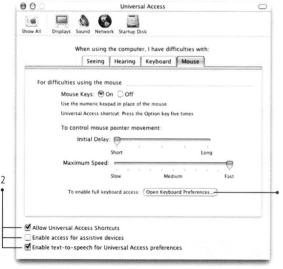

Hide and seek

This option is a great help to those who have trouble using the mouse. It allows you to:

• use the numeric keypad instead of the mouse. (It's really fun to use – choose 1 to go left and down, 3 to go right and down, 7 to go left and up and 9 to go right and up. 5 makes the selection and opens it when double-clicked).
• Fine-tune the speed and reaction of your mouse.
• Enable full keyboard access. Go to keyboard preferences first (see pages 164, 165 for details on this).

Color your World

The panels in the Hardware category control the various components attached to your Macintosh as well as the way they work together. ColorSync, which manages color across input, display, and output devices, is one such tool. And it's very complex, so pay attention! (If you don't ... check out www.apple.com/colorsync).

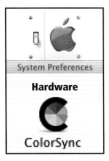

System Preferences

Hardware

ColorSync

Color Capers
Industry standard color management technology, ColorSync provides powerful control over color matching during the workflow process by using distinctive 'profiles' to describe the difference in color performance between input, output and display devices. Each device has individual color reproduction capabilities, indicated from:
• Within the relevant corresponding application (if allowed).
• Within the ColorSync Utility (Applications > Utility > ColorSync).
• Within ColorSync preferences (as indicated here).

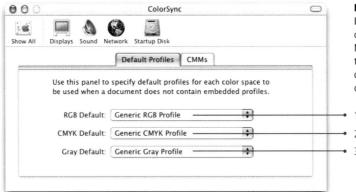

Back to basics
If a document does not contain its own profile, Mac OS X allows users to specify appropriate default profiles for each color space.

Color Set & Match
CMMs (Color Matching Methods) is the technology used to match color based on the profiles you have selected. It converts images from one color space to another (such as from RGB to CMYK). In each step of the workflow, ColorSync compensates for any variations in input, output and/or display devices. The Apple CMM is the default ColorSync CMM and is included with Mac OS. Other CMMs from vendors such as Agfa, Heidelberg, Kodak are also available.

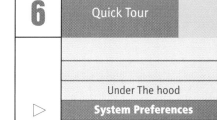

System
Preferences

1. RGB default

RGB-based color spaces are the most commonly used color spaces in computer graphics primarily because they are directly supported by most color displays. Since the colors produced by RGB specifications vary from device to device they are called device-dependent color spaces.
Some examples of RGB default profiles to choose from may include Adobe, Apple, or ColorMatch. In the example depicted (left), the generic RGB Profile has been selected.

3. Grayscale default

Gray spaces typically have a single component, ranging from black to white. Gray spaces are used for black-and-white and grayscale display and printing. In this example only the Generic Gray Profile is available as Grayscale Default.

Black   White

2. CMYK default

As with RGB, colors produced by CMYK specifications are called device-dependent color space since: • CMYK colors vary from printer, ink and paper characteristics; and • different devices have different gamuts or ranges of colors that they can produce.
Some examples of CMYK default profiles to choose from may include: ColorMatch, EuroScale, Japan Standard, Photoshop Default, Web Coated and Web Uncoated. In the example depicted (left), the generic CMYK Profile has been selected.

Key Control

Keyboard preferences (Applications > System Preferences > Keyboard) operate menus and commands on Mac OS X without the mouse. Here's how – use the Full Keyboard Access panel to ensure keyboard-controllable menus, dialog boxes, pop-up menus etc, and Repeat Rate to guard against unnecessary repetition.

System Preferences

Hardware

Keyboard

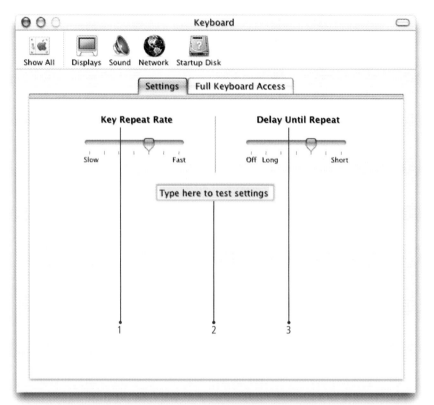

Deja vu?
If you think you've seen these preferences elsewhere in this book, you are definitely paying attention! Keyboard preferences are associated with System Preference's Universal Access and can be accessed via its Mouse and Keyboard panes. (For a quick check, turn back to pages 158-161.)

1. Repeat that, please
A repeating character is a key on the Macintosh keyboard, which when held down, continues to type its corresponding character across the page. This can be controlled by various modes of speed control – dragging the Key Repeat Rate slider from left to right will indicate exactly how slow or fast key repetition occurs.

2, Try it out
When you have chosen your desired 'Repeat Rate' and/or 'Delay until Repeat' rate, use this strip to test your settings.

3. Delayed reaction?
'Delay Until Repeat' options control the repeating procedure involved when you hold your finger on a key. It is advisable to indicate 'Long' delay settings if you're heavy on the keyboard. Select 'Off' if this option is not required.

Under the hood

System Preferences

▷

Easy access

If you prefer using keys instead of the mouse, or have difficulty with the mouse, select 'Full Keyboard Access'. This option allows you to carry out a number of actions with your keyboard, but take note – it only works in applications created specifically for OS X. To toggle between the 'Off' and 'On' control, check the indicated box or press F1.

System Preferences

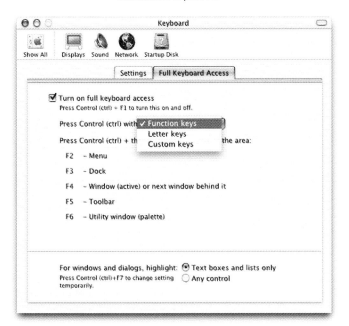

Finger fun

When the 'Full Keyboard Access' option is activated, you can press Control and your assigned key to focus on a certain part of your screen. (In this example press Control+F3 to access the Dock.)
Note: the Control Key can be used with any Function key, custom key or letter key.

Impersonate your mouse

At first, selecting and highlighting items without your mouse requires some patience. Some tips: • Use the Right Arrow and Left Arrow keys to select items from a menu;
• Use the Up and Down Arrow keys to highlight items and the Right Arrow to open a submenu – these must be from a visible menu;
• To action a selected menu command, press Spacebar; • Select the Escape key if you decide not to select anything.

Moments in time

Although you may believe that setting the date and time on Mac OS X is more a convenience than a necessity, this is not strictly true. Date & Time preferences are vital to your Mac for allocating time and date to your documents, deciding when to show you alerts and working out software download time limits. There are a whole bunch of other reasons too, so read on to find out more ...

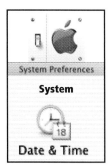

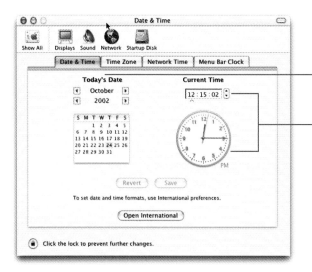

Time for a change?
Changing the date and time is really simple:
• To change the date, click the month and year arrows (either left or right) and then select a date in the calendar;
• To change the time, select the hour, minutes or seconds, then key in the new number/s or click on the arrow buttons instead. (A cute alternative is to drag the hour and minute hands around the clock and see how the time changes!). Click the Save button to confirm if you are happy with your changes.
Note: if you can't change the date and time, go to the 'Network Time' pane (discussed top right) and uncheck the 'Use a network time saver box'.

Virtual traveller
This option is helpful to anyone interested in travel or geography. Educate yourself on various time zones of different countries (simply select the continent of your choice and ensure that the drop-down menu corresponds to the country that your querying.)

CLEVER OS X
If you are in a time zone that changes to daylight savings, your clever Mac switches over automatically.

Network connect

Connect to a network time server if you have a full-time connection (for example ISDN, DSL, cable, satellite, etc.). This will ensure that your computer accurately displays the correct time.

Be aware that: (a) If you check the 'Use a network time server' box, all changes to the time in the Date & Time pane will be restricted;
(b) You should not check the 'Use a network time server box' if you have a dial-up connection.

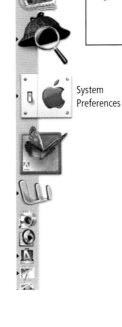

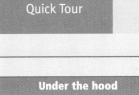 System Preferences

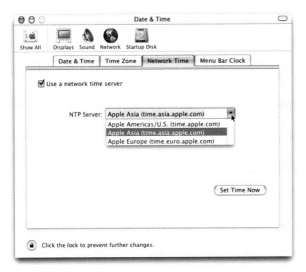

What a view!

The 'show the clock in the menu bar' option can be unchecked if you don't require the time to be shown in the menu bar. If 'show the clock in the menu bar' is checked, two viewing options are available for your convenience. Choices, choices and more choices ...

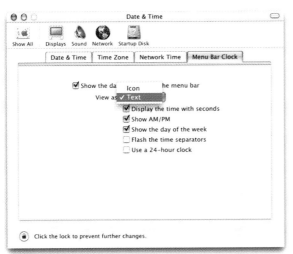

It's a small world after all

Mac OS X weaves a coat of many colors with its liberal support for international languages. Controlled through the International window, it can be accessed via System Preferences or Customize menu (find the flag, indicating International panel, to the right of the Help menu). Not only are its abilities more innovative than ever before, but it allows you to shift from language to language without reinstalling software or restarting your computer.

Multi-lingual maze
Dragging your preferred language to the top of this list will ensure that OS X and OS X-compatible software can work in other languages. Every button, menu and dialog box will be language selected.

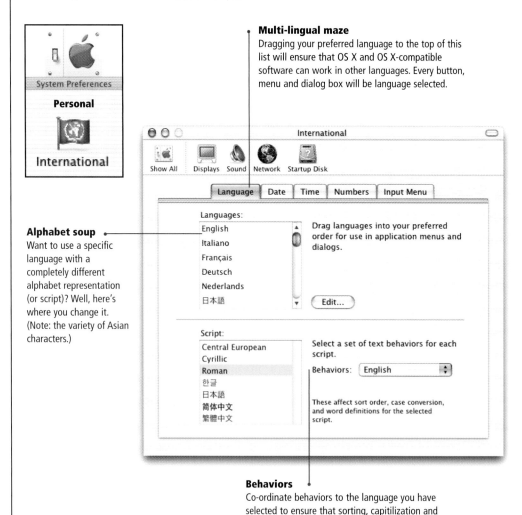

Alphabet soup
Want to use a specific language with a completely different alphabet representation (or script)? Well, here's where you change it. (Note: the variety of Asian characters.)

Behaviors
Co-ordinate behaviors to the language you have selected to ensure that sorting, capitilization and word definitions follow suit.

Pick of the crop
Selecting the Edit button from the International window allows you to choose the ones you want to appear in the Languages list .. up to 23 different languages are available.

System Preferences

TextEdit speaks Italian ... and more
After you have specified your preferred language from the International window, open a program like Internet Explorer, Stickies, Sherlock or TextEdit (if already open, quit first and relaunch). Then, notice how every menu, button and dialog box follows suit. (The only thing it doesn't do is translate, but then again you wouldn't be working in an unknown language, now would you?).

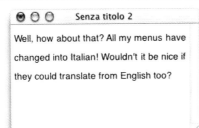

OPENTYPE AND UNICODE
Mac OS X introduces new OpenType font technology. This format takes advantage of Unicode, which, combined with the International and Keyboard preferences built into the Mac, makes your computer truly international. (See also page 191.)

SYNOPSIS

It's a small world after all (2)

Yesterday the world, today the global village. Mac OS X's International preferences pane caters for wanderlust junkies who require the date, time and/or number formatting of various regions. And it makes it really simple for each user to customize and maintain these settings separately.

System Preferences

Personal

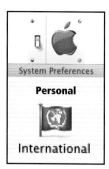

International

Date and Time

Although some users aren't too concerned about the intricacies of date and time, it is a vital part of the Mac's operating system. For example, just think where you would be if you could not locate a file because it had not been dated or time-stamped?

Time to choose

• Select whether to use a 12 or 24 hour clock here.
• Noon and midnight – how should they be indicated? It's your call.

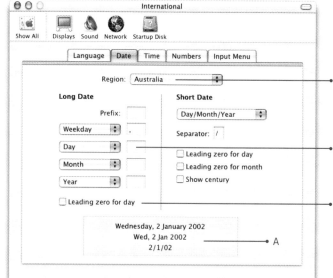

Date with destiny

• Non-US date settings and appearance can be specified here. (Note: Custom appears in the Region pop-up menu when other settings are changed in the Date tab.)
• You can add any text you want to appear before the long date by typing it in the Prefix box.
• Selecting this option enables dates prior to the 10th of the month to appear with a zero prefix.

High Noon

Set your time preferences before and after noon (am or pm) and indicate the type of separating punctuation you would like between hour and minute.

Naughts and crosses

Selecting this option enables dates prior to the 10th of the month to appear with a zero prefix.

Numbers galore

The numbers tab lets you specify: • Which characters you want to use when decimal numbers are displayed; • Your preference with regards to decimal thousands to be projected with a comma (1,000) or a point (1.000); • Region; and • Currency symbol.

System Preferences

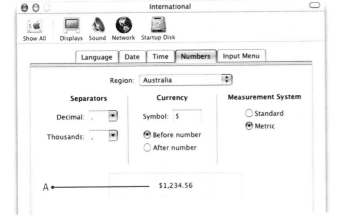

(A) Sneak peek

Results of all changes made in the Date, Time and Numbers tabs are displayed here.

Keyboard menu

Mac OS X gives you a bunch of checkboxes that determine international keyboard mapping.
(Note: that your selection will be displayed in the Finder's International menu bar too.)

Mind your language

Imagine being able to talk to your computer and get it to carry out tasks such as launching and quitting applications, opening and closing windows – even checking your e-mail. Well, in Mac OS X it has become a reality using Speech preferences. It's easy and fun to use and won't require too much gray matter to work out. Try it – you're sure to like it.

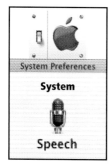

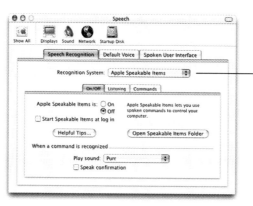

Open Speech Commands window
Speech Preferences...

Feedback Window
When 'Apple Speakable Items' is activated (see on/off pane) you will notice the appearance of a circular feedback window.
Click the arrow at the bottom of the feedback window and choose 'Open Speech Commands' window to get a list of commands.

Speech Recognition
Speech Recognition gives your Mac the ability to recognize and respond to human voices. Provided that you have a microphone (or one already built into your Mac), you can start using Speech Recognition immediately – it won't need to be 'trained' to . learn your voice.
Note: Speech Recognition can only be used on applications that support it.

Who's speaking?
1. Activate your Mac's response with the listening key (in this case Escape).
2. This 'Listening Method' indicates that the Escape key must be depressed for approximately half a second as a sign that you will soon be sending a command to your Mac.
3. Should you need to have the listening switched off at times, you can change your selection. Simply depress the Escape key for approximately a second. This will turn listening on until you hold down the key again.

On demand commands
With a program using Apple Speech Recognition, you can ask 'What time is it?' (General Speakable Items command), or open your spreadsheet by saying 'Open the February forecast', (Specific Application command), or use voice command to switch out of the game you are playing and back into Adobe Photoshop (Application switching command).

Eloquent alerts

Use the Spoken User Interface pane to select when you would like text to be converted into spoken commands from your Mac. As well as using talking alerts, you can also get your computer to speak to you when:

• an application requires your attention; • text is partially hidden due to the position of your mouse on screen; and • a certain key (your choice) is pressed. Note: different settings are demonstrated to give you a better idea of sound you are in store for.

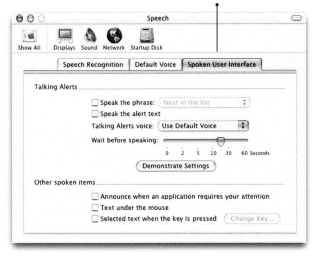

System Preferences

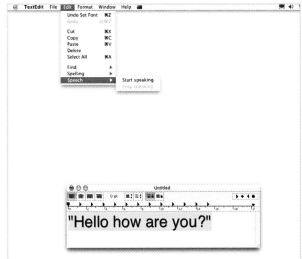

Just listen!

Once you have chosen a voice (Speech > Default Voice) for the computer to use, you can adjust the speed at which it will talk. Your nominated 'voice' will feature whenever an application is speakable. Open a document in TextEdit, select Edit > Speech > Start Speaking. Sit back and listen.

Keeping up with the Joneses

Your Mac has the ability to keep itself fit by automatically downloading software updates from the Internet. This feature is called Software Update, and you control it via the Software Update panel in Mac OS X's System Preferences.

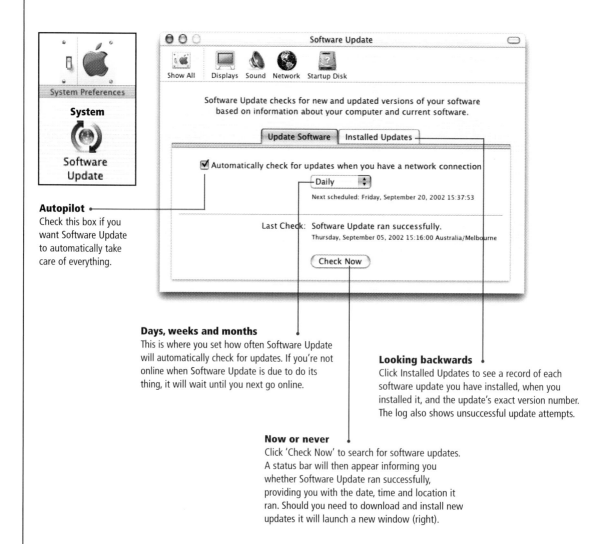

Autopilot
Check this box if you want Software Update to automatically take care of everything.

Days, weeks and months
This is where you set how often Software Update will automatically check for updates. If you're not online when Software Update is due to do its thing, it will wait until you next go online.

Looking backwards
Click Installed Updates to see a record of each software update you have installed, when you installed it, and the update's exact version number. The log also shows unsuccessful update attempts.

Now or never
Click 'Check Now' to search for software updates. A status bar will then appear informing you whether Software Update ran successfully, providing you with the date, time and location it ran. Should you need to download and install new updates it will launch a new window (right).

Time for action

When Software Updates finds an update for you to install, it presents you with this window. If any of the updates that it shows you are not relevant to your needs, select them then choose Make Inactive from the Update menu. Software Updates will no longer ask you to install them, unless you choose Show Inactive Updates from the Update menu and then reactivate the updates. Put a tick in the install box of each update that you do wish to install, and then click the Install button. You will need an administrator's password to complete the process.

System Preferences

000   Software Update

Software Update found the following new or updated software for your computer.

Click the checkbox to select the software you want to install:

Install	Name	▲ Version	Size
☑	Mac OS X Update	10.2.1	16.9MB
☑	iTunes	3.0.1	5.8MB

The 10.2.1 Update delivers enhancements and improvements to the following applications, technologies and components: Mail, Image Capture, Help Viewer, graphics, printing, networking, Rendezvous, Kerberos, USB, FireWire, SCSI device compatibility and includes additional Digital Hub peripheral device support.

Status: Not installed, restart will be required.

Updates to install: 2   (Install)

Under the hood

THE WHOLE KIT AND CABOODLE

Software Update can update Mac OS X and the programs that Apple preloaded on your Mac. However, it can't update the programs that you have added to your Mac yourself. Some of these programs will up-to-date themselves automatically. Visit: www.versiontracker.com/macosx/ to check for updates for the rest. (See also page 272.)

HOT TIP

The way things were

Mac OS X's 'Classic' environment is a bit like running the old Mac OS 9 and the new Mac OS X side-by-side on your Mac. Your Mac OS 9 programs won't benefit from Mac OS X's best features when they run in Classic mode, but at least they should run. If you can't update all your programs for Mac OS X, here's how to make the most of Classic.

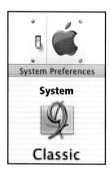

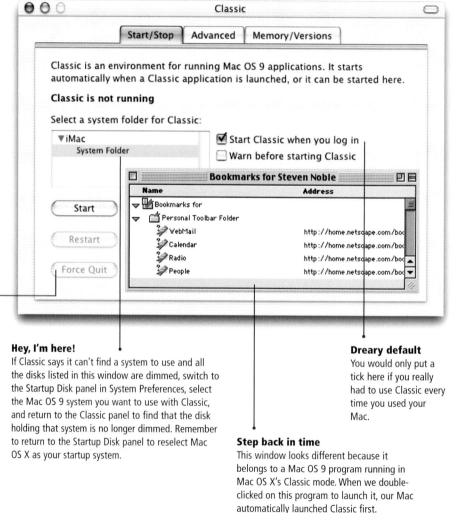

First stop, preferences
To control the behavior of Classic, visit the Classic panel in Mac OS X's System Preferences.

The traffic lights
When you're done with using Classic, click the Stop button to free up system resources. Restarting Classic could solve temporary problems with your Mac OS 9 programs, just like restarting a Mac that's running Mac OS 9. Only force Classic to quit if clicking the Stop button does not work. If Classic was not running, there would be a Start button here, not a Stop button

Hey, I'm here!
If Classic says it can't find a system to use and all the disks listed in this window are dimmed, switch to the Startup Disk panel in System Preferences, select the Mac OS 9 system you want to use with Classic, and return to the Classic panel to find that the disk holding that system is no longer dimmed. Remember to return to the Startup Disk panel to reselect Mac OS X as your startup system.

Step back in time
This window looks different because it belongs to a Mac OS 9 program running in Mac OS X's Classic mode. When we double-clicked on this program to launch it, our Mac automatically launched Classic first.

Dreary default
You would only put a tick here if you really had to use Classic every time you used your Mac.

Old problems, old fixes

Remember, running Classic is like running Mac OS 9 alongside Mac OS X. So, if Classic starts misbehaving, you have to try all those boring troubleshooting tricks that we used to depend on in the days of Mac OS 9, like rebuilding Classic's Mac OS 9 desktop database or restarting Classic with all Mac OS 9 extensions disabled. Find these tricks under the Advanced tab of the Classic panel in Mac OS X's System Preferences. Or, use Mac OS X native software exclusively and farewell all these hassles forever.

System Preferences

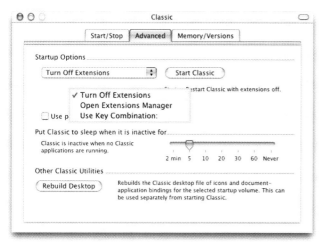

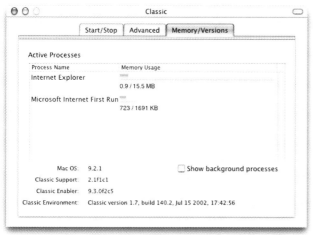

Old faithful

Mac oldies will recognize this one. The Memory/Versions pane is a sleek reconstruction of the previous operating systems' 'About this Computer' window. Use it to check memory and version information on the Classic environment, operating system, support and applications – to name just a few.

One more place at the table

If you are the appointed Administrator and plan to set up accounts for other people using your Mac, there are two preference panes you'll work with, Accounts and Login. Since we have already covered the Login preference on pages 156, 157, the Accounts pane is currently our focus. This is the place where you will not only go to create users and assign them a login picture and password, but edit and delete user accounts too.

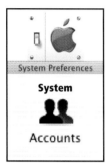

What's in a name?
In Mac OS X 10.2 you create, edit and delete accounts in the Accounts pane of System Preferences. Before Mac OS X 10.2 you would do this in the Users panel of Mac OS X's System Preferences. Same concept, different name.

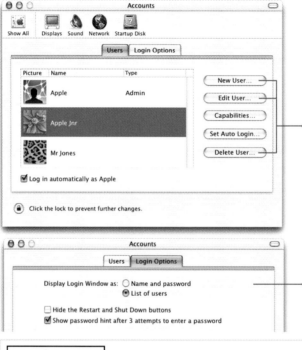

Hatch, match and dispatch
As you can see (left) three users are currently registered. The preferences for each user can be changed at any time, and new ones can be added. Any user (except the administrator) can be deleted.

At your own risk
Your Login window can display either a list of users, or the current user's name and password (only a row of bullets will be shown for obvious reasons).
You can also get your computer to provide a password hint after three incorrect attempts. The 'Hide the Restart and Shut Down buttons' box for is useful for security reasons.

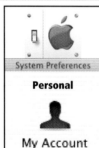

Personal Profile
To check on your account details (or to find out which user you are currently logged in as), go to System Preferences > Personal > My Account. There you will not only find the current user name but you will also have the choice of changing your password, user picture and address book card.

1. Mac of many faces
The Identity pane will pop up when you have chosen either to create a new user or edit/ delete an existing user.
• To create a new user: Select System Preferences > Accounts > Users > New User. Type in the full name in the Name field. A short name will automatically be created and is easily editable. • To edit an existing user: Select System Preferences > Accounts > Users > Edit User. Click on the name of the user you wish to change, and make changes to name or login picture as required.
• To delete an existing user: Select System Preferences > Accounts > Users > Delete User. A message will then prompt you to confirm this action and ask where the user's folders is to be moved to.

System Preferences

2. Rules and regulations
One of the administrator's duties is to oversee what facilities other users are entitled to use on the system. It is up to the administrator to allow or disallow other users to remove items from the Dock, open all System Preferences, change passwords and/or burn discs. In addition, a restriction can be placed on which applications a user can utilize.

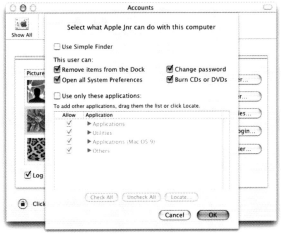

Split personality

The Internet panel of System Preferences has two purposes: to consolidate preferences for essential programs like your Web browser and e-mail program, and to sell you on Apple's optional .Mac internet service by making it easier to join, manage and use.

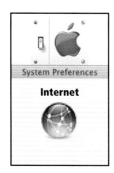

System Preferences

Internet

Off-site storage
If you sign up for .Mac, you get a 'virtual hard disk' is accessible via the Internet from any Mac.

Use the iDisk panel to view available free space on your iDisk, buy more space from Apple, and to control who can access it.

Name, rank and serial number
Once you enter your .Mac name and password, that information is available throughout your system. For example, when you click the Mail tab you'll see that your Mac can use this information to automatically connect you to your .Mac e-mail account — no fiddling required.

.Mac wants you
Apple's .Mac service isn't compulsory, but you could find it really handy. To get in on the action, click this button.

What is .Mac?
.Mac is an optional service from Apple. For an annual fee, you get a range of internet services that seamlessly integrate with Mac OS X, including:

- a virus-protected e-mail address you can take with you when you change ISPs;
- a simple, template-based Web publishing system;
- new uses for your iPhoto collection, including Web photo albums and electronic postcards;
- online storage that you can use for backups, file transfers and loads of other purposes; and
  Curious? Point your Web browser at: www.mac.com

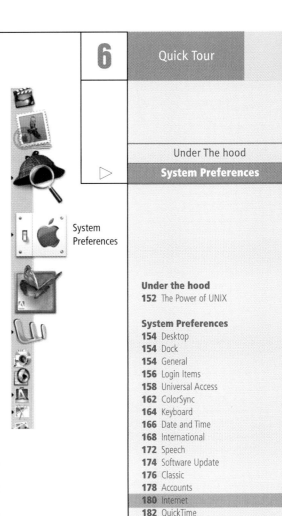

System
Preferences

Pick your provider

If you want to make Entourage or
Eudora or something else your default
e-mail program (the program that
opens when you click on an e-mail
address in a Web page), choose Select
from this menu and find your program.
If you do nothing, Mac OS X's Mail (see
pages 146, 147) will be your default.

Expanding Web

The Web panel lets you pick your
default Web browser, as the Mail panel
lets you pick your default e-mail
program. Go there too if you want to
change your Web browser's home page
or where it will save the files it
downloads.

Self-saucing preferences

Subscribed to Apple's .Mac service?
Want your .Mac account to be your
default e-mail account? If you put a tick
in this checkbox, your Mac will fill every
field in this screen, providing you with
zero-fiddle access to your e-mail.

Follow the numbers

Your ISP can tell you what to type here —
just hop on the phone and ask questions
like 'what's my incoming mail server?',
and 'what about my user account ID?'.

Digital Media Delivery

The powerful multimedia architecture of QuickTime lets you view, create, import and export media on your computer. Its free, open source, standards-based QuickTime Streaming Server delivers media either in real-time or on-demand over the Internet (data is displayed on delivery and not stored on your hard drive). This innovative application provides an abundance of media authoring capabilities, as revealed here.

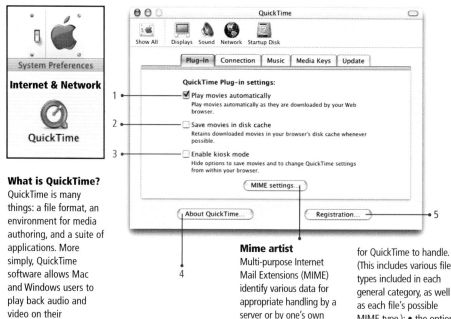

What is QuickTime?
QuickTime is many things: a file format, an environment for media authoring, and a suite of applications. More simply, QuickTime software allows Mac and Windows users to play back audio and video on their computers.

Multi-mannerisms
QuickTime plug-in settings affect the way QuickTime behaves in your Web browser. In short: **(1)** Movies are played automatically when this option is checked (Mac OS X selects it by default). **(2)** Instant replay of downloaded movies is possible when this setting is selected. (Note: to use this feature, you must have enough space in your browser's cache.) **(3)** To avoid clogging up your hard disk with big files, select 'Enable kiosk mode.' It disables the pop-up menu which usually appears when viewing a movie in a browser, hiding options to save movies (including drag and drop copying of movies).

Introducing ... QuickTime 6
When QuickTime was first released ten years ago it revolutionized the industry. Today, the revolution continues with QuickTime 6, featuring: MPEG-4; DVC Pro PAL video codec; immediate and smooth 'Instant-on' and MPEG-2 playback; skip protection; an easy-to-use 'Favorites' interface; enhanced AppleScript support; JPEG 2000 still image codec; support for Macromedia Flash 5 and a whole lot more. (Read all about it on pages 148, 149.)

Mime artist
Multi-purpose Internet Mail Extensions (MIME) identify various data for appropriate handling by a server or by one's own computer. In this example, the MIME settings pane provides:
• a list of general data type categories available for QuickTime to handle. (This includes various file types included in each general category, as well as each file's possible MIME type.); • the option to customize which file types for QuickTime to handle; and • the option to revert to the original MIME default settings.

Information kiosk
(4) Display a slide show of QuickTime developers logos and relevant Web site address details.

Officially yours
(5) Register and upgrade your copy of QuickTime online for US$29.99. Simply select this button and enter the necessary information in a separate window.

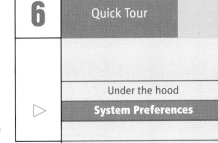

A   B

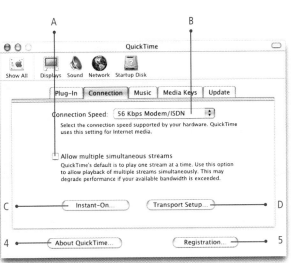

System
Preferences

Connection chaos?

This pane contains sections which effect the download, speed and quality for QuickTime media playing in a Web browser. These include:
A. Expedient media delivery (taking into account hardware limitations as well as the speed of Internet connection); **B.** Multiple simultaneous stream option, but as cautioned, this could be at the expense of performance if bandwidth is exceeded. (In most cases users would be safer to leave this option unchecked.); **C.** Instant-On. Selecting it will bring up a sheet which allows streamed media to be played automatically. Once this is enabled,there is a choice of response level, ranging from immediate to short delay. (Note: although streamed media will start playing without delay, it is important to be aware that network congestion may reduce the quality of playback.); **D.** The Transport Setup button opens a window allowing QuickTime to select preferred protocol for data transmission.

Making music

Musicians will find this option particularly useful. In addition to the QuickTime Music Synthesizer (pictured left), other newly-installed third party music synthesizers will appear in this list. To select music files handled by your synthesizer (other than the QuickTime one), make appropriate selection and choose 'Make Default'.

Digital Media Delivery (2)

Security measures and regular software updates are a vital part of Mac OS X, so it's not surprising that these concerns are addressed in many custom made applications too. Hop across to the QuickTime preference settings to manage viewing restrictions and update QuickTime and QuickTime third party software ... quick as a flash and oh, so easy!

QuickTime 6

The digital media standard.

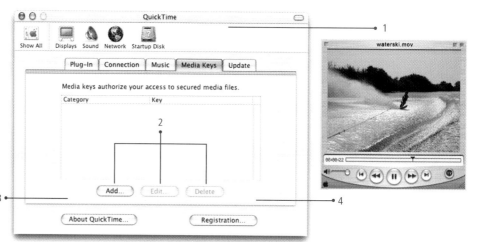

Key to security
(1) Security measures are sometimes employed on certain QuickTime files using passwords or media keys that lock the file. In order to authorize access and utilize such files, the user must enter the media key and file category information into the Media Keys pane. **(2)** Media key information can be added, deleted and edited as illustrated above.

(3) Info Kiosk
Selecting this button will display a slide show of QuickTime developers logos and relevant Web site address details.

(4) Officially yours
Register and upgrade your copy of QuickTime online for US$29.99. Simply select this button and enter the necessary information in a separate window.

QuickTime Player   QuickTime Pro   Streaming Server   Broadcaster

Introducing ... the QuickTime Suite
• QuickTime Player: for playing back audio and video files; • QuickTime Pro: for flexible multimedia authoring; • Browser plug-ins: for viewing media within a Web page; • PictureViewer: for working with still images; • QuickTime Streaming Server: for delivering streaming media files on the Internet in real-time; • Darwin Streaming Server: for delivering streaming media with Linux, Solaris, and Windows; and • QuickTime Broadcaster: for delivering live events on the Internet.
(See pages 148, 149.)

Instant connection
With a click of the 'Update Now' button you can connect to the QuickTime Web site to monitor updates and/or to install new third party software. There is also the extra facility to enable automatic updates at anytime — provided that the QuickTime Player is open.

 System Preferences

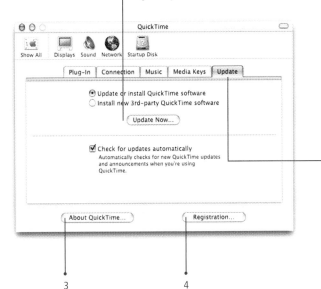

Keeping regular
The Update pane is a must-use. With it you can check online for QuickTime software updates and install QuickTime or third-party QuickTime software.

3   4

QuickTime Broadcaster

Broadcasting the digital media standard.

Share and share alike

No Mac is an island. If you want to share your files, your printer, or anything else with your friendly, neighbourhood Mac or Windows users, the Sharing panel in System Preferences is the place to do it. (Likewise if you want to keep it all to yourself.)

System Preferences

Internet & Network

Sharing

IP is everything
The services in the Sharing panel generally use TCP/IP — the networking protocol that underlies the Internet — to do their thing. Hence it's handy to see your TCP/IP address ('Network Address') in the Sharing panel, together with a direct link ('Edit...') to the Network panel, where you can change it.

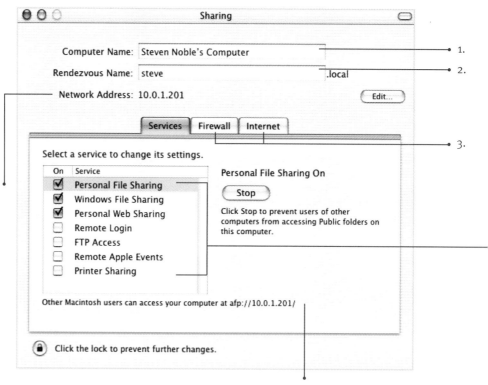

Time for action
Because we've switched on Personal File Sharing, other Mac OS X users on your local network can browse the contents of our Public folder. To do this, they would select 'Connect To Server' from the Go menu and enter the address given here.

1. Public image
If you enable Personal File Sharing, then other users will see this name when they search for your computer on their local network.

3. No extra charge
When Apple released version 10.2 of Mac OS X, it added two natty new features to the Sharing panel — a firewall, and instant Internet sharing. They're explained on (pages 266, 267).

System Preferences

2. Otherwise known as
Rendezvous is Apple's name for Zeroconf, a nifty new technology that allows computers, printers and other devices to find each on a local network without any fiddling by the user. Stick two Mac OS X 10.2 systems on the same local network, and — thanks to Rendezvous — they'll be able to instantly yak via iChat (see pages 144, 145). Stick a Zeroconf printer on the same network as a Mac OS X computer, and the Mac will be able to see and use the printer instantly.

Personal File Sharing
Provide other Mac users with access to some of the files on your hard disk.
Windows File Sharing
Give Windows users the same access.
Personal Web Sharing
Host a Web site from your Mac.
Remote Login
Connect to your Mac from another, via the UNIX command line.

FTP Access
Allow friends to download files from your Mac via the Web.
Remote Apple Events
Allow an AppleScript (see pages 298-307) running on another Mac to communicate with yours.
Printer Sharing
Share your Mac's printer with other Macs on your network.

Service checklist
Note: if you opted out of installing the BSD subsystem when you installed Mac OS X, you will not be able to use the FTP Access and Remote Login services.

TECH TIP

Doing things

Private collection

Mac OS X is a dream to use. Its Quartz rendering engine displays fonts that are beautifully rendered and anti-aliased, have automatic ligatures and kerning controls and look great onscreen and in print. Not only this, but there are a variety of free fonts to choose from and an easy-to-use user interface for font management.

Fonts & Ligatures & Filtering, Oh my!

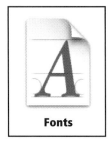

Fonts

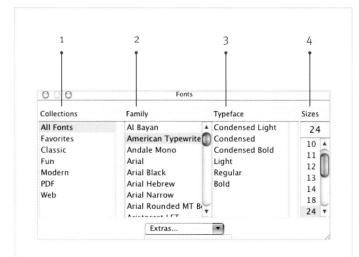

1. Collections
Several collections are made for you, and you can create your own collection of virtually any font you'd like and need quick access to. To see which group lives in which folder, simply click on a collection. Note: when you click a collection name, all of the other fonts in the list disappear. Don't worry – it's only temporary!

2. Family
The selected collection will indicate the corresponding font family. Clicking on a collection automates a dark gray selection and brings up a family's 'members' in this column.

3. Typeface
Going one step further brings up more information about the typestyle of the individual font as selected in the family column.

4. Sizes
Once the size of the font required is selected (highlighted), it appears in the text entry field at the top of the column. The text entry field has a dual purpose – it can also be modified to specify a size not displayed.

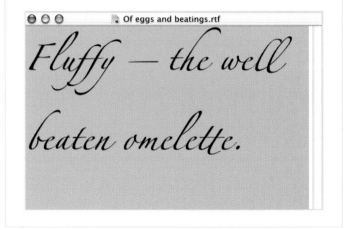

COPPERPLATE
FUTURA
Gill Sans
Helvetica Neue
Optima

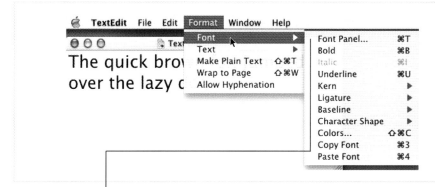

Fonts panel

Want to get immediate access to the fonts you require? This four columned Fonts panel offers a variety of ways of viewing installed fonts.

New in Mac OS X and found in Apple's Mail, TextEdit and other applications, it lets you choose fonts and colors in a consistent manner helping you become the terrific organizer you were always meant to be!

Note: your Classic Mac OS 9 fonts in your system folder are also automatically visible in the Fonts panel.

優れた表現力

Support system

Users will be delighted to find that Mac OS X has no limits on font support. In addition to maintaining the fonts Mac users have become accustomed to, there are now other font technologies to utilize. OpenType is one, and this, together with Mac OS X's in-built capabilities such as International and Keyboard preferences, provide users with a whole bunch of international fonts.

Get it 'write'

Before Mac OS X came along, it was exhausting and time-consuming to find samples of the fonts you had installed on your system. Not anymore. Apple has provided users with a Script that opens in TextEdit, and automatically types out all font samples in a flash. In addition, for those who were previously confused about font installation, the system provides you with definite guidelines, disallowing RAM abuse and providing convenience and security.

Fonts

Sampling your wares
Want to see something nifty? Go to Finder > Applications > AppleScript > Example Scripts > Info Scripts > Font Sampler.scpt. This clever little script opens TextEdit, types dozens of sentences (the same over and over again), each with its own font sample, conveniently labeled with that font name. Just what you always wanted!

COPPERPLATE
FUTURA
Gill Sans
Helvetica Neue
Optima

▷

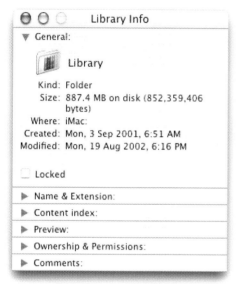

Font installation made easy

1. If you're the kind of person who likes to share things with other users, you can install your fonts in the System Library Fonts folder (this will only work if you are logged in as Administrator).
2. On the other hand, you can place any 'exclusive' fonts into the fonts folder in the Library of your Home folder. This will restrict viewing and ensure that fonts stored there are for your eyes only.
3. Fonts can also be installed into the Fonts folder in each individual user's Home folder. But in this case those fonts will only be seen by the particular user in question.
4. Things are just the same in Mac OS 9, and if you are a user that still accesses a lot of Classic applications you can install fonts to your heart's content just as you always did.

Note: never put fonts in the main system Library fonts folder. (Nothing drastic will happen – the system will simply stop you from going any further.)

Mac OS X font technology
In addition to maintaining the fonts Mac users have become accustomed to, there are now other font technologies to utilize. In a nutshell:
• PostScript Type 1: printer and screen fonts alike;• Mac TrueType: distinguished by TT;
• Mac.dfonts TrueType fonts with the extension .dfont: accessible on various platforms; • Mac OpenType fonts (.otf): embraces the OpenType and Unicode technology, essential for Korean and Japanese languages; • Windows TrueType fonts (.TTF), and Windows OpenType fonts (.OFT): excellent for cross-platform work (you can use the same font for both platforms). However, ensure that it works first before experimenting!

HERCULANUM
American Typewriter
Marker Felt
Papyrus
Zapfino

Extra fun with fonts

Mac OS X's all-new font panel, found in TextEdit and Mail (Format > Font > Show Fonts) comes complete with an 'Extras' pop-up menu that allows you to add fonts (complete with style and size) to Favorites, edit existing Collections, add color and buy new fonts. With such ingenuity you can see why ATM (Adobe Type Manager) is no longer part of the system.

Fonts

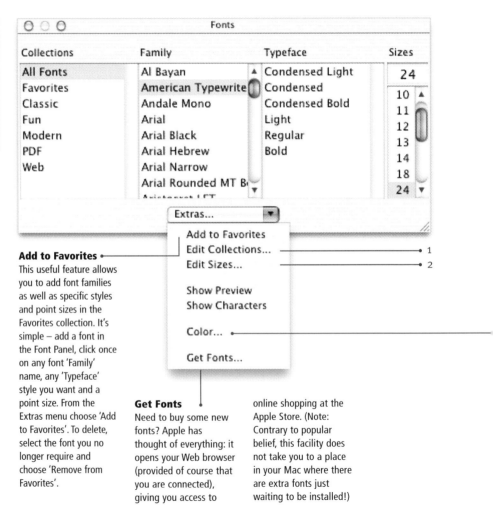

Add to Favorites
This useful feature allows you to add font families as well as specific styles and point sizes in the Favorites collection. It's simple – add a font in the Font Panel, click once on any font 'Family' name, any 'Typeface' style you want and a point size. From the Extras menu choose 'Add to Favorites'. To delete, select the font you no longer require and choose 'Remove from Favorites'.

Get Fonts
Need to buy some new fonts? Apple has thought of everything: it opens your Web browser (provided of course that you are connected), giving you access to online shopping at the Apple Store. (Note: Contrary to popular belief, this facility does not take you to a place in your Mac where there are extra fonts just waiting to be installed!)

COPPERPLATE

FUTURA

Gill Sans

Helvetica Neue

Optima

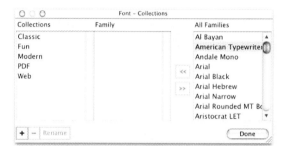

1. Edit Collections
Create and remove your font collections, using Edit Collections. To add, choose 'Edit Collections', select collection and go to the column entitled All Families. Select font and click on the black arrow button to move in Family column. To delete, choose 'Edit Collections', click on the collection name (far left), select font in 'Family' column and click on the black arrow button.

Font Management

Other subjects of relevance

2. Edit Sizes
A quick and easy way of editing preset font sizes and entering new sizes, 'Edit Sizes' lets you change the Sizes control so you can drag a slider to resize your selected text. As you drag, notice an increase or decrease in text.

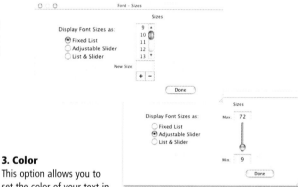

3. Color
This option allows you to set the color of your text in a very sophisticated way. Choose from either the Color wheel, Color Palettes, Color Spectrum and/or modes such as RGB, CMYK and Hue, Saturation and Brightness. Colors can either be dragged and dropped to highlighted text or Applied. Favorite colors can be kept in an eight slot mixer palette and dragged out at random.

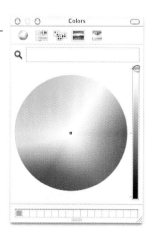

ATM no more?
Because Mac OS X takes care of font rendering on the screen and to the PostScript printer so well, Adobe's (ol' faithful) Type Manager is no longer needed. It seems that Adobe has so much confidence in OS X's type management ability that it is planning to discontinue the ATM line of products.

SYNOPSIS

Installing Mac OS X

If you are installing Mac OS X on your G4, there are a number of issues you should consider. You may need to update your computer's firmware. The updates may be on the installation CD. Your computer should have at least Mac OS 9.1 and 128Mb of RAM. There should be internal monitor support, or an Apple supplied IXMicro, ATI or nVidia video card installed, as well as at least 1.5Gb of disk space.

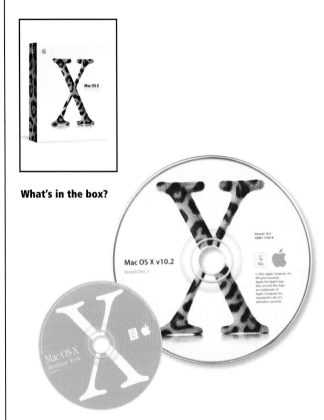

What's in the box?

Developer Tools
This CD contains software and documentation for developing applications on Mac OS X. Only install this if you intend to develop applications.

The System
The latest version of the Mac OS X system is delivered on a single disc. Follow the prompts, choose where to install and the system is installed automatically.

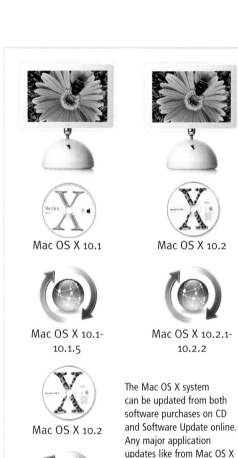

Mac OS X 10.1

Mac OS X 10.2

Mac OS X 10.1-10.1.5

Mac OS X 10.2.1-10.2.2

Mac OS X 10.2

Mac OS X 10.2.1-10.2.2

The Mac OS X system can be updated from both software purchases on CD and Software Update online. Any major application updates like from Mac OS X 10.1.5 to 10.2 are available on CD. However, security, networking and other firmware updates can easily be downloaded.

Authenticate
When you install Mac OS X, you need to create a user account. This must be an administrator. As the administrator, user accounts can be added, you can change certain system settings, set up for multiple users and have greater access to the system settings.

License agreement
The license agreement covers the rights and restrictions pertaining to the use of the software.

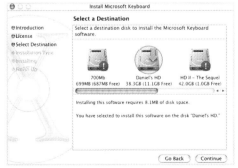

Select a destination
A destination for the Mac OS X system can be the same place as Mac OS 9 if you choose. Alternatively, you may choose to install Mac OS X on a separate, dedicated partition on your hard drive. Click the 'Install' button and after a short while, it is done.

Installing an application

There are two basic strategies by which applications are installed. There is the drag-and-drop method where the disk image is simply dragged to the required location. The second way is using the Apple Installer. You could install it in your Home directory, but no one else can use the application once the installation is there. To allow all users to be able to access and use the application, install it in the Applications directory. To do this, you must be logged in as an Administrator.

Authenticate
Enter your name and password to authenticate your use of the computer. You can do most things as a User, but need to be logged in an as Administrator to install the software. The installation process will begin automatically once your identity has been authenticated.

License agreement
This agreement covers the legal and copyright points pertaining to the application as it arrives on your computer.
It is best to read these just so you know.

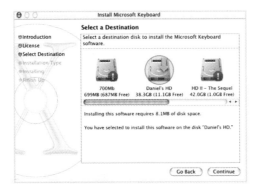

Select a destination
Applications can be installed in any location if you are logged in as an administrator.
As a user, it is best to install them in the 'Applications' folder, so everyone can see and use them. The Apple Installer will take you through similar panels as the Mac OS X installation and install it painlessly.

Installation successful

Under the Admin log-in, applications can be installed in one of two ways. You can use the installer application as shown, or you can drag the disk image straight to the Applications folder on the drive.

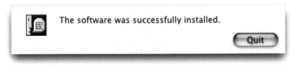

If all goes well, this is the dialog that appears.

Classic applications

When installing applications to be used only under the Classic environment, you may want to install them in the 'Applications (Mac OS 9)' folder. If you find there are problems installing the application where you want to, log in as Administrator if you are able. As you can install the application anywhere you like. If you find there are other problems installing Classic software while using Mac OS X, boot up your computer using Mac OS 9 (Systems Preferences > Startup Disk) and then install the software.

Alternate installation method

Under the Admin log-in, applications can be installed in one of two ways. You can use the installer application as shown, or you can drag the disk image straight to the Applications folder on the drive.

Root user installation

On rare occasions, some high-end applications may only be installed by going through to the 'root user' level. Administrator level command line moves such as this are best done with a steady hand. (Read more about this operation on pages 248, 249.)

UPDATE TIPS

You can save updates to install on a network of computers. This want to install the update on them without accessing the Internet for each time you need an update.

HOT TIP

Updating Mac OS X

Unless you have the updates on the CD in your hand, the Internet-based Software Update will allow on-line updating to your system. A new Apple installer, which opens and distributes to the appropriate directories is settled neatly in the Applications > Utilities folder sporting a '.pkg' extension. This installer assists in the updating of Mac OS X via the Software Update System Preferences panel.

Software updates
Software Update can be set to check automatically for updates on a regular basis. You can also click the 'Update Now' button to check for updates whenever you require. Software Update uses an Internet connection to check for updates so you will have to be on-line at the time.

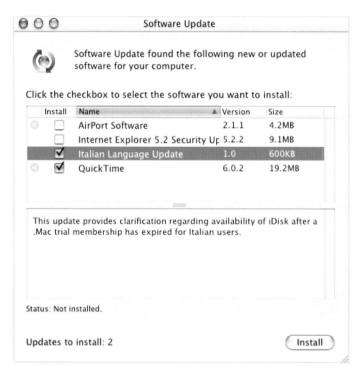

Software Update

Software Update found the following new or updated software for your computer.

Click the checkbox to select the software you want to install:

Install	Name	Version	Size
☐	AirPort Software	2.1.1	4.2MB
☐	Internet Explorer 5.2 Security Up	5.2.2	9.1MB
☑	Italian Language Update	1.0	600KB
☑	QuickTime	6.0.2	19.2MB

This update provides clarification regarding availability of iDisk after a .Mac trial membership has expired for Italian users.

Status: Not installed.

Updates to install: 2   (Install)

Customized update
To customize the operation of the Software Update, open the System Preferences panel and find the Software Update icon along the bottom of the window. Once launched, Software Update will display options for collecting updates. (See page 174.)

Software
Update

Authenticate
To run a Mac OS X update, or most applications for that matter, you need to authenticate with your login and password.

License agreement
The license agreement covers the rights and restrictions pertaining to the use of the software.

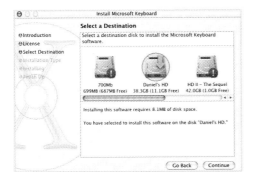

Select a destination
A destination for the Mac OS X system update is limited to locations where you have installed Mac OS X previously. Be aware that some updates will require a recent Mac OS X system such as Mac OS X 10.2.

That was then
This is now

About this Mac
[See also pages 76, 77]

	OS 9		OS X	
	In OS 9 if you need to find out how much memory your Mac has and how much it is using, you simply go to the Apple menu and select 'About	this Mac' to see available memory and how it is utilized.	You will still find 'About this Mac' in the Apple menu in OS X, but it has a different function – it will display the amount of memory available on your	system, not the way it is utilized, as well as processor information, serial and build numbers.

Aliases

Make an alias by pressing Command+ Option and drag or Command+M (shortcut File Menu > Make Alias.)

Make an alias by pressing Command+Option and drag or Command+L (shortcut File Menu > Make Alias.)

AppleScript
[See also pages 298-307]

AppleScript can be found in System Folder > Extensions.

AppleScript has been enhanced and lives in the Applications folder in OS X as well as in AppleScript Studio on the Developer Tools CD.

Application information

To view basic information on a current OS 9 application, go to the Apple menu. 'About this Mac' changes to 'About [Application Name]'.

To view basic information on a current OS X application, go to the Finder menu. 'About this Mac' changes to 'About [Application Name]'.

Application menu

In Mac OS 9 this menu is located in the right hand corner of the screen.

This menu no longer exists in OS X, but you can select the new Finder menu to hide/show applications, or go to the Dock to monitor running applications and/or items.

Applications running

All applications currently running in OS 9, will be listed in the Applications menu.

You can view running applications, preferences and/or minimized documents on the Dock. They are the ones with a small black triangle to the right, left or beneath the application icon (depending where your Dock is positioned.)

	OS 9		OS X	
Chooser [See also pages 256, 257]	Go to the chooser to select a printer or activate AppleShare in OS 9.		The Chooser is no longer a feature of Mac OS X, the alternatives are: • Print Center to select network printers; and	• Connect to Server (File > Go menu) to connect to a server or shared folder.
Contextual menus 	Contextual menus are available in OS 9 (while holding down the Control key, point to an item and click).		Contextual menus are still available in OS X, with the exception of labels. (Labels has been omitted in OS X, so it's obviously not a	contextual menu option.) These capabilities extend to the Dock – select any icon in it while holding Control and a contextual menu will also appear!
Control Panels [See also pages 64-73 and 154-187]	Control Panels are found in your System folder in OS 9.		Many Control Panels in OS 9 have undergone a facelift and been moved to the System Preferences in OS X. These include • Appearance: some of these can be found in Personal; • ColorSync; • Date & Time; • Energy Saver; • Internet; • Keyboard: keyboard layouts Script moved to 'International'; • Monitors: renamed 'Displays' in Mac OS X; • Mouse; • Multiple Users: renamed 'Users' in OS X; • Numbers: absorbed into 'International' in OS X; • QuickTime Settings: renamed 'QuickTime'; • Software Update: moved to System folder > Library> Core Services; • Sound; • Speech; and	• Startup Disk: this is where you will select whether to start up in Classic or OS X. Control Panels no longer in OS X include: • Apple Menu Options; • Control Strip; • Launcher; • Memory; • Text; and • General Controls. Control Panels absorbed into Internet and Network System Preferences include: • AppleTalk; • Configuration Manager; • DialAssist; • Extensions Manager; • File Exchange; • File Sharing; • Location Manager; • Modem; • Remote Access; • TCP/IP; • USB Printer Sharing; and • Web Sharing. The Keychain Access Control panel is now located in Utilities in OS X.

That was then

This is now

OS 9	OS X

Desk Accessories
[See also pages 90, 91 and 100, 101.]

Calculator, Key Caps and Stickies are convenient desk accessories that live in the System Folder > Apple Menu Items in OS 9.

In OS X, Calculator and Stickies have moved to Applications and Key Caps has moved to Utilities.

Desktop

The OS 9 desktop consists of disk icons and a trash can. The current date, international settings and Applications menu are located to the top right of the screen. The Apple menu to the far left of the screen is represented by a colored Apple icon.

In OS X, disk icons may or may not be visible, depending on what you have selected in Finder preferences. The Date & Time, Monitor and Sound settings are located on the top right of the screen. Although the menus are to the left, the Special menu is gone and there's a new menu – Finder.

At the far left, the Apple menu is represented as typically aqua by a translucent blue Apple icon. The new Dock may or may not be visible, and if so, it may be located to the left, bottom or right of the screen – again, depending on the Finder preferences you have selected.

Dock
[See also pages 122-125 and 155]

Mac 'oldies' used the Application menu, Apple menu, Launcher, Chooser and Control strip to share files, quickly launch applications, identify and toggle between currently running applications, open recent documents and gain fast access to items such as Remote Access, Finder, printer/s, general settings and utilities.

The Dock combines the functions of OS 9's Application menu, Launcher, Chooser and Control strip. It contains a unique strip of icons that can be uniquely controlled, and easy-to-see triangles below or beside the icons (depending on Dock placement) show you what applications are running at a glance.

Finder

Finder is located in the Applications menu in OS 9. (When toggling between applications it serves as a navigator from desktop to other windows.

In Mac OS X the term Finder refers to a variety of items. These are:
• the finder window that appears when you have

selected Finder on the Dock;
• Mac OS X's new-look windows; and
• the all-new Finder menu.

OS 9		OS X	

Finder windows
[See also pages 84-87]

Windows are not known as finder windows in Mac OS 9. Typically, they contain:
- two grey buttons (to the top right) – to adjust the height or width of the window; and
- one grey button (to the left) used for closing the window.

Clicking on a window's title bar minimizes it so that only the title bar can be seen.

To see a window in list, icon or view, go to Finder > View menu. OS 9 windows are not equipped with a toolbar.

Finder Windows refer to the new-look windows in OS X. Attractive and easy-to-use, they consist of:
- a new Show/hide button at the top right of the window for displaying or hiding the toolbar;
- a toolbar, consisting of buttons that take you to the areas you use the most, such as Home, Computer and Favorites. It can be customized and has a nifty Search facility;
- 3 colored buttons to the left of the window. These close (red),

minimize, move to dock (yellow) and adjust (green) the window. A window can also be minimized and moved to the dock by double-clicking on its title bar;
- View panel: choose from Icon view, List view, and the all-new Column view, which displays folders in multiple levels, providing thumbnails of icons and photos; and
- a new Back button to transport you to the folder window you were viewing prior to the current one.

Folders
[See also pages 78-81]

To make a new folder, select Command+N or go to File > New.

The concept of spring-loaded folders was introduced in OS 9.

Making a new folder still available from the File menu but the shortcut is now Apple+Option+N. Jaguar has re-introduced spring-loaded folders,

available in Icon, List and Column view. (This feature was omitted in early versions of OS X.)

Fonts
[See also pages 190-195]

Collections	Family	Typeface	Sizes
All Fonts	Al Bayan ▲	Condensed Light	24
Favorites	American Typewrite	Condensed	
Classic	Andale Mono	Condensed Bold	10 ▲
Fun	Arial	Light	11
Modern	Arial Black	Regular	12
PDF	Arial Hebrew	Bold	13
Web	Arial Narrow		14
	Arial Rounded MT B ▼		18
			24 ▼

Mac OS X's all-new Font panel comes complete with an 'Extras' pop-up menu that allows you to add fonts (complete with style and size) to Favorites, edit existing Collections, add color and buy new fonts.

With such ingenuity you can see why ATM (Adobe Type Manager) is no longer part of the system.

That **was then**

This is now

OS 9		OS X	

Force Quit]
[See also pages 43, 102, 103, and 124, 125]

Command+Option+Esc causes you to Force Quit an application when it's giving you trouble. This does not always isolate the problem and often you have to restart your computer anyway.

You can still press Command+Option+Esc to Force Quit an application. However, you can also go to the Apple Menu > Force Quit, or hold down the Option key and press the application icon in the Dock.
Force Quit also works differently in Mac OS X. Darwin allocates a unique

memory space for each application. This means that if something goes wrong, your computer won't need to be restarted. When Force Quit is selected, OS X simply shuts down the troublesome application without harming other applications or the system itself.

Getting information [See also pages 94 - 97]

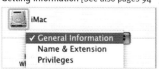

For details on your selected icon, go to File > Get Info (Command+I). An application's memory can be adjusted using Get Info.

Get Info was changed to Show Info in OS X, and reverted to Get Info in OS X 10.2. The File Menu and shortcut key command remain

unchanged, but you can no longer adjust memory in OS X using this option – it is no longer necessary (see also pre-emptive multi-tasking).

Labels

View > Labels is a nifty feature in OS 9 that allows you to assign text labels and colors to files for easy identification. They can be customized

and files can be sorted and searched for in label view.

The Labels feature no longer exists in OS X.

Networking
[See also pages 248 - 261]

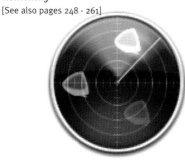

In Mac OS 9, use:
• the Internet Control Panel to enter settings such as your e-mail address, preferred e-mail application, and Web browser;
• the AppleTalk, Modem, Remote Access, and TCP/IP Control Panels to set up network connections;

• in Mac OS X, use the Internet pane in System Preferences for Internet settings; and
• Mac OS X has consolidated AppleTalk, Modem, Remote Access, and TCP/IP settings into the Network pane in System Preferences.

Finding lost treasures

	OS 9		OS X	
Pre-emptive multi-tasking [See also pages 40, 41]	In Mac OS 9, it's often necessary for a user to set preferred memory requirements for each application (See also	'Getting information') Because applications are actually sharing the system's processing time, it's common to have to quit the application and increase the amount of memory assigned to it. Not only this but complex tasks fully consume the processor until complete, forcing other tasks to be put on hold.	In OS X there's no more quitting an application so that others can run. Thanks to Darwin, memory for each application is automatically adjusted and whenever more memory is needed, it allocates exactly the amount required. Darwin also knows how	to give priority to your primary application, but still crunch away at other jobs in the background. With Mac OS X pre-emptive multitasking, the system remains responsive, so you can do a whole bunch of other things while processing the task in the background.
Printing Windows **Page Setup… Print Window…**	File > Print Window is a handy features in OS 9 that lets you print out information on the content of your Finder windows.		File > Print Window is not featured in OS X.	
Recent Applications, Documents and Servers		In OS 9 you can go to the most recent applications, documents and servers by selecting Apple Menu Items > Recent Applications.	To select recent applications, documents or servers in OS X, go to Recent Items in OS X's Apple menu. A new feature, Recent Folders, is	available in the equally-as-new Go menu.
Sherlock [See also pages 268, 269]		Sherlock is located in the Applications folder on OS 9. (Command+F) provides a quick alternative to launching it.	This personal search detective has had a radical makeover in OS X 10.2. Located in the Applications folder, it can no longer be accessed by	Command+F. (Instead, this shortcut command now launches Mac OS X 10.2's Find command (Finder menu).
Special menu [See also pages 102-113]	This well-used menu carries out regulars tasks such as emptying trash, ejecting and erasing a disk and burning a CD.	The Sleep, Restart and Shut Down commands can also be found in the Special menu .	This is no longer a feature of OS X. Instead, Sleep, Restart and Shut Down are located in the Apple menu. Burn CD has	moved to the Edit menu, Empty Trash has moved to the Finder menu and Eject has moved to the File menu.

That **was then**

This is now

OS 9	OS X

System Folder
[See also pages 92, 93]

In OS 9, the System Folder is easily located on your hard disk. Many items in the System Folder can be modified to keep the operating system running smoothly.

OS X does not have the kind of System Folder you got used to in its previous systems. The folder named 'System' has more files than it did in OS 9 and is not accessible unless you are logged on as root user.

Trash
[See also pages 208, 209]

The OS 9 trash can serves many purposes:
- trash items in OS 9 by dragging them to the Trash Can or selecting the Move to Trash or Put Away options. (Found in the File menu or on a contextual menu when Control is pressed);
- choose whether or not you would like to be

warned before emptying the trash by clicking on the trash can and selecting the File > Get Info menu option.
- The trash can is also used as a medium from which to eject discs, CDs etc.
- Empty the trash by going to the Special menu.

In OS X a few things have changed:
- the trash can is located in the Dock;
- the Put Away command (and its shortcut keyboard combination) no longer exist;
- you now empty the trash via the new Finder menu;

- To be warned of the Mac's intentions to empty the trash, go to Finder preferences and not Get Info; and
- although media can still be dragged to the trash can for ejecting, the trash can icon changes its appearance when this occurs.

Undo

In OS 9, the Undo command (Edit menu) undoes your last occurring editing action.

In OS X, the Undo command's editing action abilities extend to a variety of desktop actions. These include dragging an icon into a different folder

or to the Trash, renaming a folder, etc.

Users [See also pages 178, 179, 250-253]

User accounts are optional in OS 9 and the login screen is quite sophisticated – a user name can be selected from an existing list and your voice can be used instead of a password.

Mac OS X makes some aspects of using a Mac a bit more complicated due to improved security measures. Each user has to set up at least one user account. In short, a name and password must be recorded for at least one user of the computer.

OS 9		OS X	
Utilities [See also pages 90, 91] 	Utilities for fonts, printers, preparing, fixing and compressing discs are all available in OS 9.	The utilities in OS X have undergone some changes: • Drive Setup, Disk First Aid, Disc Burner (Utilities in OS 9) have been merged into Disk Utility; • The Print Center utility	has taken over the Chooser in OS 9. It manages anything and everything to do with printing (see pages 256, 257). Note: see also pages 90, 91 for an entire new range of available utilities.
View menu > View Options [See also pages 114, 115] 	OS 9 provides numerous options to view windows and columns, such as date, folder sizes, origins, labels, icon size and arrangement.	All options in OS 9 are available in OS X apart from Labels. It is now easier to manipulate to icon size and arrangement, and	you now have you the choice to make global view changes to your window and to adjust your windows background color.
Window ... or multi Windows? 	The Mac pioneered a graphic user interface with folders and windows: • double-clicking a folder in OS 9 causes another window to open automatically; • if a file is brought forward in OS 9, any other files relating to the source application follow, hiding all other applications;	Mac OS X extends the usefulness of the graphical environment. • it is not necessary to open another window when you double click on a folder OS X. You can either set a preference to disallow this or work in Column view; and • in OS X, an application's individual windows can	be brought forward without bringing all windows pertaining to that application forward too. (Note: press the Command key while double-clicking the folders icon to turn off multi-windows temporarily. See also page 47.)
Word processing 	SimpleText, the free and simple word processing application in Classic, is now called TextEdit in Mac OS X and is very much more sophisticated.	TextEdit creates standard Rich Text Format files which you can open in other programs. It opens text, RTF and documents created with other	applications, find, replaces and formats text, checks spelling and can have pictures added to it.

Cool new things
What's new in OS X?

About this Mac
[See also pages 76, 77]

To see the amount of memory available on your system, as you have always done, select 'About this Mac'. OS X no longer displays the way memory is utilized, but gives information on your processor and current version of system software. (Note: if you hold down the Control key and click on the version number, the OS X build number appears.)

AppleScript enhanced
[See also pages 298-307]

AppleScript in Mac OS X version 10.2 delivers more power, more features and more speed while retaining its ease of use and flexibility.

CD burning
[See also page 138]

In OS X, everything you need to burn a CD is built-in to the system. You can prepare a disc for burning via Disk Utility and go to the Finder menu to burn it. It's that simple. (Note: CD burning has also been added to iTunes.)

Desktop
[See also pages 80, 81]

The desktop is quite different in OS X. Disk icons may or may not be visible, date and time, monitor and sound settings are located on the top right of the screen. The Finder menu on the left replaces the Special menu and the Apple menu icon is now translucent aqua. The new Dock may or may not be visible, and if so, could be located to the left, bottom or right of the screen – depending on your preferences.

Digital Hub

With Mac OS X and applications like iMovie, iDVD, iTunes and iPhoto, Apple has pioneered the 'digital hub' makes the digital lifestyle possible. In short:
- iPhoto helps you save, organize, share and enjoy digital images;
- iDVD takes advantage of the power and stability of Mac OS X to make DVD creation faster and easier;
- iTunes music software converts music from audio CDs, lets you search and browse your entire music collection, and download songs to MP3 players;
- iMovie 2 lets you edit movies, adding professional-quality effects;
- QuickTime supports MPEG-4, the new standard for playing and viewing pro-quality audio and video over the Internet.
(See also pages 128-149 for full details on this.)

Dock

[see also pages 155 and 122-125]

The Dock contains a unique strip of icons of frequently used applications, files, utilities and preferences. You can magnify items on it, add to/remove from it, set preferences, resize it, reposition it, make it disappear and reappear, and immediately notice existing items that are active.

Eject icon

[see also pages 104 and 105]

The Trash icon transforms to an Eject icon when File > Eject (Comman+E) is selected, or removable media is dragged towards the trash.

Filenames

[see also pages 46 and 96]

Mac OS X supports very long filenames on both Mac and Windows platforms.

Finder

[see also pages 80, 81]

In OS X the term Finder refers to a few things: the Desktop; the Finder window that appears when you have selected Finder on the Dock; Mac OS X's new-look windows; and the all new Finder menu, complete with preferences. It has undergone a complete redesign, resulting in a composite of technologies from the original Finder and from the NeXTSTEP file viewer.

Finder menu

[see also pages 104, 105]

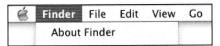

This new menu has taken a few items such as 'About the Finder', 'Hide others' and 'Move to Trash' from other menus in OS 9 and tidied them up into the Finder menu. It has a cool new option called Services that lets you mix and match spelling checkers, drawing tools and calculation methods between Cocoa applications, as well as the ability to set up your Finder using the Finder preferences menu.

Cool new things

What's new in OS X?

Finder views [see also pages 86 and 87]

A new Finder view is added to Mac OS X 10.2. The new Column view makes file navigation a breeze and previews pictures and movies.

Finder preferences let you view discs, media and servers on your desktop, Home or Computer details and file extensions.

Finder windows

[see also pages 80, 81 and 84]

Windows in OS X are dissimilar to anything that has ever been seen before. They:
- don't flicker and flash when dragged/resized;
- have alpha channel support and smooth edges thanks to Quartz;
- have curved interface elements, courtesy of Aqua;

- contain the assembly of 'drawer and parent' which can be added to applications using Cocoa;
- have believable shadows (which individual programs written for OS X now have too);
- feature transparency on windows and pull-down menus;

- can be brought forward without all windows relating to that application following suit;
- contain all-new Sheets;
- have spring-loaded folders in Finder views;
- include customizable tool bars; and
- come equipped with both a back and forward button.

Fonts

[see also pages 190-195]

Working with fonts in OS X is a breeze:
- The Quartz rendering engine displays and

Fonts & Ligatures & Filtering, Oh my!

prints beautifully rendered and anti-aliased fonts with automatic ligatures and kerning controls;
- a variety of fonts are

now free;
- the font panel helps you add, edit and color fonts and purchase new fonts on the Internet.

- a new Script opens in TextEdit to demonstrate Font samples;
- It's easy (and safe) to install fonts.

Free Applications

[see also pages 98,99]

Mac OS X comes with a bunch of free software you can use as soon as your new system software is installed. This includes:
- the system wide Address Book;
- Clock: an alternative to the time display in your menu bar;
- Sherlock 3: which locates hard-to-find

information, delivers the latest news, up-to-the-minute flight status details, stock prices, addresses, maps and driving directions;
- TextEdit: Apple's latest word processing application; • Preview: views, opens and prints PDFs and graphics files;
- iChat: the instant

messenger for chatting with your AOL and Mac.com buddies;
- Image Capture: transfers images from your digital camera to your computer;
- Internet Explorer (IE): Microsoft's Web browser for the Mac ships free with Mac OS X; • Internet Connect: dials your ISP or

connects to AirPort or Ethernet; • Chess: computerized chess;
- Mail: Mac OS X's standards-based e-mail program; • Inkwell: built on Apple's Recognition Engine, Inkwell's handwriting recognition turns text written on a graphics tablet into typed text.

Go menu [see also pages 118, 119]

Go	Window	Help	
Back			⌘[
Forward			⌘]

It's all systems go, with new Go menu, which:
- provides users with an alternative to the Window toolbar – go to various locations (such as Home, Favorites) instead of physically finding and clicking on the icon in a window;
- helps users access shared files; and
- provides a list of recently used folders users can go to, by text entering instead of pointing.

Internet
[see also pages 262-269]

- In Mac OS X, the Internet pane in System Preferences is used for Internet settings.
- Mac OS X's BSD networking stack makes it easier for developers to publish UNIX-style network programs on Macintosh. It provides built-in support for various ways of connecting to the Internet, including dial-up modem (PPP), cable modem, DSL (including PPPoE), built-in Ethernet and AirPort. It allows for the use of standard Internet services as well as Apache, the open source web server technology that runs more than 50 percent of the Web sites on the Internet. BSD also enables the Perl, Telnet and FTP command-line utilities.
- access to a .Mac account is built into Mac OS X, so users don't have to install a thing.
- Mac OS X provides users with all the applications required to access the Internet right away, such as: AirPort Assistant; Internet Connect; Mail; Microsoft Internet Explorer for Mac OS X with Java 2; iChat; and Address Book; and
- new Sherlock 3 (Mac OS X 10.2 only) can be used in place of a Web browser. It provides flight information, access to Web search engines, stock art libraries, a dictionary and Apple's technical support library to name just a few.

iTools online collection
[see also pages 118, 119]

This collection is exclusively accessible to Mac users. It consists of:
- iDisk: comprises 20Mb of personal storage space on Apple's Internet servers as well as an FTP site for file sharing with other users;
- iCards: electronic postcards that can be customized;
- Email: a free e-mail service; and
- Homepage: a free customizable Web site for Macintosh users only.

Library [see also pages 88, 89]

Mac OS X Library folders:
- hold information the Mac needs to run each user's environment, fonts and applications;
- contain folders for Favorites, Internet Search Sites, Web browser plug-ins, cached Web pages, keyboard layouts, and sound files etc; and
- are personalized individually. There are three of them on the system and not all can be accessed by everyone.

Cool new things
What's new in OS X?

Networking & Communications

[see also pages 248-261]

Mac OS X offers a solid foundation for networking and communications including:

- BSD (Berkeley Standard Distribution) makes it easier for developers to publish UNIX-style network programs on Macintosh. It supports DHCP, BootP and manual network configurations, making it easy for users to integrate Mac OS X computers into existing local area networks;

- consolidation of: AppleTalk, Modem, Remote Access, and TCP/IP settings into the Network pane in System Preferences. It is here that you can connect your Mac to the Internet, your corporate network, or even the old PC Network.

(This panel also helps your Mac to automatically use whichever connection methods are available at any time: Ethernet, modem, Airport, or Bluetooth modem.);

- Rendezvous, the new networking technology that uses the industry-standard IP networking protocol. It allows for automatic creation of a network of computers, printers and other peripheral devices over Ethernet, AirPort, Bluetooth, USB or FireWire- without manually configuring drivers or settings;

- a number of technologies that make it simple to integrate the Mac into cross-platform networks; and

- automatic switch

over to the Ethernet network if you connect to Ethernet using AirPort. What's more, you can log on to new Airport networks and Mac OS X enters the password for you.

New Applications

[see also pages 100, 101]

Applications

Mac OS X has inspired the application developer community to embrace its new graphic interface. technology. Leading developers have

demonstrated their support and numerous native products are currently available, or in the process of being made available, to run

on Apple's new UNIX-based operating system.

New Folder shortcut
[see also pages 108, 109]

All Mac users take note: making a new folder is slightly different in OS X. The shortcut keyboard command is no longer Command+N.

Instead, it is now Command+Option+N. Although it takes a bit of getting used to at first, users who use the File menu will be relieved to

discover that this remains File > New Folder.

Online software updates
[see also pages 48, 174, 175, 294, 295 and 200, 201]

Mac OS X has the ability to download software updates automatically, including the latest security updates (automatically installed

through the Software Update mechanism) via System Preferences > Software Update.

PDF: a common file format for Mac OS X
[see also pages 45 and 152, 153]

Thanks to Quartz, PDF is a common file format for Mac OS X. Any PDF file saved in Mac OS X can be opened, viewed, and

printed using PDF-compatible tools including Adobe Acrobat Reader 5 – on all supported platforms.

Pre-emptive multi-tasking
[see also pages 40, 41]

Thanks to Darwin, pre-emptive multitasking: memory for each application is automatically adjusted

and the system remains responsive, so you can turn your attention to other things while processing the task in

the background. (No more quitting an application so that others can run.)

Printing

Printing from Mac OS X is a simple process. Any printer purchased from a major manufacturer will probably have software built into Mac OS X. This

can be turned on in Utilities > Print Center and hey presto! you're ready to print.

Public and Shared Folders
[see also pages 92, 93]

Public Folder: other users can view your files here; Drop Box folder: other users can leave files for you here.

Shared folder: 'free for all'. Other users can copy to it, but only the originator can move, trash or change it.

Cool new things
What's new in OS X?

Stability (crash-resistant computing)
[see also page 43]

If an application attempts an illegal operation in OS X (for example, taking up too much memory), the operating system simply shuts it down. This has no affect on the rest of the system.

If the application you are working on in OS X stops responding, you can Force Quit the application without harming other applications, so there is no need to restart your computer.

Symmetric multi-processor support

Much of Mac OS X is multi-threaded, so applications that use system services such as sound, graphics, and networking accrue the benefits of dual-processors. Symmetric multiprocessing takes advantage of dual-processor systems.

System Preferences
[see also pages 154-187]

Mac OS X has a whole range of new System Preferences (formerly known as Control Panels, and found in the System Folder in OS 9). These are divided into the following categories for ease of reference:
• Personal: Desktop; Dock; General; International; Login Items; My Account; Screen Effects; Hardware: CDs & DVDs; ColorSync; Displays; Energy Saver; Keyboard; Mouse; Sound
• Internet & Network: Internet; Network; QuickTime; Sharing; and
• System: Accounts; Classic; Date & Time; Software Update; Speech; Startup Disk; Users; Universal Access.

Many of these have been greatly improved in the transition from OS 9's Control Panels including: General; International; ColorSync; Displays; Date & Time; Energy Saver; Mouse; Sound; Keyboard; Internet; Network; Startup Disk; Sharing; and Users. The following preferences are new to OS X:
• Desktop: customize your desktop pattern;
• Dock: to set size, position and visibility;
• Screen Effects: to changing Screen Effects modules; and
• Classic: helps users run both Mac OS 9 and Mac OS X.
Universal Access preferences have been greatly modified since the first version of OS X.

The latest offerings for speech, sight, hearing, keyboard and mouse, courtesy of Mac OS X 10.2 are:
• innovative settings to assist with reading text and seeing pictures and graphics (i.e. higher screen contrast displays);
• Speech Recognition in place of keyboard or mouse;
• displaying a flashing screen rather than hearing an alert;
• use of the numeric keypad in place of the mouse; and
• sequential modifier keys for those with keyboard difficulties.

Toggling between Classic and OS X

[see also pages 72, 73 and 176, 177]

• Choose whether to start up from OS X, Classic or another CD via System Preferences > Startup Disk; • Choose System Preferences > Classic when you need to adjust settings for Classic, such as getting Classic to start automatically when a Classic application is launched.

Undo [see also pages 36, 37 and 112, 113]

Edit	View	Go	Window	Help	
Undo Move of "NEW FOLDER"				⌘Z	

Edit > Undo can undo your last desktop action such as dragging an icon into a different folder or to the Trash, renaming a folder, etc.

UNIX [see also pages 152, 153 and 270, 271]

Mac OS X is made up of a unique combination of technical elements, these include:

• **Aqua:** thanks to Aqua, the Mac user interface has had a facelift. Transparent, shiny and droplet-shaped elements, drop shadows and sheets all contribute towards OS X's new look;

• **Classic:** most Mac OS 9 compatible applications will run side-by-side with Mac OS X applications thanks to Classic;

• **Carbon:** system elements that work in both Classic and OS X;

• **Quartz:** this unique system in Mac OS X uses PDF as the basis of its imaging model. It delivers crisp graphics, anti-aliased fonts, and blends 2D, 3D and QuickTime content with transparency and drop shadows;

• **Darwin:** the industrial-strength, UNIX-based foundation lies beneath Mac OS X's interface. It features a protected memory architecture and gives priority to a primary application, but still lets the user work on other jobs in the background (preemptive multitasking).

• **Open GL:** specifically designed for any application that requires a sturdy framework for visualizing shapes in 2D and 3D;

• **Java:** the Java application environment exists to develop and carry out Java programs on Mac OS X, including Pure Java applications and applets; and

• **Cocoa:** this application, descended from NeXTSTEP, is designed specifically for Mac OS X-only native applications.

Users concept

[see also pages 178, 179 and 250, 253]

Mac OS X has secure file access with built-in support for multiple users. Every user on the system has a secure login account and a Home directory for storing personal files, preferences, and system settings. When users log into their personal accounts on a Mac OS X computer, they can access the Macintosh, with their customized desktop, Finder, Dock, and applications, as well as all their personal files.

Cool new things

What's new in OS X?

Utilities [see also pages 90, 91]

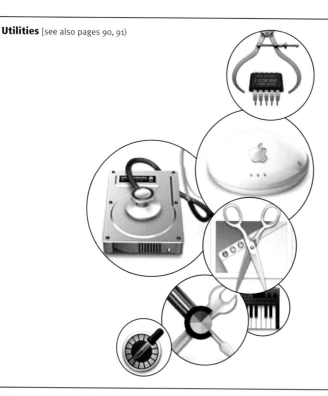

There are an entire new range of utilities available in OS X. Some that may be commonly used are:

• **ColorSync Utility:** which works with ColorSync preferences to specify accurate color profiles;

• **Disk Utility:** combines the functions of Drive Setup, Disk First Aid, Disc Burner (utilities in OS 9);

• **Display Calibrator:** resurrected from much older versions of Mac OS, this utility adjusts your monitor to provide you with accurate color;

• **Grab:** takes screen snapshots;

• **Print Center:** the Print Center has taken over the Chooser in OS 9. It manages anything and everything to do with printing;

• **Bluetooth File Exchange:** used to transfer files between one or more Bluetooth-enabled devices.

• **Key Caps:** perfect for finding the right keyboard combinations.

• **StuffIt Expander:** a quick, easy and very useful decompressor for compressed file formats.

• **Disk Copy:** required to open or create a disk image, which, in theory, looks and acts like a real disk but is actually a file.

Windows compatibility
[see also page 34]

Point-and-click Windows file sharing makes it easy to connect to Windows servers and PCs. OS X comes with Active Directory interoperability, and with a PPTP-based virtual private network (VPN) client that allows Mac users to connect remotely to Windows corporate networks.

Windows-style (three-letter) filename suffixes
[see also pages 38 and 98, 99]

Mac OS X uses Windows-style (three-letter) filename suffixes to identify the application needed to launch a document, and provide a preference for users to hide the suffixes if so desired allowing them to continue to have a name-only relationship with their files.

Third parties

CorelDRAW Graphics Suite 11

It's time to get excited. CorelDRAW Graphics Suite 11 is the design package that lets you enjoy what you do. Equally intuitive and creative, it makes design an experience — not a process. This comprehensive suite — CorelDRAW 11 (page layout and illustration), Corel PHOTO-PAINT 11 (image-editing) and Corel R.A.V.E. 2 (vector animation) — is carbonized for Mac OS X and features the sleek Aqua user interface.

Why buy?

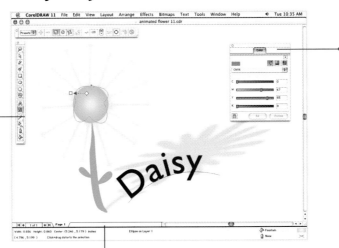

Interactive Tools and Live Effects
- Manipulate and view graphics in real time.
- Experiment until you find the right look without repeatedly starting from scratch.
- Fast and easy-to-use interactive tools allow you to apply effects such as drop shadows, fills, vector extrusions and envelopes.

Professional Color Management and Output Features
- All essential color management options appear in one dialog box.
- Offers you three predefined styles — for the Web, desktop printing and professional output.
- Also includes ICC profile options, Apple ColorSync technology and new PANTONE color palettes.

Tight Integration
- Move between applications seamlessly.
- All three applications share a commonality between user interfaces and tools.
- Familiar environment reduces the learning curve and lets you get the job done faster.
- Easily transfer raster images between CorelDRAW 11 and Corel PHOTO-PAINT 11.

OTHER REASONS TO BUY
- Extensive Compatibility — support for more than 100 import and export filters.
- Customizable Workspace — customize everything from menus and toolbars to status bars and dialog boxes, increase productivity, work uniquely.
- Printing and export preflight warnings.
- Network Installation made easy with Microsoft Installer.

SUMMARY

PRICE	DISTRIBUTION	SYSTEM REQUIREMENTS	NOTES
Full: US$529.00, A$1,031, NZ$1,265 **Upgrade:** US$249.00, A$485, NZ$596	You can purchase Corel Graphics Suite II from www.corel.com/ graphicssuite11/	Mac OS 10.1: Power Mac G3 or higher 128Mb RAM, mouse or tablet, 1,024 x 768 screen resolution, CD-ROM drive, 250Mb hard disk space	For more info see: www.corel.com/ graphicssuite11/

Details reflect Australian criteria. May differ for other countries.

Why upgrade?

Already own a previous version of CorelDRAW Graphics Suite? Upgrade to Version 11 and you'll quickly discover all the new features you're missing out on. In addition, it offers increased efficiency and responsiveness, ultimately making the design experience even more enjoyable.

Corel R.A.V.E. 2: Web graphics & animation
• Real Animated Vector Effects — add animations to your Web designs in minutes.
• New Symbols — optimize Flash file sizes by referencing objects or animated symbols.
• Enhanced Flash filter — produce compact animations for the Web.
• Enhanced Behavior Support — add a greater level of interactivity to Flash animations, etc.
• New Animate or Tween — animate text of a path and use customizable shapes to create animations quickly with tween Perfect Shapes.

Photo Editing with Corel PHOTO-PAINT 11
• New CutOut tool — quickly mask complex objects.
• Enhance Image Stitching — create seamless panoramas with multiple images or objects.
• New Image Slicing — load large images on a Web page faster by breaking them into segments.
• New Rollovers — add dynamic effects to Web graphics.
• New Red Eye Removal tool — merely brush over problem areas to correct your photos.
• More than 100 effects.

CorelDRAW 11
This intuitive graphic design package for print and the Web, has a variety of great features. Some of these are:
1. New Polyline tool — create curves and lines in one stroke, using one tool.
2. New 3 Point Ellipse,

Rectangle and Curve tools — create exact size and rotation of these shapes in two easy clicks.
3. New Roughen and Smudge brushes — easily edit curves with these pressure-sensitive tools with full tablet support.

4. Live Effects — work freely and efficiently with real-time feedback.
5. Enhanced SVG support — create data-driven, graphics using SVG.
6. Customizable workspace — design a workspace that suits your personal needs.

Extensis Portfolio 6

Extensis Portfolio 6 for Mac OS X is the fastest way for creative professionals to share, organize, retrieve and distribute the digital files they create and use every day. It takes the grunt work out of organizing files and removes the chaos for creative workgroups and enterprises alike by providing instant visual access to digital photos, scans and other media files. In short, Portfolio 6 lets you focus on creating art while it creates the order.

Create stunning visual catalogs of your images to share over a network or publish on the Web.

Add customized keywords to each individual entry for faster searching.

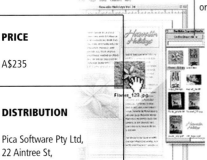

PRICE

A$235

DISTRIBUTION

Pica Software Pty Ltd,
22 Aintree St,
Brunswick, VIC 3056

Tel: (+61) 3 9388 9588
Fax: (+61) 3 9388 9788

E-mail: info@pica.com.au,
Web site: www.pica.com.au

SYSTEM REQUIREMENTS

32Mb RAM

NOTES

Portfolio 6 for Mac OS X is available in Spring 2002. Free upgrade of Mac OS X version for registered users on offer.

In Mac OS X, Portfolio 6 allows you to:
• Search and provide information on files stored on CD or other removable media, not only on your hard drive or network.
• Scan multiple catalogs at once to instantly locate your images based on any criteria.
• Work with different file formats such as PDF and MPEG, not just JPEG or GIF.
• Easily build Web pages

based on your catalog contents, using professionally designed templates.
• Copy and catalog files automatically for CD distribution with Collect & Publish.
• Have instant visual access to your files from anywhere on your system.
• Add more copies of Portfolio as your workgroup expands.

Easily create a catalog of all your images.

PORTFOLIO SERVER FOR WORKGROUPS
• Workgroups of over five users can use Portfolio Server to share and distribute catalogs with client/server speed.
• Portfolio Server can also connect to and serve as a front-end for larger SQL databases with Portfolio SQL Connect software (sold separately).
• Both Portfolio and Portfolio Server provide robust scripting capabilities for building customer solutions, database publishing, Web publishing and more.
• The Portfolio family of products takes the complexity of asset management solutions out of the equation.

SYNOPSIS

Details reflect Australian criteria. May differ for other countries.

Extensis Suitcase 10

In the past, ensuring you obtain the font you need when you needed it may have meant storing in excess of 200 fonts on your computer. This may also have meant a dramatic slow down of your system's performance and potential output problems with font conflicts or missing/corrupt fonts. But this was way before Extensis Suitcase and Mac OS X entered the scene ...

Quick and easy font management

Mac OS X has a minimum of four different System Font folders for font storage, making font management more of a challenge than ever before. The solution? Extensis Suitcase 10 — it lets you activate only the fonts you need for all applications (Cocoa, Carbon and Classic). Regardless of the applications you use, Extensis Suitcase 10 will save you valuable time and system resources and make fonts easier than ever before to use.

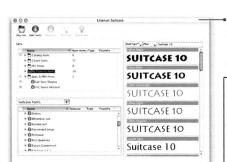

Extensis Suitcase 10 is packed with automated features that make previewing, organizing and activating fonts a snap.

In Mac OS X, Suitcase allows you to:
• Quickly activate only the fonts you need, making your system run faster and smoother.
• Activate fonts for all applications (Cocoa, Carbon and Classic) no matter what environment you are operating in.
• Auto-activate fonts for Classic applications and Carbon applications, such as Adobe Illustrator 10.
• Detect and fix font

conflicts and corrupt fonts before they cause you trouble, using FontDoctor.
• Preview fonts side-by-side for easy selection.
• Print type pages with font samples using the included LemkeSoft FontBook.
• Use several different supported font types in Mac OS X including OpenType, Windows TrueType and Apple's new dfont format.

PRICE

A$515

DISTRIBUTION

Pica Software Pty Ltd,
22 Aintree St,
Brunswick, VIC 3056

Tel: (+61) 3 9388 9588
Fax: (+61) 3 9388 9788

E-mail: info@pica.com.au,
Web site: www.pica.com.au

SYSTEM REQUIREMENTS

32Mb RAM (Mac OS 8.6 to Mac OS 9.2.2)
128Mb RAM for (Mac OS X)
14Mb free hard drive space.

NOTES

Free 30-day evaluation download at www.pica.com.au

SUITCASE SERVER FOR WORKGROUPS

SYNOPSIS

Suitcase Server is compatible with Mac OS X Server and its cross-platform support allows client workstations to connect and share fonts whether they are using a Mac or Windows workstation. Automatic synchronization makes it easy for entire workgroups to access the same set of fonts and workgroup members can control which fonts are downloaded or subscribed to, so they get only the fonts they need when they need them.

Office v. X for Mac

Office X builds on the renowned success of Office 2001 for Mac, by offering Microsoft Word, Excel, PowerPoint and Entourage — all Carbonized exclusively for Mac OS X. Rather than just 'porting' to Mac OS X, all four applications in the suite have been completely rearchitectured, and now offer many new and improved features that are a delight to try and easy to use.

Details reflect Australian criteria. May differ for other countries.

SYNOPSIS

SUPPORT FOR KEY MAC OS X TECHNOLOGIES

Office v. X continues to be at the forefront of supporting Mac OS technology, by adding functionality for Sheets, Quartz 2-D Drawing Technology and Carbon Events. Office users will also find that the same features they have come to know and expect are in Office v. X as well. These include: • Carbon Events Framework; • Sheets; • Quartz 2-D Drawing Technology; • Mac OS X Native Navigation Services; •Native Mac OS X controls; • QuickTime movies and transitions; and • drag and drop.

OS X look and feel

All four applications in Office v. X have been given a complete Aqua overhaul. Office v. X applications include a bold and classy new visual appearance. Every visual nuance in Office v. X has been completely redesigned to make the user interface identical to Mac OS X. In fact, more than 800 dialog boxes, toolbar icons and alerts have been changed in Office v. X to match the liquid blue appearance of Mac OS X's new Aqua interface. In addition to this:

• Within each Office v. X application, components such as toolbars have been redesigned to offer larger and easier-to-read buttons.

• More than 700 new icons have been added that use Anti-Aliased graphics for a cleaner appearance and enhanced discoverability.

• All the applications and supporting features such as the formatting palette have been designed to 'Genie' to and from the Dock.

• No other Mac OS X application can boast as much Aqua development work as Office v. X.

PRICE		DISTRIBUTION	SYS REQUIREMENTS
Microsoft Office v. X for Mac:		Available from your local Apple Centre.	Mac OS X 10.1 or later
Full Version:	$999.00*		RAM (minimum): 128Mb
Upgrade Version:	$619.00*		HD space (minimum):
Academic Version available on request.			160Mb: drag-and-drop
(* = Recommended Retail Price)			75Mb: custom install

Formatting palette

All formatting tools throughout Office X are found on a single, improved, context-sensitive palette. As users work on different parts of a document, the Formatting Palette adapts and shows appropriate tools for the task at hand. Words, tables, lists, pictures and the overall document can therefore be edited quickly and easily.

In addition, many discoverability features of Mac OS X have been included throughout Office v. X, such as the Genie Effect.

SOME OTHER COOL NEW THINGS

STABILITY AND RESPONSIVENESS: Office X uses key components of the modern Mac OS X architecture, resulting in a suite of programs that are more stable and responsive than ever.

HELP IMPROVEMENTS: Help now includes the full-text search feature to look for Help topics containing specific words by simply typing a word or two.

COMPATIBILITY: Office v. X users can easily exchange files across platforms. It is cross-platform compatible with Office for Windows XP, Office for Windows 2000 and Office for Windows 97 and works seamlessly with Office 2001 for Mac and Office 98 Macintosh Edition.

TOOLS ON THE WEB: Office Tools on the Web offers electronic services from the Microsoft Office Web site. Other resources in Tools on the Web include online templates, clip art, and reference services.

PROJECT GALLERY: The task-based Project Gallery helps find the right document, template, or wizard for creating any Office X project. (The new Based on Recent category is a must-use to base new documents on those already created.)

SWITCHING IDENTITIES IN OFFICE X: Separate identities can be set up in Office X so that each person can configure unique settings — individually used in each Office program.

Collect and paste

The Office Clipboard allows Word X users to easily collect and copy multiple blocks of text or pictures from one or more of their documents, e-mail messages, Web pages, presentations or other files. Users can then paste these blocks into any Office v. X application, either individually or all at once using the handy Paste All feature.

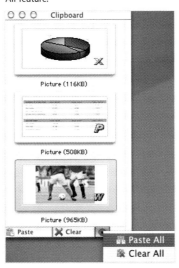

Excel X for Mac

Excel X for Mac is the newest update to the Mac community's most useful and feature-rich analysis and spreadsheet application. Assisting Mac OS X users to improve productivity, Excel X now offers an array of new tools, embraces Quartz 2-D Drawing Technology, has improved compatibility with support for third-party applications, is cross-platform with PC users and shares files with both Mac and PC users running Office 98 Macintosh Edition and Office 2001.

Transparent Charts and Anti-Aliasing

Through the power of Quartz 2-D Drawing Technology, users have the ability to create stunning transparent charts. From 3D graphs to pie charts, Excel X takes charts to a new level. What's more, Quartz makes the border and lines in spreadsheet graphics such as pie charts clean and smooth thanks to Anti-Aliasing.

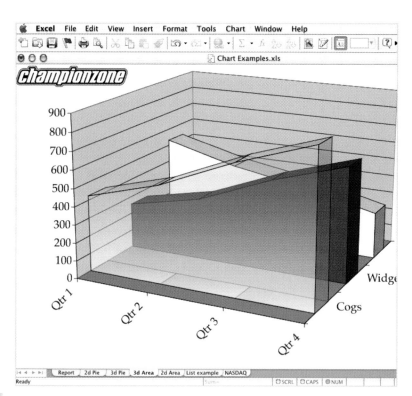

PRICE		DISTRIBUTION	SYS REQUIREMENTS
Microsoft Office v. X for Mac:		Available from your local Apple Centre.	Mac OS X 10.1 or later
Full Version:	$999.00*		RAM (minimum): 128Mb
Upgrade Version:	$619.00*		HD space (minimum):
Academic Version available on request			160Mb: drag-and-drop
(* = Recommended Retail Price)			75Mb: custom install

Customize Keyboard

Categories:

All Commands
File
Edit
View
Insert
Format
Tools

Tools

Spelling...
 Dictionary
AutoCorrect...
Share Workbook...
Highlight Changes...
Accept or Reject Changes...
Merge Workbooks...

Current keys:

F7

Remove

Press new shortcut key:

Command+2

Add

Currently assigned to: Unassigned

Description

Starts spelling checker

Reset All...   OK

Customizable keyboard shortcuts
Set the keyboard shortcuts to function as they did in Excel 98, or customize to personal preference.

Preferences

View
Save
Calculation
Edit
General
Transition
Custom Lists
Chart
Color

Settings

☑ Save AutoRecover info

Every: 5 ⟳ minutes

SOME OTHER COOL NEW THINGS

HELP IMPROVEMENTS: Help now includes the full-text search feature to look for Help topics containing specific words by simply typing a word or two.

LIST AutoFill: List AutoFill automatically extends the list's formatting and formulas, saving the user steps and helping ensure greater accuracy.

REALbasic INTEGRATION: Migrate from Visual Basic to REALbasic, a powerful and easy-to-use tool for creating your own applications. Excel X contains a trial version of REALbasic in the Value Pack.

CALCULATOR: A first-for-the-Macintosh feature, Excel X's calculator makes it easier for users to work with simple formulas and link to other cells or use precompiled functions to do their work.

LIST MANAGER: Excel X offers the List Manager to simplify the chore of managing simple lists. It anticipates the intent to create a list and automatically offers to convert the cells into a manageable, sortable list.

Auto Recover
AutoRecover is a new default feature in Excel X that automatically saves a working document every 10 minutes. If a user loses a document (e.g. via power outage or system crash) Excel will proceed to AutoRecover all files in reverse save order so that the focus will be on the file that was saved last. AutoRecover can also be customized to save more frequently if a user chooses.

Calculator

=D12/E13+E12

Answer: 303.4375

Place in cell: G28

Clear   ÷   x
7 8 9 −   If...
4 5 6 +   Sum...
1 2 3 (More...
0 .)

?   Cancel   OK

Entourage X for Mac

To become more organized in today's increasingly busy work environment, it is vital to streamline communication and systematize personal information. This is where Microsoft's Entourage X comes into play. Improved for Office v. X, this innovative, e-mail application and personal information manager now has a newly-designed user interface and improved functionality, providing users with faster communication and greater efficiency than ever before.

Entourage:mac

1. Help Improved
Find help faster with the new improved Help feature in Entourage X. Help now includes full-text search, a feature that lets you search for Entourage Help topics containing specific words. And when you find the topic you're looking for, you can print it for quick-and-easy reference.

2. OS X look and feel
Entourage takes advantage of the fresh, new design of Mac OS X. More than just 'Aquafied', the Entourage X user interface now features a centralized collection of intuitive buttons for easy access and navigation, such as the Mail, Address Book, Calendar, Notes, Tasks and Custom Views buttons. There are also several new OS X keyboard shortcuts available (such as Command+M to minimize open document to the Dock). Through the Preview Pane, users can display the entire e-mail message without the need to open separate windows.

Redesigned Calendar
To improve the way people make appointments, keep track of tasks and manage daily activities, Entourage X offers a newly redesigned and enhanced calendar and improved versatility. Users can now switch between Day, Week, Work Week, and Month view and track to-do lists at a glance with a new Tasks pane that keeps current tasks visible as events are checked in any Calendar view.

In addition, through automatic international time zone adjustments, Entourage X makes it easy to co-ordinate schedules and setting reminders for important events worldwide.

PRICE	DISTRIBUTION	SYS REQUIREMENTS
Microsoft Office v. X for Mac: Full Version: $999.00* Upgrade Version: $619.00* Academic Version available on request (* = Recommended Retail Price)	Available from your local Apple Centre.	Mac OS X 10.1 or later RAM (minimum): 128Mb HD space (minimum): 160Mb: drag-and-drop 75Mb: custom install

Details reflect Australian criteria. May differ for other countries.

▷ **Software for Mac OS X**

Hardware for Mac OS X

Peripherals for Mac OS X

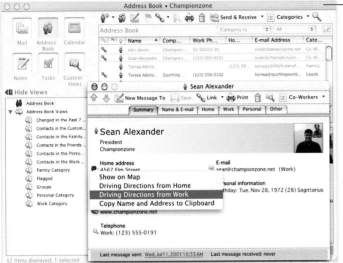

Address Book

The Entourage X Address Book offers:
• Improved support for international contacts.
• The ability to view all contact information and access the selected contact's last e-mail message — thanks to Summary view. • Easy exchange of personal and business information across networks, courtesy of vCard. • Action buttons to carry out common tasks, such as finding directions.
• The ability to view complete contact information in the Address Book using the Preview Pane without opening a contact.

Rich Content

Movies, pictures and sound files can now be attached or inserted within an Entourage X e-mail message thanks to rich content support in messages, signatures, and notes.

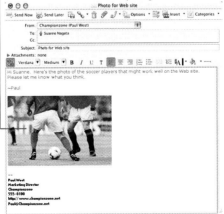

SOME OTHER COOL NEW THINGS

NEW MAC OS KEYCHAIN SUPPORT:
Entourage X smartly adds saved password to the user's Mac OS keychain.

IMPROVED CUT/COPY/PASTE: Pasted text (including fonts, font colors and sizes, bulleted lists, numbering, and alignment) retains selected formatting options from the text cut or copied from original document.

PERFORMANCE ENHANCEMENTS: In Entourage X, data storage has been greatly enhanced for quick and efficient operation.

OFFICE NOTIFICATIONS: Timely reminders are displayed in a single, easy-to-view window — even if Entourage or other Office programs are not currently running.

IMPROVED CUSTOM VIEWS: With predefined custom views, Entourage X helps users become familiar with the various ways of creating and saving personalized views.

TASKS: Entourage X Tasks is now even easier to access than before. It provides a seamless way to create lists of tasks, with built-in reminders to keep track of individual projects.

231

PowerPoint X for Mac

With PowerPoint X for Mac, starting and completing a slide show is a snap. Users will find many new features and improvements to deliver their presentations, including in person during meetings, on the Web, and by using QuickTime movies. And, as demonstrated throughout the entire Office v. X suite, it also provides the ability to leverage Quartz 2-D drawing technology, making for very rich and compelling presentations all round.

PowerPoint:mac

PowerPoint Packages •

The new PowerPoint Package option allows users to pack their presentation and all linked files into one folder. Now movies, sounds and images intended for use in a presentation can be saved, stored in an individual folder and transferred intact to other users' machines, CD-ROMs or a network share.

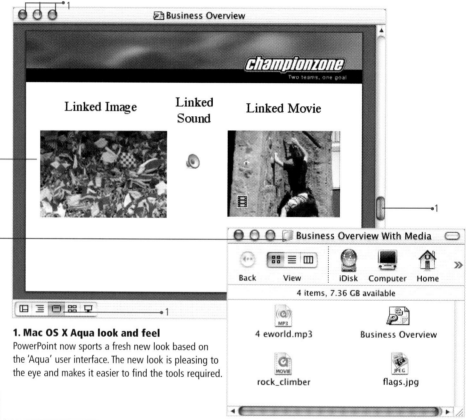

1. Mac OS X Aqua look and feel
PowerPoint now sports a fresh new look based on the 'Aqua' user interface. The new look is pleasing to the eye and makes it easier to find the tools required.

PRICE	DISTRIBUTION	SYS REQUIREMENTS
Microsoft Office v. X for Mac: Full Version: $999.00* Upgrade Version: $619.00* Academic Version available on request (* = Recommended Retail Price)	Available from your local Apple Centre.	Mac OS X 10.1 or later RAM (minimum): 128Mb HD space (minimum): 160Mb: drag-and-drop 75Mb: custom install

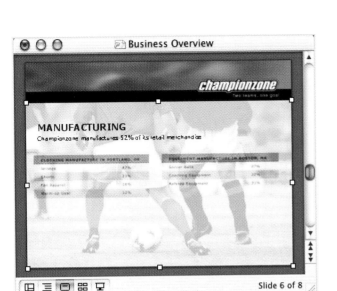

True Transparency

PowerPoint X provides even more image manipulation power by allowing you to decide just how transparent any drawing or shape available in Office Art should be. Thanks to Quartz 2-D Drawing Technology, users can lay shapes and images on top of text or one another for a truly amazing effect in their presentations.

SOME OTHER COOL NEW THINGS

POWERPOINT MOVIES: Users can now include any combination of animations, slide transitions, and interactive features such as action buttons and hyperlink in their PowerPoint movies.

QUICKTIME TRANSITIONS: • With full support for Apple QuickTime, PowerPoint X for Mac can use QuickTime Transitions to move between slides in a presentation; • Quartz 2-D transparency features in PowerPoint X enable users to create new Fade In and Fade Out effects between slides.

HELP FULL-TEXT SEARCH ENGINE: Help now includes the full-text search feature to look for Help topics containing specific words, by simply typing a word or two.

MULTIPLE LANGUAGE SUPPORT: PowerPoint provides full support for Mac OS X language settings using the Microsoft Language Register tool. Full support for Euro currency values is also provided.

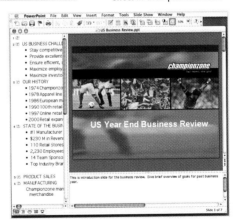

Multiple slide masters

Like PowerPoint 2001, PowerPoint X supports the use of more than one slide master and title master in a presentation. Through Multiple Master, users apply slide masters and title masters to single slides or multiple slides at a time. If slides from one presentation need to be copied to another, PowerPoint can be set to copy the slide and title masters along with the slides.

Word X for Mac

A native Mac OS X business productivity application, Word X for Mac offers a number of advanced features and timesaving tools that make it even easier to create professional documents, letters, Web pages, and other printed or online material. Its seamless compatibility with Word XP, Word 2000 and Word 97 for Windows, and the way it embraces Mac OS X technology and compatibility, makes this popular word processing application more desirable to Mac users than ever.

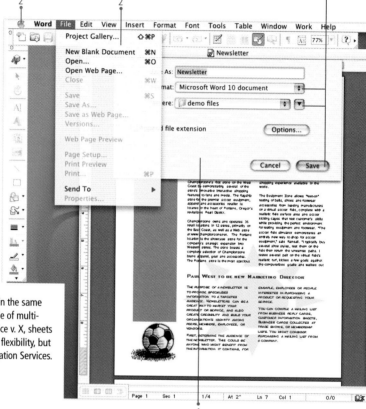

1. Sheets

Sheets replace alerts and dialog boxes in Word X, providing an immediate visual connection between a dialog box and the respective document that it affects. So, if a sheet is open, users can ignore it temporarily and continue working on other documents in the same applications (a perfect example of multi-tasking). Seen throughout Office v. X, sheets not only provide freedom and flexibility, but also offer added Native Navigation Services.

2. Aqua Interface

Word X offers a bold and brilliant new Aqua interface that perfectly matches Mac OS X's new look — as does all in the Office v. X suite. It includes Mac OS X-specific features (such as transparent drop down menus) that leverage the architecture of the new operating system.

PRICE		DISTRIBUTION	SYS REQUIREMENTS
Microsoft Office v. X for Mac:		Available from your local Apple Centre.	Mac OS X 10.1 or later
Full Version:	$999.00*		RAM (minimum): 128Mb
Upgrade Version:	$619.00*		HD space (minimum):
Academic Version available on request			160Mb: drag-and-drop
(* = Recommended Retail Price)			75Mb: custom install

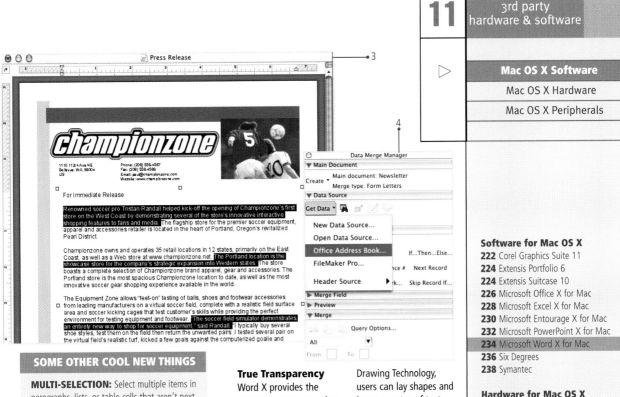

SOME OTHER COOL NEW THINGS

MULTI-SELECTION: Select multiple items in paragraphs, lists, or table cells that aren't next to each other. (Ideal for finding and replacing text or formatting).

CLEAR FORMATTING (3): Removes any manually-applied character and paragraph formatting, and resets the default text style.

OFFICE ADDRESS BOOK: • New and convenient integration features with Microsoft Entourage X for Mac; • use the Contact toolbar to: manage contacts in the Office Address Book, insert contact information directly into documents; send information in e-mail using Word's new Data Merge Manager.

DATA MERGE MANAGER (4): Simplifies creating form letters, labels, envelopes, catalogs, and other documents you want to share with others within one window.

HELP IMPROVEMENTS: Help now includes the full-text search feature to look for Word Help topics containing specific words.

True Transparency
Word X provides the power to create stunning graphics by allowing users to set a specific percentage of transparency to any drawing or shape available in Office Art. Thanks to Quartz 2-D

Drawing Technology, users can lay shapes and images on top of text or one another for a truly amazing effect. In addition, professional publishing-quality graphics can be added to any Office v. X document.

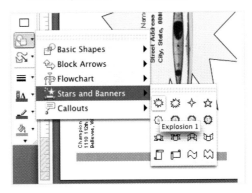

Six Degrees™

Timefreeing technology is how Creo's Six Degrees ™ software is described. In keeping with the theme of 'six degrees of separation', this e-mail driven productivity tool remembers all related e-mail threads, including document and recipient's name, and considers them part of the same project. Six Degrees software helps organize your desktop, creates dynamic, self-updating projects and finds documents, messages and contacts with ease ... instead of having to launch Sherlock or scroll aimlessly through your e-mail.

Messages Button

Clicking the Messages Button displays e-mail messages that are related to the item you are focusing on.

Legend

When Six Degrees is started, the Legend automatically displays all e-mails, files and people related to what you are focused on.

Focus Field

Displays what the Legend is currently focusing on. In this case, (item **3**), the focus relates the documents threads and people to this file.

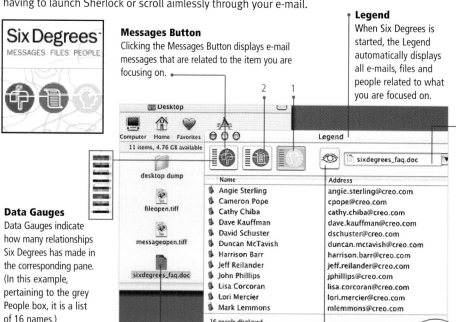

Data Gauges

Data Gauges indicate how many relationships Six Degrees has made in the corresponding pane. (In this example, pertaining to the grey People box, it is a list of 16 names.)

Watch Applications Button

Control how the Legend focuses on items with the Watch Applications button.

• When the eye is open (default), the legend automatically changes focus as you open messages and files.

• Click the button to close the eye, and the legend holds its current focus.

DOUBLE-CLICK DOES THE TRICK ...

When you double-click on an item in the legend list, note the following:

• Native application will be launched when a **File** is selected.

• Contact information will be displayed when a **Name** is selected.

• E-mail client will open when a **Message** is selected.

1. People Button

Clicking the People Button displays the people related to the item you are focusing on. In this illustration notice that the People button is grey and 16 names are listed. (It is important to note that the grey area highlights the current area of focus in the legend.)

TIP: Select a person from the list and drag their name to the desktop. This creates a 'Person file' on your desktop. Double-click this icon to see all items related to that person right from your desktop!

2. Files Button

Clicking the Files Button displays the files that are related to the item you are focusing on.

Note that Six Degrees software can locate files with similar names or file revisions anywhere on your system.

PRICE	DISTRIBUTION	SYS REQUIREMENTS	NOTES
Special introductory offer — $99 US	You can purchase Six Degrees from Creo's eStore: www.creo.com/sixdegrees	Mac OS X, using Microsoft Entourage as e-mail client.	Free 30-day evaluation download at www.creo.com/sixdegrees

Symantec

Protect your Macintosh from Internet threats with Symantec, the Internet security technology specialist with a broad range of content and network security software for individuals, enterprises and service providers. Symantec products ensure that you receive secure and protected information and that your Macintosh runs smoothly, reducing stress levels and saving you time.

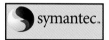

Internet Security

A firewall is your first line of defense against hackers and can be controlled with Norton Personal Firewall. It's available on its own or as part of Norton Internet Security suite which also includes:

- Norton AntiVirus for virus protection (also available for purchase on its own).
- Norton Privacy Control for keeping personal information private.
- Aladdin iClean — for freeing disk space and removing Internet clutter.
- Who's There? Firewall Advisor (from Open Door) for information on hacking attempts.

Norton Utilities

Forgot to make a backup and suddenly found your files damaged? Try Norton Utilities. It attempts to repair damaged files and disks, using:

- Norton Disk Doctor — for finding and repairing disk problems.
- Speed Disk — for optimizing your drive by reorganizing and defragmenting files.
- Norton FileSaver — for taking a snapshot of your drive's file directories.
- Volume Recover — for restoring crashed or accidentally erased disks.
- UnErase — for recovering virtually any accidentally deleted file.

Norton SystemWorks

Protect your data with Dantz Retrospect Express, the most popular backup program for the Macintosh. It's available as part of the Norton SystemWorks suite, including:
- Norton Utilities for optimizing performance and solving problems easily (also available for purchase on its own); • Norton AntiVirus for virus protection (also available for purchase on its own); • Alsoft Disk Warrior for recovering data in emergencies; and • Aladdin Spring Cleaning for safe uninstallation of old programs and Internet clutter removal.

TAKING CARE OF OS X
We provide more in-depth information about Norton Antivirus, Norton Disk Doctor, Norton Personal Firewall, Norton Utilities and Norton Speed Disk on pages 266, 267, 290, 291 and 294-297.

HOT TIP

Details reflect Australian criteria. May differ for other countries.

▷

PRODUCT	PRICE & SYS REQUIREMENTS	SOFTWARE INFORMATION
Norton Internet Security	ERP (inc GST): A$159 Upgrade (inc GST): A$97.90 ***Mac OS X:** 128Mb of RAM 25Mb of available hard disk space ***Mac OS 8 and Mac OS 9:** 24Mb of RAM, 25Mb of available hard disk space, Internet connection for LiveUpdate	Essential Internet protection for your Macintosh, this suite comprises Norton AntiVirus, Norton Privacy Control and Norton Personal Firewall in one convenient package, as well as two bonus applications, Aladdin iClean and Who's There? Firewall Advisor from Open Door.
Norton Personal Firewall	ERP (inc GST): A$109 Upgrade (inc GST): A$75.90 ***Mac OS X:** 128Mb of RAM 10Mb of available hard disk space ***Mac OS 8 and Mac OS 9:** 24Mb of RAM, 10Mb of available hard disk space. Internet connection for LiveUpdate	Norton Personal Firewall provides maximum defense against hackers. It: •keeps data private and secure; • prevents hackers by monitoring all incoming access attempts to your Mac and blocking unauthorized connections; • is easy to install and customize; and • supports Mac OS X.
Norton AntiVirus	ERP (inc GST): A$129 Upgrade (inc GST): A$86.90 ***Mac OS X:** 128Mb of RAM 15Mb of available hard disk space ***Mac OS 8 and Mac OS 9:** 24Mb of RAM, 10Mb of available hard disk space, Internet connection for LiveUpdate.	This antivirus software: • supports Mac OS X; •automatically removes viruses without interrupting your work; • detects viruses in e-mail attachments and Internet files during download; •eliminates macro viruses; • includes Exclusive Live Update technology for easy software updates via the Internet.
Norton SystemWorks	ERP (inc GST): A$199 Upgrade (inc GST): A$130.90 ***Mac OS X:** 128Mb of RAM 30Mb of available hard disk space ***Mac OS 8 and Mac OS 9:** 24Mb of RAM, 30Mb of available hard disk space. Internet connection for LiveUpdate.	This suite provides five leading utility products in one convenient package and supports Mac OS X. It consists of: • Norton Utilities; • Norton AntiVirus; • Retrospect Express Backup from Dantz; • Alsoft Disk Warrior; and • Aladdin Spring Cleaning.
Norton Utilities	Full version: A$149 Upgrade: A$97.90 ***Mac OS X:** 128Mb of RAM 15Mb of available hard disk space ***Mac OS 8 and Mac OS 9:** 24Mb of RAM, 15Mb of available hard disk space, Internet connection for LiveUpdate.	Norton Utilities optimizes performance and solves problems easily. It supports Mac OS X and includes: • Norton Disk Doctor; •Speed Disk; • Norton FileSaver; and • Volume Recover.

DISTRIBUTION: Available through the Apple reseller network. For upgrades, please call 1800 810 101.

*Further details re: recommended Mac processors can be obtained from www.symantec.com.au or 1800 680 026.

HP Photosmart c812

Snap, share and store images easily with the sleek and modest HP Photosmart c812. With its advanced features and easy-to-use photo and imaging software, it defines digital diversity. And that's not all. HP Instant Share Technology lets you select where you want your photos to go — right from your camera. PC, Mac, or the Photosmart 8881 digital camera dock? It's your call.

Memory card reader
Integrated digital memory card slot makes it easy to save and store more photos and accommodates SecureDigital (SD) memory cards (16Mb SD card included).

Automated advantage
Exposure levels, red-eye reduction and the flash are all enabled automatically.

LCD screen
The 1.5 inch color LCD screen allows you to see, share photos and save or delete photos on-the-fly, and has 4x magnification.

Digital zoom
The Pentax lens provides 21x total zoom (3x optical zoom and 7x digital zoom), f-stop versatility, auto-focus for close-ups and panoramics and has 4.13MP resolution.

Sleeping Beauty
Small, sleek design.

Camera dock
Connect your camera to the Photosmart 8881 digital camera dock. You can instantly send and view photos and recharge batteries with it. (Note: camera dock comes standard with the Photosmart 8881 when purchased in Australia.)

Audio/Video features
You can record video clips up to 30 seconds per image with audio, by simply switching from camera to video mode.

PRICE & WARRANTY
Suggested Retail: $1,299
1 year hardware warranty

DISTRIBUTION
Hewlett-Packard Australia
(see also www.hp.com)

SYSTEM REQUIREMENTS
(Macintosh): 233 MHz Power PC processor, 64Mb RAM, 150Mb free hard disk space, 800 x 600 16-bit color display, CD-ROM drive, USB port, Mac OS 9.0, 9.1, or OS X 10.1 or higher.`

MORE COOL FEATURES

- With HP InstantShare you can send photos to your connected PC, Mac, or digital camera dock. (Select up to 14 destinations, including e-mail addresses, printers, and more.)
- Works with USB compatible PCs and Macs equipped with Microsoft Windows XP, 98, 2000 Professional, Me, and Mac OS 9.1 or higher and OS X 10.1 and higher.
- Easily print photos directly from your camera to an HP Photosmart or Deskjet printer with USB connectivity — no PC required!

Details reflect Australian criteria. May differ for other countries.

HP PSC 2210

Don't let looks deceive you. The HP PSC 2210 may be small but it's innovatively versatile and cleverly compact. With HP's PhotoRet4 color layering technology you can achieve outstanding output quality for printing, scanning, copying and faxing. You can also print photos directly from your digital camera memory card without using a PC. Sounds all too easy? Well, it is.

Peak copy productivity
Make up to 99 copies from one original at 17cpm (black) and 12cpm (color) and enlarge from 25 to 400 percent.

Versatile flatbed scanning design
Makes scanning and copying existing photos and 3D objects easy, with results up to 1,200 x 2,400 dpi (optical) and 19,200 dpi (enhanced).

Sharper images, more intricate details
The HP PSC 2210 delivers up to 4,800-optimized dpi mode and HP Photo Paper makes images sharper and more intricate. This alternative printing mode is ideal for high-resolution source images up to 1,200 x 1,200 dpi.

Creative features
Create instant projects with the 'creative copying' feature — without a PC; • reduce or enlarge images from 25 to 400 percent of the original size; • image can appear multiple times on one page with the new Clone feature; • new tiled poster feature enlarges originals up to 400 percent; • Mirror image reverses your picture or photo image for iron-on transfers.

MORE COOL NEW FEATURES
- Compact product — fits in anywhere.
- Easy installation: all software on one disk.
- Memory card slots for *CompactFlash, *SmartMedia, *Secure Digital and *Sony Memory stick.
- Scan-to-e-mail, Share-to-Web.
- 100 sheet input tray, 50 sheet output tray, single envelope slot.

Preview photos from digital camera
Print preview (HP Photo Sheet) directly from your digital camera's memory card slots* without a computer, to make your choice of image/s.

Fast color faxing
Fax transmission is faster thanks to built-in 33.6kbps modem. Speed dial buttons ensure that color faxes are sent with ease.

PRICE & WARRANTY	DISTRIBUTION
Suggested Retail: $749 1 year hardware warranty (See also www.officejetsupport.com)	Hewlett-Packard Australia: www.hp.com.au

SYSTEM REQUIREMENTS

(Macintosh): G3 processor; Macintosh OS 9.0, 9.1 (64Mb RAM), and OS X (128Mb RAM); 100Mb available hard disk space, plus 50Mb for full-color scanning; CD-ROM drive; 800 x 600 and 256-color display; sound card and internet access recommended, local connect requires available USB port.

Nikon COOLPIX 4300

High quality digital to go — that's the Nikon COOLPIX 4300 digital camera with its 3x Optical Zoom-Nikkor Lens and 4.0 effective megapixels housed in a portable design. But don't be fooled — it's more than just a pretty face. This little masterpiece will enhance your inventiveness and make transferring images to your Mac a breeze. And let's not forget its ability to take pretty pictures too.

Stunningly Crisp, Colorful Images
The 3x optical zoom-Nikkor lens, offering a focal range of 8-24mm (equivalent to 38-114mm in 35mm [135] format), and 4.0 million effective pixels combine to give you sharp, vivid images in living color — from breathtaking open landscapes to fabulous close-up photography.

Shutter speeds
From 1/1000 to 8 sec.

Multi Autofocus
5-Area Multi Autofocus for versatile photo composition.

Take Great Pictures Easily
Start up your digital photography with the COOLPIX 4300's Auto mode and then progress to the 12 programmed Scene Modes. The camera automatically makes adjustments for your choice of specific situations such as Portrait, Landscape, Sunset and Museum, letting you easily turn great scenes into memorable photographs. There's also Manual mode, which gives you control over exposure value and various settings.

SYSTEM REQUIREMENTS

Mac OS 9.0 — 9.2 (only built-in USB ports supported), Mac OS X (10.1.2 or later); **Models:** iMac*, Power Macintosh G3 (Blue/White), Power Mac* G4 or later; iBook*, PowerBook G3 or later only built-in USB ports are supported; **RAM:** 64Mb or more recommended,
Hard Disk: 25Mb required for installation, with additional amount equivalent to twice the capacity of the camera memory card plus 10Mb required when Nikon View 5 is running; **Display:** 800 x 600 with thousands of colors or millions of colors recommended or higher; **CD-ROM** drive required for installation.

PRICE	DISTRIBUTION	NOTES
Suggested Retail: $1,199	Leading camera stores. All enquiries to1300 366 499.	For more information, visit www.coolpix.com.au

Portability and Comfort

The COOLPIX 4300's compact, lightweight design makes for a camera that goes anywhere. Its smooth, friendly contours offer a secure, comfortable grip with a modern look. And the clear, sensible ergonomics make all buttons and controls easily accessible.

One-Touch Upload

The COOLPIX 4300 makes transferring images from your camera to your computer one-button easy, letting you share them with family and friends sooner — via e-mail or a Web site. The supplied Nikon View 5 software turns your computer into the most versatile photo album ever, and the camera's Small Picture function enables the creation of a reduced-size copy within the camera making images easier to e-mail.

SOME OTHER COOL NEW THINGS

- Macro shooting at minimum distance of 4cm.
- Best Shot Selector (BSS) automatically chooses the best shot in continuous mode.
- Versatile white balance settings and White Balance Bracketing.
- Noise Reduction Mode.
- Movies (up to 35 sec.).
- Quick Review button to review images and keep/delete, without interrupting shooting.
- Longer battery life of approx. 90 min with Li-ion rechargeable battery EN-EL1.
- Plug-and-play USB interface for smooth connection to a computer (USB Mass Storage Class or PTP).
- Compatible with Nikon Telephoto, Wideangle and Fisheye Converter Lenses, and Slide Copy adaptor (requires optional Step Down Ring Lens Adaptor UR-E4).
- All-in-one package provides everything required for immediate use, including Lens Cap, Hand strap, Video Cable, 16Mb CompactFlash Card, USB Cable UC-E1, Rechargeable Li-ion Battery EN-EL1, Battery Charger MH-53, Nikon View 5 CD-ROM image management software.

Wacom graphics tablets

Wacom graphics tablets are the fastest, most comfortable way to work with your computer. Providing something for every creative 'dabbler' from novice to graphic designer, page layout artist to 3D animator, CAD modeler to photographer, these tablets are changing the way the digital world works.

intuos2

Intuos2 product line
Intuos2 is the professional graphics tablet that turns on the full power of Photoshop's 19 pressure-sensitive tools. With its comfortable Grip Pen and feature-packed mouse, you have the control and power you need to really get the most out of all your graphics applications. Available in 5 sizes, Intuos2 is both Mac and PC compatible. (iMac and Power Mac users require Mac OS 7.1 or later (Serial version) or Mac OS 8.0 or later (USB version) to utilize Intuos2.)

Menu Strip
Programmable Menu strip on all models.

Tilt Sensitivity
 +/- 60% all sizes support tilt angle and tilt direction, particularly useful when using calligraphy pen and airbrushing.

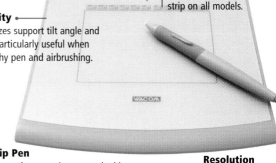

Resolution
2450 lpi

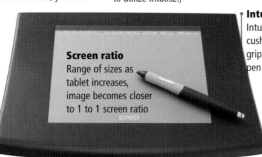

Screen ratio
Range of sizes as tablet increases, image becomes closer to 1 to 1 screen ratio

Intuos2 Grip Pen
Intuos2 enlarges the pen grip area and adds a cushioned rubber sleeve to minimize the required grip pressure by up to 40 percent. In addition, the pen and eraser has 1024 pressure levels.

Ambidextrous Abilities
Use two Intuos2 devices at the same time with Dual Track for 6 x 8"and larger. The mouse can be held in one hand to orient an object in 3D space, while the other hand can paint it with the Intuos Pen.

4D Mouse
Intuos2 4D Mouse: Wacom's redesigned 4D Mouse comes with Intuos2 9 x 12 sized tablet. It gives users rotation control, five customizable buttons and a programmable thumbwheel.

TABLET SIZES
4 x 5": Smallest tablet, comes with Intuos2 pen.
6 x 8" (Approx. A5): fits neatly on your desktop, lap or briefcase, comes with Intuos2 pen.
 9 x 12": Perfect size for professional computer imaging. Matches aspect ratio and size of most monitors, includes Intuos2 pen and 4D mouse.
12 x 12" (Working area is approx. A4): Perfect for full page creation or tracing at scale, or graphics that require a full arm motion.
12 x 18"(Working area is approx. A3:) High resolution, 1 to1 scaling ratio options, for precise, accurate work.

b

Adobe
Photoshop Elements 2.0

a

Software Included
Intuos2 is bundled with the following software (PC and Macintosh-compatible): • procreate Painter Classic (a) Expression 2 Lite, • Adobe Photoshop Elements (b) — 6 x 8 size only.

SYNOPSIS

Cintiq

Cintiq product line
Cintiq offers a powerful new way to work directly on the screen, combining the advantages of an LCD monitor with the control, comfort and productivity provided by a Wacom tablet.

LCD monitor
The LCD monitor (available in black or cream) has a highly durable glass surface, 16.7 million colors and 1,024 x 768 resolution. The Cintiq 15x has a full 15" diagonal viewing area, while the Cintiq 18sx has a full 18.1" high resolution display.

Batteryless and cordless pen

Pen used directly on screen

Removable pen holder

Pen includes DuoSwitch as well as pressure-sensitive eraser

Adjustable, removable stand

Pen has 512 levels of pressure-sensitivity

Cintiq 18x pen and stand

graphire2

graphire2 product line
Have fun with your digital photos with graphire2's new and improved tablet. It's perfect for the digital photographer, budding videographer and computer graphics enthusiast.

Choose from three translucent colors — white, graphite silver or sapphire blue.

Pressure-sensitive pen technology. Works with Mac OS X.2's handwriting recognition software, Inkwell.

Removable pen stand.

Clear overlay for tracing.

Software Included
graphire2 is bundled with procreate Painter Classic (see (a) left) and Expression 2 Lite and Pen Plus Personal (Annotation software).

PRODUCT	PRICE & COLOR
Graphire 2	4 x 5 with pen: $182 Available in white, graphite silver or sapphire blue
Intuos 2	4 x 5 with Pen: $440 6 x 8* with Pen: $682 9 x 12* with Pen and 4D Mouse: $924 12 x 12 with Pen: $924 12 x 18 with: $1,320 All models in ice blue (* = also in deep purple)
Cintiq	Cintiq 15x: $4,620 Cintiq 18sx: $9,020 LCD monitor available in black or cream

DISTRIBUTION
VideoBytes Australia: http://www.videobytes.com.au

More
technical

One root to rule them all

In Mac OS X, one user account can do anything: create, change
and delete any file; start, stop or alter any program; and connect
or disconnect any user. This user is called 'root', and its absolute
power can corrupt your system absolutely. Only enable and use
the root user if you must, and you know exactly what you're
doing. The majority of administration can be achieved without
enabling the root user at all.

Net Info Manager

First things first
Before you can use the root user in Mac OS X, you will
have to enable it. Do this using NetInfo Manager,
which is in Utilities in Mac OS X's Applications folder.

Moving target
Before Mac OS X 10.2, these functions were under the
Security submenu of the Domain menu. Now, Security
is a menu of its own.

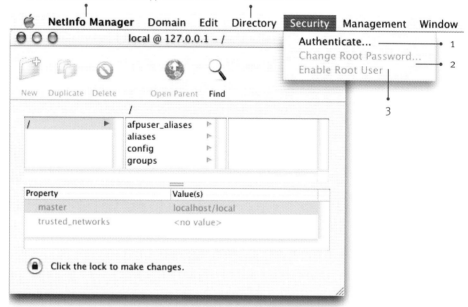

1. Who goes there?
You will have to
'authenticate' (provide
your Admin username
and password) before
you can enable the root
user. In fact, you'll
probably have to
authenticate more than
once.

2. Password protect
Your root user password
should be different to
your ordinary Admin
password, and
impossible to guess.
Note: the system only
checks the first eight
characters of your
password.

3. Shut the gate
when you leave
This menu item changes
to Disable Root User
after you enable root.
Disable the root user as
soon as you're finished
with it.

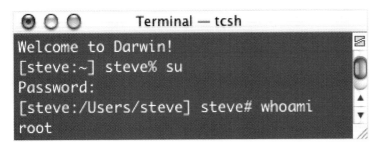

```
⊖ ○ ○              Terminal — tcsh
Welcome to Darwin!
[steve:~] steve% su
Password:
[steve:/Users/steve] steve# whoami
root
```

Superuser ahoy

After you've enabled the root user, there are two ways you can login as root. First, you can choose Log Out from the Apple menu and log back in the root. This will require you to type 'root' as your username, so click the Other button if you're presented with a list of users rather than username and password fields. Once you login as root, you will be able to do anything. For example, you can delete corrupt files that otherwise refuse to budge, but you can also drag vital system resources to the Trash, so be careful. If you are comfortable using Mac OS X's command line (see pages 292, 293), you can login as root through the Terminal. Just type 'su', then give the root user's password when prompted. Then type 'whoami' to confirm you're now the root user. You are only the root user within that particular Terminal window, so to end your root user session, close the window.

WARNING
Never create a user account with the name 'root', as conflicts between this account and the real root user can make your computer behave strangely.

WARNING

Everyday admin

When you first used Mac OS X, your Mac created an admin account in your name. This account has administration privileges, which means it can do anything from installing new software, to creating and deleting accounts for non-admin users, to passing oneself off as the all-powerful root user (see pages 248, 249.)

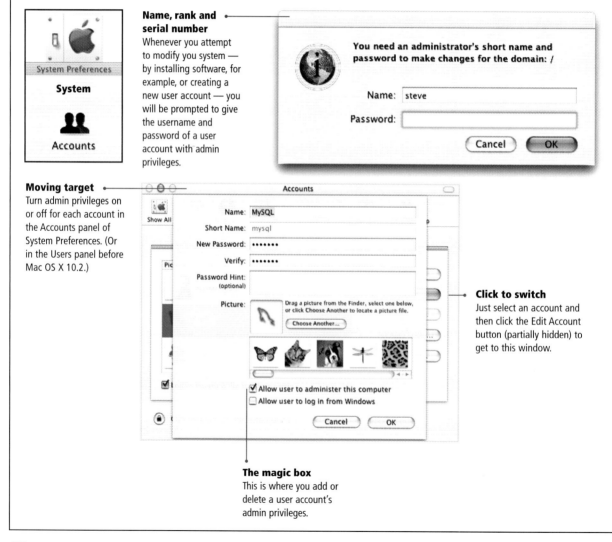

Name, rank and serial number
Whenever you attempt to modify you system — by installing software, for example, or creating a new user account — you will be prompted to give the username and password of a user account with admin privileges.

You need an administrator's short name and password to make changes for the domain: /

Name: steve

Password:

Cancel   OK

Moving target
Turn admin privileges on or off for each account in the Accounts panel of System Preferences. (Or in the Users panel before Mac OS X 10.2.)

Accounts

Name: MySQL
Short Name: mysql
New Password: ••••••
Verify: ••••••
Password Hint: (optional)
Picture: Drag a picture from the Finder, select one below, or click Choose Another to locate a picture file.

Choose Another...

☑ Allow user to administer this computer
☐ Allow user to log in from Windows

Cancel   OK

Click to switch
Just select an account and then click the Edit Account button (partially hidden) to get to this window.

The magic box
This is where you add or delete a user account's admin privileges.

System Preferences

System

Accounts

```
000                    Terminal — tcsh
Last login: Tue Oct 22 11:02:49 on ttyp4
Welcome to Darwin!
[steve:~] steve% cd /private/var/root
[steve:/private/var/root] steve% ls -l
total 0
drwx------   9 root   wheel   306 Aug 19 10:23 Desktop
drwxr-xr-x   5 root   wheel   170 Aug 21 21:16 Library
[steve:/private/var/root] steve% ls Desktop
ls: Desktop: Permission denied
[steve:/private/var/root] steve% sudo ls Desktop
Password:
Picture 1.tiff   Picture 3.tiff   Picture 5.tiff   Picture 7.tiff
Picture 2.tiff   Picture 4.tiff   Picture 6.tiff
```

Skeleton key
The user account 'steve' has admin privileges, so it can use the sudo ('superuser do') command to perform any other action as if it was the root user. Just place 'sudo' before any command that requires root user privileges and give your admin password (no — you don't even need the root user's password) when prompted. In this case, we used sudo to view the contents of /private/var/root/Desktop. The directory contained seven pictures in TIFF format.

Access denied
In short, this transcript shows that the /private/var/root/Desktop directory belongs to the all-powerful root user (see 'One root to rule them all', page 248, 249), and no other user is permitted to view this directory's contents.

Avoiding Problems
To reduce the risk that you'll accidentally damage your system, you should create a non-admin account for your day-to-day work, and only use your admin username and password when necessary.

TECH TIP

Accounting for difference

You might think you own one Mac, but actually you own a thousand. Each of these 'Macs' is actually a different account on your Macintosh, and each of these accounts can have its own secure area to store its owner's documents (the place you go when you click the Home button), its own e-mail address, its own desktop picture — even its own language.

System

Accounts

1. Initial account
When you first run Mac OS X, its set-up program will ask you for your name and address, and create a default account to match.

2. What's in a name?
In Mac OS X 10.2, you create, edit and delete accounts in the Accounts panel of System Preferences.
Before Mac OS X 10.2, you would do this in the Users panel of Mac OS X's System Preferences. Same concept, different name.

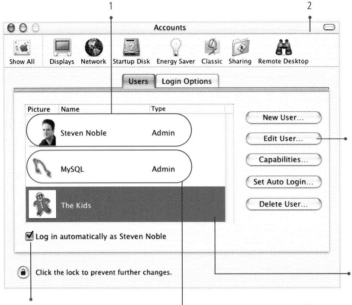

Edit the user
Click this button to change an account's name or password. Note: Mac OS X only pays attention to the first eight characters of the password. This is also where you can grant or revoke an account's Admin privileges (via the 'Allow User To Administer This Computer' checkbox) and change the small picture that represents the account in the login screen.

Out of harm's way
Notice that the user account called 'The Kids' does not have admin privileges. If this is the only account that your children can access, they will not be able to install software, delete your Internet password or make other potentially catastrophic changes.

Avoid the hassle
Put a tick in this checkbox if you don't want to have to select your default account and enter your password every time you fire up your Mac. You can still make your way to the login screen by choosing Log Out from the Finder's Apple menu. To change the user account that automatically opens when you start-up your Mac, select a new account in this window, click the 'Set Auto Login' button, and then give the new account's password when prompted.

Accounts aren't just for people
If you do serious web development using a program like MySQL, you might want to create a secure account for that program alone. That way, if a hacker seizes control of the account that drives your Internet database, they don't have automatic access to the rest of your Mac.

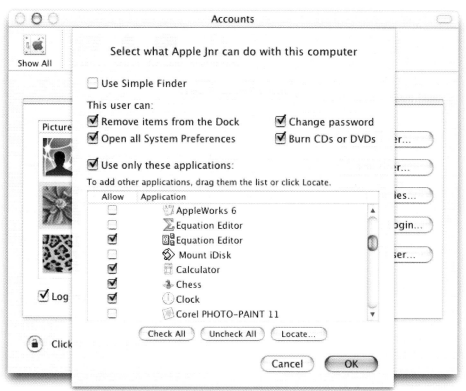

Set the rules
You, as an admin user, can control how a non-admin account's ability can and cannot use your Mac. Just select the account in the Account panel's main window then click the Capabilities button to come to this window. If you put a tick in the Use Simple Finder checkbox, the non-admin account will employ a child-like version of the Mac OS X interface. To create a My Applications folder for this user that only contains the applications you want this account to use, use the 'Show These Applications In "My Applications" folder' checkbox and the controls that are below it.

King of the castle

Under Mac OS X, if you are the owner of a file or application or your user account has administration privileges, you are king. You can decide whether you will use, change or delete the file, and you grant these 'permissions' (as they are known) to any other user — or revoke them at will.

Hard Disk

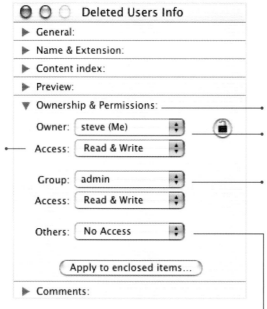

Permission central
To view or modify a file's permissions, click it once in a Finder window to select it, then select Get Info from the File menu. In the palette that appears, click the Ownership & Permissions disclosure triangle to view these controls. Note: before Mac OS X 10.2, the menu item was called Show Info not Get Info, and there was a pop-up menu rather than a disclosure triangle.

What's mine is mine
From this menu, you can change the file's owner. Mac OS X marks your own user account with '(Me)'.

Group therapy
Most users belong to several Unix 'groups', which are a handy way of granting permissions to a group of users simultaneously. For example, to grant certain permissions to every user with Admin privileges, you would select the wheel group, to which all Admin users belong.

Reading, 'riting and 'rithmatic
Allow the owner of this file to use it without changing it (select 'Read Only' from the pop-up menu), to use and change it ('Read & Write'), or neither ('No Access').

Catchall category
This is where you determine whether 'everyone else' may read or alter the file.

Drill down
If you are modifying a folder rather than single file, the 'Apply to enclosed items' button will appear here. Note: clicking this button only applies your permission changes (the changes to the Owner, Group and Others pop-up menus) to the enclosed items. It does not apply any ownership changes (the changes to the two Access pop-up menus). To apply ownership changes to enclosed items you must either modify them one by one, or use the Unix 'chown' command (see 'In command', pages 292, 293).

Final piece in the puzzle

Programmers are used to thinking in threes: read, write and execute. Yet Mac OS X's Get Info command only lets you specify whether you can read or write a file. To make a script executable (or vice versa), use Unix's 'chmod' command (see 'In command', pages 292, 293).

Handle with care

Needless to say, changing a file's ownership or permissions can be quite dangerous. Only change ownership or permissions if you must do so, you understand what you are doing, and you've got a backup of your system. Apple has provided tools for returning all permissions to their default settings if you (or some renegade software) make an error in this area. However, restoring all settings to their defaults can be dangerous too, as it can override settings that certain programs require. To restore the default settings in Mac OS X 10.2 or later, go to the First Aid tab of Disk Utility (Applications > Utilities), and click the Repair Disk Permissions button.

To restore the default settings in Mac OS X 10.1.5, download the Repair Privileges utility from Apple Support (www.apple.com/support). If you are using an earlier version of Mac OS X, upgrade to 10.1.5 via Software Update (see 'Keep up with the Joneses', pages 174, 175), and then use the Repair Privileges utility.

Commit to print

Printing from Mac OS X couldn't be simpler. If you buy a new printer from a major manufacturer, chances are you'll find that software for using the printer is already built into Mac OS X. Just turn on your printer's software in Print Center (Applications > Utilities), and you're ready to print from just about any program on your Mac.

Print Center

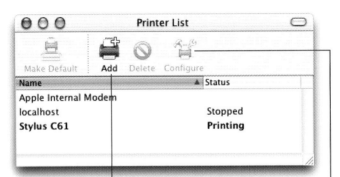

Pick your printer
The printer that you made the default printer in Print Center will appear here first.

Add a printer
If you don't see your printer, click the Add button, choose a connection method from the pop-up method, select your printer when it appears, then click the Add button. If your printer does not appear, check your printer's installation CD-ROM or its manufacturer's Web site for Mac OS X printing software.

More than this
Clicking this button does more than enable you to configure your printer. Mac OS X also includes software for maintaining the ink cartridges and nozzles of many popular printers, and you access these features by clicking the Configure button.

US Letter or A4
It's also worth visiting Print Center's Preferences (from the Print Center menu) before you start printing.

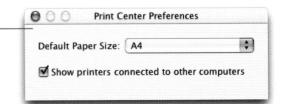

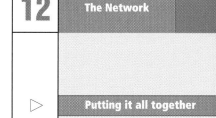
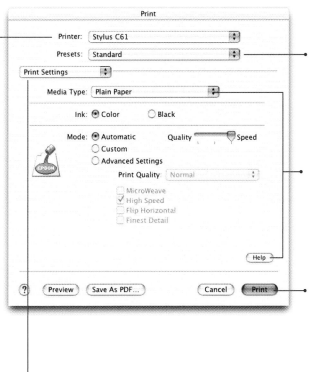

Time saver
If you find yourself using the same print settings repeatedly, save them by selecting Save from the Presets pop-up menu. If you create several presets for different tasks (in-house drafts, official correspondence, photographs), you can toggle between them with this menu.

Just for you
Chances are, your printer will add a panel to Mac OS X's Print dialog box, too. The Epson Stylus C61 added this panel, which makes it easy to save time and ink when you can afford to wind back quality, or to maximize quality when that is most important.

Central station
Select Print from almost any Mac OS X program's File menu to come to a Print dialog box like this one.

Endless options
Use this pop-up menu to switch between the Print dialogue box's many settings panels, where you will be able to determine how many copies you will print and many other matters.

The program that you are printing from will probably insert its own panel, too. For example, Internet Explorer's Print dialog box panel allows you to override a Web site's background pattern when you print it.

Straightforward scanning

A desktop scanner is great for bringing photos and documents into your Mac. In fact, some people even use them to scan flowers, hands and other found objects. If Mac OS X drivers came with your scanner or are available online, using a scanner with your Mac is simplicity itself. Here's how:

Scanning

TWAIN's the name of the game
As long as it has Mac OS X-ready TWAIN driver software, you can use your scanner with any TWAIN-ready program, including Image Capture, which is included free with Mac OS X. We downloaded drivers for the Epson Perfection

1660 scanner from Epson's support web site (www.epson.com/support), but you could find them on the scanner's set-up CD-ROM or on a Mac OS X downloads site like VersionTracker (www.versiontracker.com/macosx/). Before you buy a scanner, check that Mac OS X drivers are

available. If you don't see a window like this one in Image Capture after you install the Mac OS X TWAIN drivers, select Preferences from Image Capture's Preferences window, put a tick in the 'Use TWAIN Software Whenever Possible' checkbox, then quit and relaunch Image Capture.

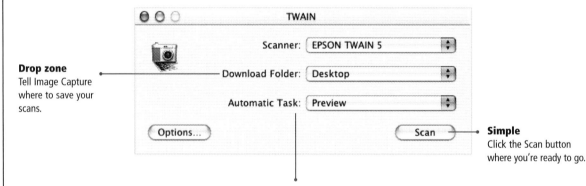

Drop zone
Tell Image Capture where to save your scans.

Simple
Click the Scan button where you're ready to go.

Do as I say
If you wish, you can tell Image Capture to automatically open your scans in a graphics program, like Mac OS X's Preview.

▷ **Putting it all together**

TWAIN for action
Once you click the Scan
button, the TWAIN driver
will take over.

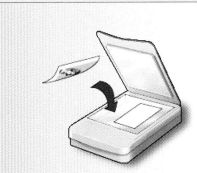

EPSON TWAIN 5

EPSON

To scan in Full Auto mode, place the
document on the document table, then
click Scan.

To switch to Manual mode, click Manual
Mode.

Close   Manual Mode...   Scan

☑ Specify Document Source for Full Auto Mode
   ● Reflective   ○ Film

☑ Specify Resolution for Full Auto Mode
   Reflective [300] 🔼   Film [300] 🔼

Finer detail
If you're scanning for the
Web, scan at 72dpi. If
you're scanning for print,
scan at your printer's
maximum resolution or
300dpi — whichever is
less. If you want to
enlarge the image,
increase the scanning
resolution
proportionately. For
example, if you wish to
print a scan at twice the
size of the original
image, scan at 600dpi.

See right through you
As our Epson model can scan both
reflective material (such as photographs)
and transparent material (like film), the
driver allows us to select the appropriate
scanning mode.

Blue in the tooth

Sometimes we don't need fast networks and fancy features. Sometimes we just want to connect two nearby devices so they can exchange small quantities of data. Bluetooth is the answer, especially if you have a Bluetooth-enabled mobile phone or handheld computer that you can connect to your Mac. Here, we show how to beam a file from one Bluetooth-enabled Mac to another.

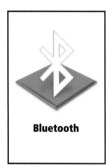

Bluetooth

Instant Bluetooth
With Mac OS X 10.2, you need only plug the D-Link DWB-120M USB Bluetooth Adapter into a spare USB port on your Mac and this Bluetooth panel will appear in System Preferences. (Quit and relaunch System Preferences if necessary.) To access this panel with earlier versions of Mac OS X, you should upgrade to Mac OS X 10.1.5 via Software Updates (see pages 174, 175), and then download Apple's Bluetooth software from Apple support (www.apple.com/support).

Arrivals desk
Tell the Bluetooth software where it should save incoming files, whether it should ask you before receiving them, and whether it should open the files when they hit your hard disk.

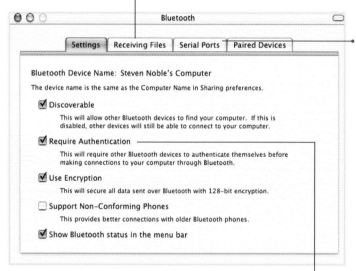

Bonus software
The Serial Ports tab is designed to help you synchronize your Mac with a handheld computer (see pages 140, 141). You don't need to use it to send a file to another Mac via Bluetooth.

BSD subsystem install
Note: If you did not install the BSD subsystem (it's installed by default when you install Mac OS X), you will have to install it before you can use Apple's Bluetooth software.

Joined at the hip
If you select this option, 'pair' your Mac with another (via the Paired Devices tab) before you attempt to send a file to the other Mac using the Bluetooth File Exchange utility. (Two Macs should be able to exchange Bluetooth 'passkeys' without being paired, but pairing was necessary when we tested Mac OS X Bluetooth Technology Preview 2.1.)

Departure lounge
Drag any file onto the Bluetooth File Exchange icon (Applications > Utilities) to open this window, which allows you to send the file to another Bluetooth-enabled Macintosh.

Destination Macintosh
This window will show every discoverable Bluetooth device within range, and every device in your Bluetooth Favorites list.

○ ○ ○   Send File: rules_of_footy.pdf

Select one or more recipients:

Recipient
iBook

(Search) Idle.

(Add to Favorites)   (Cancel) (Send)

Phone a friend
Click Search to find all discoverable Bluetooth devices within range.

My favorite Macs
When you find a Bluetooth device that you want to connect to regularly, click it once and then click Add to Favorites to have it automatically appear in this window without searching.

Final farewell
Choose a device and then click Send to send it the file.

Warning
One of the promises of Bluetooth is wireless printing. But before you invest in a Bluetooth adaptor for your Mac and Bluetooth-enabled printer to match, check whether the Mac OS X Bluetooth software has begun to support wireless printing. The version of the software that was current at the time of writing (Technology Preview 2.1) did not include this ability.

Get on the net

There are dozens of ways you can connect your Mac to the Internet, but most of them are fairly straightforward. One method — signing up with the ISP that has agreed to provide Internet access to Apple customers in your country of residence — is so simple that it requires virtually no technical knowledge.

Internet

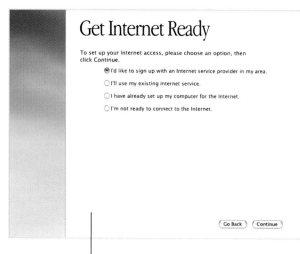

Get Internet Ready

To set up your Internet access, please choose an option, then click Continue.

- ● I'd like to sign up with an Internet service provider in my area.
- ○ I'll use my existing internet service.
- ○ I have already set up my computer for the Internet.
- ○ I'm not ready to connect to the Internet.

(Go Back) (Continue)

A, B, C, 1, 2, 3
When you first run Mac OS X on your Mac, it will walk you through the Internet set-up process. Easy.

Path of least resistance
In many countries, Apple has partnered with a major ISP to provide reliable Internet access to its customers. Signing up with this ISP is the simplest method of getting online. Just connect a telephone jack to your Mac's modem port (marked with a telephone handset symbol), then start your Mac or Mac OS X for the first time, and Mac OS X's Setup Assistant will launch automatically. When you reach its Get Internet Ready panel, select 'I'd like to sign up with an Internet service provider in my area', then click Continue. Your Mac will automatically download the contact details for Apple's ISP partner in your country, then walk you through the simple sign-up process.

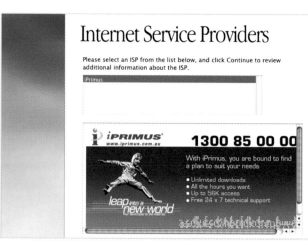
SYNOPSIS

INFINITE POSSIBILITIES
Having your Mac's modem dial into an ISP is only one of a dozen ways you can connect your Mac to the Internet. Other options include AirPort (which is wireless) and broadband (which is much faster than a modem). Whether you want to upgrade to AirPort or broadband or you simply want to switch to a cheaper ISP, the Network panel of System Preferences (see pages 66, 67) is where you will enter most of your new Internet settings.

Modem: Idle

Connect

USB Bluetooth Modem Adaptor
✓ Internal Modem

✓ Show time connected
✓ Show status while connecting

Open Internet Connect...

Connect, disconnect
Once you have setup your account with an ISP, you can connect and disconnect via Internet Connect (in Mac OS X's Applications folder). But with Mac OS X, Apple introduced a far more convenient option – inconspicuous menus that can appear in the top-right corner of your screen. To add one of these menus to your menu bar, just select 'Show status in menu bar' in the appropriate panel of Internet Connect. To connect to the Internet or disconnect, select Connect or Disconnect from the menu.

Checklist
If you want to use an ISP other than Apple's preferred partner in your country, you'll need some information from your ISP before connecting to the Internet:
• Your username and password;
• Your ISP's local dial-up number in your city or town;
• Whether to configure TCP/IP manually or using PPP, plus your IP address if you are to configure it manually; and
• The address of your ISP's domain name system (DNS) server. Once you have all this, go to the Get Internet Ready panel of Mac OS X's Setup Assistant, select 'I'll use my existing Internet service', then click the Continue button. The Setup Assistant will help you to configure your Mac to use this account. Later, enter this information in the Network panel of System Preferences. (See pages 66, 67.)
Note: the Get Internet Ready panel also contains the option 'I'm not ready to connect to the Internet', should users not have the necessary information.

Here, there, everywhere

If you continually move your Mac between work, school and home, there's no need to manually update your network/Internet settings each time. Instead, Mac OS X allows you to record the settings required for each location, and toggle between them with a single click.

System Preferences

Internet & Network

Network

Automatic ease
When you first set up your Mac for Internet or network access, Mac OS X stores your settings in a default location file called Automatic. To edit the network/Internet settings for that location, choose it from the Location pop-up menu, then reconfigure any part of the Network panel of System Preferences. To edit another location's settings, select it instead before you start making changes.

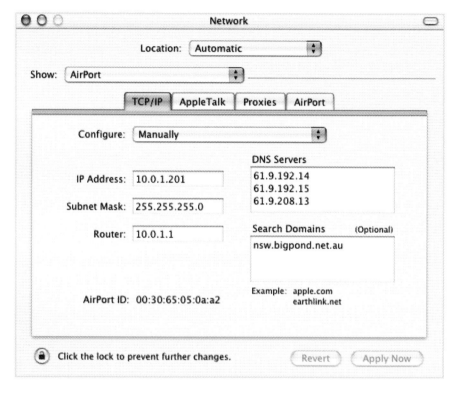

Beyond Mac OS X
Mac OS X's Locations feature allows you to automatically change your Internet/network settings when you move your Mac. However, the version of Mac OS X that was current when this book went to press (Mac OS X 10.2) could not automatically select a new default printer, time zone or email address for each new location. That's where Location X steps in — it can switch all these settings and more. This program is shareware, meaning you can download a demonstration version to try before you buy from: homepage.mac.com/locationmanager/

Courses for horses

If your Mac is set up to access the Internet at work and you want to use it to connect from home as well, select Edit Locations from the Location pop-up menu to come to this window. Give the new name 'Work' to Automatic, duplicate that location, rename the duplicate location 'Home', and start editing Home's settings.

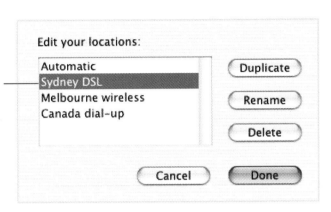

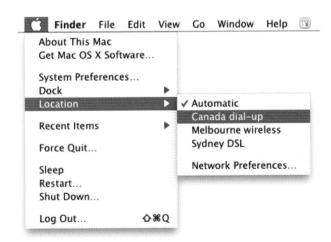

Instant switch

Once you've created a group of network/Internet settings for each location, switching between them is just a matter of selecting the current location from the Apple menu's Location submenu. Mac OS X takes care of the rest.

Friends and foe

There's a flipside to connecting your Mac to the Internet. While it allows you to access a world of information, it can also give hackers the opportunity to break into your Mac. Luckily, Mac OS X includes a firewall — the traditional tool for guarding against intruders — and Mac OS X 10.2 makes it much easier to use.

Firewall

At your service

Mac OS X provides a range of networking 'services', such as the ability to share files with Mac users ('Personal File Sharing'), PC users ('Windows File Sharing'), and as Web pages ('Personal Web Sharing'). To allow or block access to these services from other computers, go to the Services panel, select the service in question, and click Start or Stop. Mac OS X will take care of updating the firewall's settings.

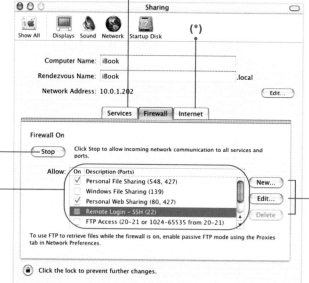

(*) Share you protection

With Mac OS X providing a secure connection to the Internet, the obvious next step is to share that connection with the other computers in your home or business. Interested? Jump to the Internet panel.

Relax

The firewall is on, so you're protected. You can click Stop to turn it off and Start to switch it on again.

Selective access

This firewall is configured to allow other computers to access the Mac's web pages and shared files. At present, it does not allow Windows file sharing, remote login, or FTP access.

Provide a passport

If the firewall is on, it blocks all incoming network traffic that it has not been told to allow. To allow a new form of incoming network traffic, click the New button. If the service you wish to permit is listed in the Port Name pop-up menu, select it then click OK. Otherwise, select Other from the pop-up menu. Enter a name and port number for the service.

Finding port numbers

You can find the usual port number for most services in the Internet Assigned Numbers Authority's list (www.iana.org/assignments/port-numbers). For example, to allow Rendezvous traffic when the firewall is enabled, you would enter Other, 5298, and Rendezvous. A Mac-specific list of port numbers is also available in the Apple Knowledge Base (kbase.info.apple.com).

```
●  ○  ○                    Terminal — tcsh
IPFW(8)                 System Manager's Manual                    IPFW(8)

NAME
     ipfw - IP firewall and traffic shaper control program

SYNOPSIS
     ipfw [-q] [-p preproc [-D macro[=value]] [-U macro]] pathname
     ipfw [-f | -q] flush
     ipfw [-q] {zero | resetlog | delete} [number ...]
     ipfw [-s [field]] [-aftN] {list | show} [number ...]
     ipfw [-q] add [number] rule-body
     ipfw pipe number config pipe-config-options
     ipfw pipe {delete | list | show} [number ...]
     ipfw queue number config queue-config-options
     ipfw queue {delete | list | show} [number ...]

DESCRIPTION
     ipfw is the user interface for controlling the ipfirewall(4) and the
     dummynet(4) traffic shaper in FreeBSD.

     Each incoming or outgoing packet is passed through the ipfw rules.  If
     host is acting as a gateway, packets forwarded by the gateway are pro-
     cessed by ipfw twice.  In case a host is acting as a bridge, packets for-
:
```

Firewall and a half

While the Firewall pane in the Sharing panel in System Preferences is easy to use, it lacks many features found in commercial products, such as the ability to be remain silent during intrusion attempts (rather than sending back 'access denied' messages). One means of increasing your control of Mac OS X's firewall is to open Terminal (Applications > Utilities folder), type 'man ipfw', and follow the instructions. Another is to use a commercial firewall, like the one included with Norton Internet Security.

Find stuff fast

If you want to track an international flight or translate 'dia de los muertos' from Spanish to French, you don't have to open a Web browser in the hope of eventually finding a Web site that can help you. Instead, get Sherlock 3, built into Mac OS X 10.2 and later, to do the legwork for you.

Sherlock

Channelling Sherlock
Click here to view all the channels available through Sherlock 3. (Tip: to alter which channels you view permanently in the toolbar, select 'Customize Toolbar' from Sherlock 3's View menu.)

Finders keepers
Enter a departure city and an arrival city and click the green search button, and this Sherlock 3 channel will find all known flights that match. Note: your search can be restricted to a particular airline or flight number.

Pick your channel
Sherlock 3's built-in channels can provide quick access to Web search engines, stock art libraries, online auctions, a dictionary, an automatic language-translation service, and Apple's technical support library.

Lost and found
Sherlock 3 is a completely different beast to Sherlock 1 and 2. Apple has moved the ability to search for files according to their name or their content (yes — you can search for screenplays containing the work 'rosebud') from Sherlock to the Finder's Find command.

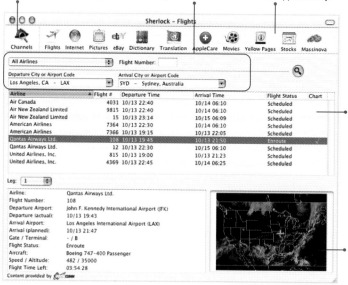

Instant results
Sherlock found 9 flights that matched our criteria. For each flight, Sherlock provides a summary of the available information, such as the airline and flight number. Click a flight once to view all available information about the flight in the two panels below.

Find detail
Our search for Los Angeles-to-Sydney flights turned up this aircraft, which departed from New York and is traversing the United States before setting down in Los Angeles.

Changing channels
To show or hide channels that are relevant to certain countries only, adjust the settings in the Countries panel of Sherlock's Preferences.

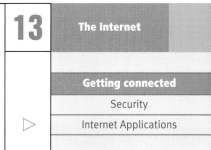

Fast find
Give Sherlock's Internet channel a 'natural language' query (like 'Why is the sky blue?') and it will scour the Internet for the most useful response.

Sherlock 2 vs Sherlock 3
You may notice that Sherlock 3 does not support Sherlock 2 channels. Sherlock 3 channels are built using a new technology that communicates directly with XML servers, which are multiplying at an astonishing pace. Hopefully, the number of Sherlock 3 channels will soon grow just as rapidly.

Mix 'n Match

Mac OS X has changed the way we look at things – even popular applications seem to be different somehow. In some cases, it's because they have been developed via the Cocoa environment or written for the Carbon environment. In others, it's because they haven't been changed at all but need to be launched in the Classic environment. But how do you know which application belongs to which format? Read on and we'll explain ...

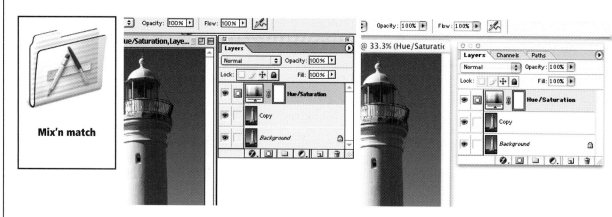

Mix'n match

Classic

Though you may have a soft spot for it, it's time to accept that Mac OS 9, now known as 'Classic', is last century's operating system. It served admirably through the 90s, and it inspired many of the features you now see in Mac OS X.

Mac OS X allows you to run your 'Classic' applications under Mac OS X effectively running Mac OS 9 as a separate application. Unfortunately, Classic apps don't take advantage of Mac OS X's Aqua interface, so they will appear exactly the same as the would under OS 9.

Mac OS X native

Applications that are Carbonized or Cocoa-developed take full advantage of Mac OS X's modern features such as the Quartz rendering engine that delivers the Aqua-interface. Advanced Aqua features include transparency, drop shadows, interleaved windows, and special effects such as the Genie effect when you move windows to the Dock. The overall effect is an interface that is easier on the eyes.

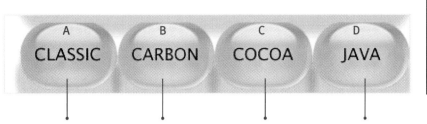

A	B	C	D
CLASSIC	CARBON	COCOA	JAVA

Classic applications
These applications can run under previous versions of Mac OS as well as Mac OS X — thanks to its Classic environment.

Mac OS 9.2

Carbonized applications
Many Mac OS 9 applications were carbonized to become Mac OS X applications at the initial stages of the OS X inception, so Carbonized applications work in both operating systems. Software developers can choose how much of the look and feel of OS X to embrace, hence some applications will have the look and feel of the Aqua interface more than others.

Cocoa applications
These applications take advantage of Mac OS X's advanced features — thanks to the Cocoa programming architecture. Because Cocoa applications have to be written from the ground up in the new environment, the finished application runs only in Mac OS X.

TextEdit

Java applications
Sun Microsystems' Java. is generally known as a programming language used by certain Web sites and accessed only from a Web browser. This is not strictly true – Java software can be created to run independently of a browser, and Mac OS X has plans to do just this. By converting its Aqua interface into Java code, the Java application of the future will appear distinctively like an OS X application. In addition, because Java is platform-independent, the newly-developed software will be able to run on any computer that supports Java. At present there aren't that many Java applications available for Mac OS X, but existing programs written in Java can be run on the system.

UNIX applications
Because UNIX is at the core of OS X, a large number of UNIX applications can be run on your Mac using the command line. Not only this but developers can customize and enhance relevant applications using Darwin.
Two examples of these are Apache Web Server and Samba file server for Windows. (See also pages 52, 53.)

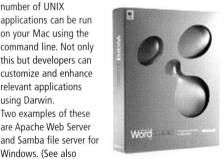

JAVA HELP
Mac OS X has two utilities that work with Java – Applet Launcher, which allows you to run Java applets without opening a Web browser, and Java Web Start which launches Java applications platform independently via any browser anywhere on the Web.

SYNOPSIS

Application Updates

Your system is a bit like you. In the way that you require nutrition, it requires top quality software and media, regular system maintenance and of course, vigilant checks for application updates. Apart from using Software Update (Applications > System Preferences) for preloaded programs and system software, there are a number of ways to ensure that you are running the most up to date programs.

Application Update

If you turn to pages 174 and 175, you'll find out all about Software Update (Applications > System Preferences). Although it's a great tool for updating Mac OS X and the programs that Apple preloaded on your Mac, it can't update the programs that you have added to your Mac yourself. Unfortunately, you will have to do this alone. But wait – there's help at hand ...

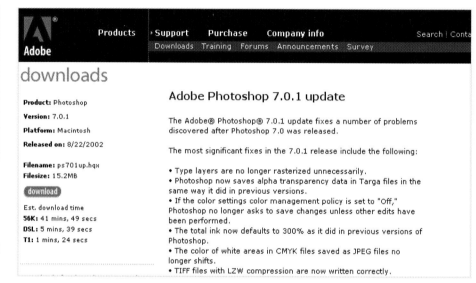

downloads

Product: Photoshop
Version: 7.0.1
Platform: Macintosh
Released on: 8/22/2002

Filename: ps701up.hqx
Filesize: 15.2MB

[download]

Est. download time
56K: 41 mins, 49 secs
DSL: 5 mins, 39 secs
T1: 1 mins, 24 secs

Adobe Photoshop 7.0.1 update

The Adobe® Photoshop® 7.0.1 update fixes a number of problems discovered after Photoshop 7.0 was released.

The most significant fixes in the 7.0.1 release include the following:

• Type layers are no longer rasterized unnecessarily.
• Photoshop now saves alpha transparency data in Targa files in the same way it did in previous versions.
• If the color settings color management policy is set to "Off," Photoshop no longer asks to save changes unless other edits have been performed.
• The total ink now defaults to 300% as it did in previous versions of Photoshop.
• The color of white areas in CMYK files saved as JPEG files no longer shifts.
• TIFF files with LZW compression are now written correctly.

Software publishers' Web sites

Software updates are announced (and ready to be downloaded) on respective Web sites. Note: the applications themselves may direct you to a Web site for online patches, automatic or manual updates and/or information about new versions.

Version Tracker:

Visit www.versiontracker.com/macosx/ to check for application updates and patches that do not generate automatically in Mac OS X.

MacMinute

Last Updated: Tuesday, November 19, 01:44 EST (06:44 GMT)

📧 Send Your News   💬 Site Comments   ☕ Reader Café   📣 Advertising

Apple posts NVIDIA firmware update
November 19 - 01:44 EST Apple has released NVIDIA Graphics Card Firmware Update for "customers using Mac OS X version 10.2 (Jaguar) or later with an Apple Cinema HD Display and a Power Mac G4 with one of the following NVIDIA graphics cards: GeForce2 MX, GeForce2 MX TwinView, GeForce3, or GeForce4 MX. These cards require the update to support the high resolution of the Cinema HD Display."
[Email this Story | Rate this Story : 1 2 3 4 5 | Rating : · · · · ·]

  Taming Jaguar – Understanding and Administrating Mac OS X
OSXFAQ: Everything you ever wanted to know about OS X and more...

⨯ IdeaResources releases irEdit 1.5
November 19 - 00:45 EST IdeaResources today released irEdit 1.5, an update to its popular text-editing software for Mac OS X. Version 1.5 adds built-in FTP support, performance improvements, and the option of setting your deafult window size. The update also allows Mac OS X 10.2 (Jaguar) users to choose which window style they would like to use — standard white-striped windows or textured windows like iTunes and iCal. irEdit is US$20 shareware.
[Email this Story | Rate this Story : 1 2 3 4 5 | Rating : · · · · ·]

Apple updates Hot Deals section
November 19 - 00:04 EST Apple has updated its Hot Deals section with the latest offerings from B&H Photo and Video, CompUSA, and J&R. Great prices can be found on a large selection of digital cameras from Canon, Olympus, Nikon, Fuji, and Sony, and an equally large selection of digital video cameras from Sony and Canon. Other Highlighted deals include the Altec Lansing multimedia speaker system, color inkjet

Search MacMinute [Go]

Advanced Search
Top Rated Stories
View Current Headlines

Recent News Items

This week
Apple Specialist Hot Deals
Apple after–Thanksgiving event
Mac OS X Up-To-Date extended

Last week
De La Soul "Switch" ad
Roxio to acquire Napster
Yo Yo Ma "Switch" ad
Denver, CO Apple Store
Tony Ho, Apple VP of Asia Pacific
Apple UK "An Offer of No Interest"
Apple releases Sherlock 3 SDK
WebObjects 5.2
iPod engraving price lowered
Emeryville store opening changed
Mac OS X 10.2.2

Latest Software Updates

This week
NVIDIA Firmware Update
irEdit 1.5
OmniOutliner 2.1.1
Art Director's Toolkit 3.1

Mac news sites

Mac news and information on application updates can be found on a number of Mac news sites and mailing lists. Visit: www.macminute.com, www.macsurfer.com, or www.maccentral.com

ORGANIZING APPLICATIONS

One of the things that most Mac users complain about is the fact that it is often difficult to locate application registration and serial number details. If you are the elected system administrator it may be a good idea to make this information as accessible as possible – as a start, compile a list of relevant information and keep it in a logical place. This won't only be a great timesaver but also very impressive to your disorganized colleagues!

Polish that Apple

Maintaining your disks is a must to maximize performance and prevent problems. Mac OS X system administrators will find Disk Utility (Applications > Utilities) perfect for basic disk maintenance and repair as well as more advanced disk optimization like defragmentation and partitioning.

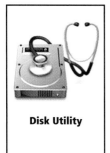

Disk Utility

What's cooking?
Disk Utility provides information on any mounted disk. Details such as size, available space and the amount of files and folders stored on the disk are all readily available here.

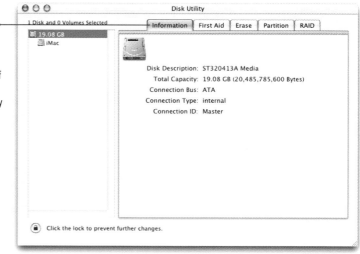

Split levels
The partition feature is useful for splitting very large disks into several volumes.

Drive partitioning: why do it?
Partitioning divides a drive into two or more separate volumes and causes them to behave as though there are actually different drives rather than just the one. The advantage of this is that, should you be having trouble with one, you can restart with the other. Note: a good idea is to install Mac OS X and Mac OS 9 on separate volumes.

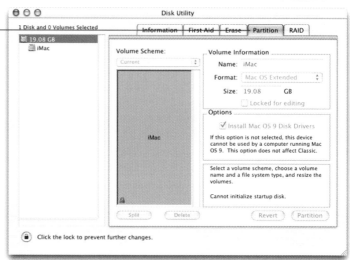

Eraser 'tool'
Erase removable disks and any partitions (apart from the startup disk) with this feature. But handle with care – erasing actually destroys all the data on the disk.
Note: Erase is the initial part of the process of reformatting CD-RW discs.

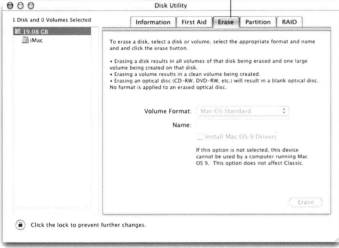

Storage solution
If you don't know what RAID is, you probably won't need to use this feature, but we'll tell you anyway. RAID (redundant array of independent disks) is a multiple disk storage solution that deposits the same data in different places. The operating system recognises the multiple disks as one hard disk.

Rescue remedy
When things become a bit strange in the OS department, it's a good idea to go to First Aid, which checks repairs and verifies problems on any mounted disk (apart from the startup disk) and media.
Note: you can test and repair your Mac OS X startup disk by inserting your Mac OS X installation CD and restarting while depressing the C key.

Apple Psychology

When things go wrong with your system, your first reaction may be to hire a resident Apple psychologist. Jokes aside, system glitches can frustrate you beyond belief. The good news is that many of the problems you encounter may be resolved with a little of your own preventative maintenance ... understanding the cause may remedy the effect and in turn save you a lot of grey hairs.

Problem	Details
Not following the correct instructions.	Failing to follow software and hardware instructions is more than often the cause of many problems. If you stick to them dutifully you should not have any difficulty.
It just won't work!	Design flaws, manufacturing problems, system conflicts or bugs could be the cause. In this case, refer to your Apple Support contact.
System maintenance – what's that?	Ignoring system maintenance is similar to neglecting your health. With system preferences such as Software Update and the ease in which you can update applications thanks to the efforts of software publishers and the Internet, you now have no excuses for not keeping your system up-to-date. Run a disk utility over your disk before any upgrade.
Not enough space to store your files.	This problem is common to most users. It's easy to get bogged down with everyday tasks and forget to keep an eye on your hard drive. As it's a particular problem in Mac OS X (virtual memory is always on and low disk space can cause problems related to insufficient RAM), it's best to keep a watchful eye out for this.

Problem	Details
Some programs aren't compatible with others.	System conflicts are not as common in Mac OS X as they were previously thanks to protected memory. This is not to say that there is no longer the potential for conflict between software that may modify the system and the core OS. There is, so be aware of it.
Outside system attacks.	Outside attacks on your system can be carried out by viruses or hackers. Anti-virus software and as much security as possible are both solutions. Symptom awareness is vital.
Hardware failures.	Brand new hardware or that which is on its last legs can sometimes cause problems, particularly when there have been system upgrades.
Refusing to acknowledge your Mac's limitations.	Certain applications require the right amount of processing power to run effectively. There is no way around this. If you attempt to run your favourite program on an under-equipped Mac, the writing's on the wall!

Look, don't touch

Making changes to Mac OS X can be fun and powerful, but it can also foul things up if you're not sure what you're doing. Here are some areas to handle with care—or to avoid altogether.

Alert !!!

Not for ten

Control Panels allow you to make changes to Mac OS 9 in the same way that System Preferences allows you to make changes to Mac OS X. You can open these Mac OS 9 Control Panels in Mac OS X, but you should not. Making changes to Mac OS 9 Control Panels from Mac OS X can confuse your Mac and cause unexpected trouble.

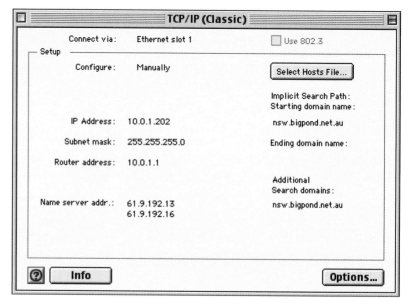

Classical treasures

Mac OS 9 users can get in the habit of trolling through their System Folder, deleting any files that look out of place, and seeing what happens. Don't do this in Mac OS X. 'Classic', the feature that enables you to run Mac OS 9 alongside Mac OS X, depends on a suite of files that it places in the Mac OS 9 System Folder. If you delete them, you won't be able to use Classic.

Too much power

The Utilities folder in Mac OS X's Applications folder is full of utilities that allow you to view and change almost every aspect of your system. Terminal and NetInfo Manager are the two most powerful utilities in this team, and the two most dangerous. Do not even look at them unless you're sure that you know what you're doing, or if a Mac OS X expert is guiding you through the process.

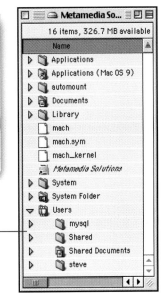

Suddenly revealed

When you restart in Mac OS 9, you'll see some files required by Mac OS X's Mach kernel. Leave them alone. You might also be tempted to try to delete a Mac OS X user while you are running Mac OS 9, either by dragging the user folder to the Trash or via the Multiple Users control panel. Again, don't do this. The only place you should try to delete a Mac OS X user is the Accounts panel in Mac OS X's System Preferences.

Invisible UNIX

Mac OS X usually does a grand job of hiding UNIX folders such as 'bin', 'etc', 'sbin', 'usr' and 'var' from you, the user. If these folders suddenly become visible, don't be alarmed—just leave them alone, because fiddling with them could damage your system.

The run down

Apple System Profiler (Applications > Utilities) can make your Mac stand up straight, push out its chest, and provide a lot more information than just its name, rank and serial number. In fact, using Profiler, almost any question about your Mac can be answered.

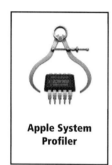

Apple System Profiler

Memory is made of this

For everyday bragging, you only need to know that your Mac has 320Mb of RAM (memory). However, if you're thinking of buying extra RAM, you must know what kind of RAM your Mac requires and whether you have any vacant slots that could take additional DIMMs (memory chips).

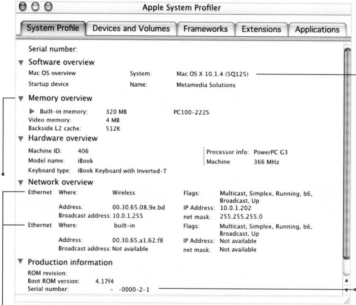

System build

Usually, you only need to know that you're running, say, Mac OS X version 10.1.4. However, sometimes a technician might ask you for your operating system's exact build number: in this case, SQ125.

Name, rank, serial number

Remember to jot down your Mac's serial number before it gets stolen.

Where on Earth ...?

Your Macintosh can connect to almost any network using Ethernet. Every single computer that has an Ethernet port also has its own, unique MAC address —that's short for 'media access control', not Macintosh. Find your MAC address here, if your network manager asks you to provide it.

Share your profile

The simplest way to send someone a snippet from your profile is to drag the information from an Apple System Profiler window to the body of a new e-mail message. If you wish to save your entire profile, select New Report from the File menu, customize the report if you wish, and then click the OK button. When the report appears, choose Save As from the File menu. The report is just a text file—to open it, drag it onto Apple System Profiler or any word processor or text editor.

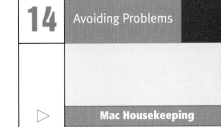

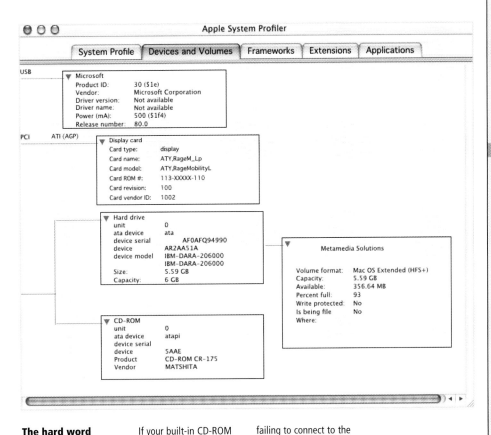

The hard word on hardware

Pretty much any hardware that's in your Mac or connected to it should appear in this window.

If your built-in CD-ROM drive stops working, look for it here. If Apple System Profiler doesn't know that your CD-ROM drive exists, you could have a loose wire that's failing to connect to the drive.

But if Profiler does know that your drive exists, your Mac can 'see' the drive, so problem is elsewhere.

Tender loving care

Apple's legendary ease of use combined with its new rack-optimized server, Xserve, and the AppleCare Premium Service and Support Plan provide users with expert service and support. And because both your Xserve hardware and Mac OS X software come from Apple, there's one number, and one number only, to call when you need responsive and reliable technical support.

Taking care of your system

What is Xserve?

Xserve combines phenomenal processing power, massive storage capacity, high bandwidth I/O and remote management tools with remarkable performance and stability thanks to its UNIX-based server operating system, Mac OS X Server. Its IU rack-optimized design lets you stack 42 performance units in an industry-standard 8-foot tall rack with up to 630 gigaflops of processing power. The units feature powerful PowerPC G4 processors, hot-pluggable drives, RAID solutions, remote management tools and the ability to boot up and run without a monitor.

Because Xserve is designed for quick and easy swapping of crucial parts; no special training or certification is required. Combined with the AppleCare Premium Service and Support Plan and an AppleCare Service Parts Kit and you'll see how easy it is to fix a problem.

Often you'll find that Apple experts can troubleshoot your system right over the phone.

AppleCare Premium Service and Support Plan

The AppleCare Premium Service and Support Plan for Xserve provides up to three years of expert telephone/e-mail support and on-site hardware service, and covers Xserve hardware and Mac OS X Server and delivers:

- expert telephone and e-mail support with 30-minute response time — 24 hours a day, seven days a week to help you determine if it's a hardware failure or a Mac OS X Server configuration issue.
- 4-hour on-site response during business hours and next-day on-site response after business hours (terms apply).
- assurance that Apple-authorized technicians will perform repairs using genuine Apple parts.

Because both your Xserve hardware and Mac OS X software come from Apple, there's only one number to call when you need support. For further AppleCare information, including Professional Services, visit: www.apple.com/support/products/

AppleCare Service Parts Kits

To minimize downtime, Apple also offers AppleCare Service Parts Kits for Xserve, made up of a logic board, a power supply, a blower, and an Apple Drive Module. AppleCare Service Parts Kits let you keep key modules handy to address the most common hardware failures.

AppleCare Web site support

The AppleCare support Web site, with its training and support resources can help you keep your Xserve system running smoothly. It features in-depth product information, training on hardware and software installation and configuration. Technical resources include the AppleCare Knowledge Base discussions, and downloadable software on Apple's Featured Software Web site.

Kingdom of the Keys

All you know about Mac Os X's Terminal application is that it's located in the Utilities folder. You may have also heard that it's a gateway to UNIX, and thus the keyboard is the only tool you'll need to utilize its command line interface. At this stage, you are terrified and don't know where to begin. Which is where we come in, and show you that it's really not as bad as it looks. Ready?

Utilities

What a welcome
When you launch Terminal you'll notice a simple window containing this friendly little greeting.

Made to measure
Terminal windows are no different to other Mac OS X windows and can be resized with ease. When resizing, the title bar will display the width and height of the window separated by an X.

Reaching Darwin
When the Mac OS X system boots up, the first thing it does is load Apple's Darwin operating system which runs silently in the background, and can only be reached on the command line via the Terminal program.

Quick crossover
When using the Terminal program you are logged in as the same specific user indicated in the Mac OS X GUI. But there's one essential difference that's prominent when using UNIX commands – you can change user identity for part of your Terminal session by typing in 'su' (switch user).

Mistaken identity?
If you are a little forgetful, the command line prompt will cleverly remind you who you are. In addition, you can type the 'whoami' command and the shell discloses your identity.

Identity access
Typically, you cannot access other identities in Terminal until you create other accounts or enable root login in NetInfo Manager.

HOT TIP

LOGIN WITHOUT LOGOUT
Using Terminal to execute a few commands as another user means that there is no need to toggle between Login and Logout. Simply switch user (su) on the command line, execute required commands and terminate the shell session.

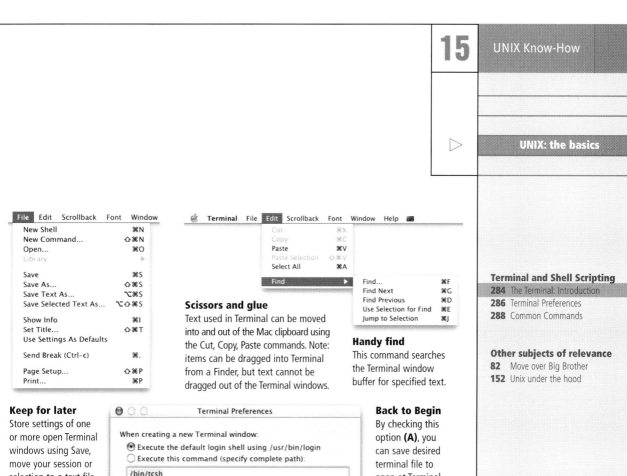

Scissors and glue
Text used in Terminal can be moved into and out of the Mac clipboard using the Cut, Copy, Paste commands. Note: items can be dragged into Terminal from a Finder, but text cannot be dragged out of the Terminal windows.

Handy find
This command searches the Terminal window buffer for specified text.

Keep for later
Store settings of one or more open Terminal windows using Save, move your session or selection to a text file using the Save as Text and/or Save Selection as Text commands.

Back to Begin
By checking this option **(A)**, you can save desired terminal file to open at Terminal commencement.

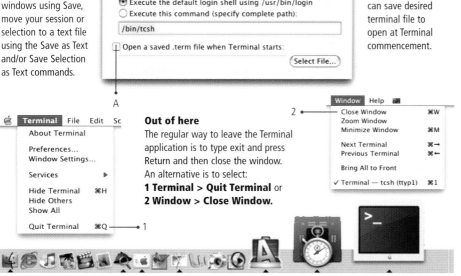

Out of here
The regular way to leave the Terminal application is to type exit and press Return and then close the window. An alternative is to select:
1 Terminal > Quit Terminal or
2 Window > Close Window.

Terminal Preferences

Mac OS X provides a range of options for using shell commands and terminal emulation which are convenient and easy to use. These include the ability to: • split view for quick reference to past history while texting; • select text and drag it to another application or to the desktop as a clipping; • apply transparency to terminal window/s; • turn anti-aliasing on or off; and • adjust character spacing thanks to better font control. But wait! There's more ...

Utilities

1. Verbosity
Previously users were only able to type 80 characters per command line but this has been greatly increased.

2. Wrap up
By checking this wrap option, window lines are wrapped to width. Note: leaving this option unwrapped could mean scrolling horizontally to have a full line of text in view.

Source for preference
Set general Terminal Preferences from the Terminal menu to select which shell to use and execute a login script at shell start up. To control more specific preferences go to File > Get Info. The Terminal Inspector will appear, complete with a pull-down list of preferences (namely Shell, Processes, Emulation, Buffer, Display, Color, and Window).

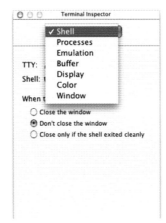

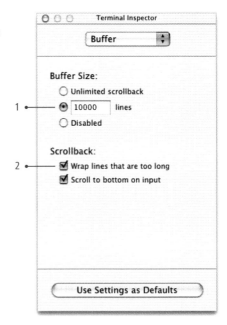

Improved functionality
Preferences seen here will help to improve the functionality of Terminal as it emulates a teletype device. (If you are using Telnet, you may need to adjust the settings in this window. If you do not know what these settings mean, do not change them.)

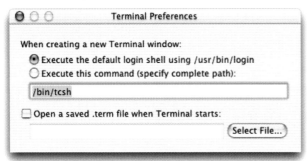

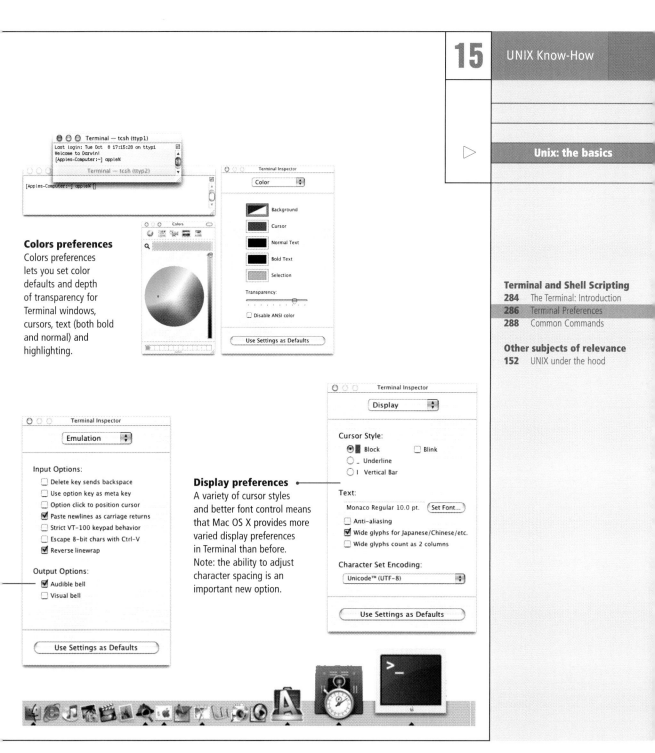

Colors preferences
Colors preferences lets you set color defaults and depth of transparency for Terminal windows, cursors, text (both bold and normal) and highlighting.

Display preferences
A variety of cursor styles and better font control means that Mac OS X provides more varied display preferences in Terminal than before. Note: the ability to adjust character spacing is an important new option.

Common commands

Together with programs like Telnet and FTP, Darwin provides commands for Mac OS X navigational assistance, which carry out similar functions established by the Mac Finder, such as moving folders as well as copying, pasting and deleting files and directories. For the purposes of this Visual Companion, we have chosen not to blind you with 'command' science. Instead, we'll give you just a bit of the basics ...

Utilities

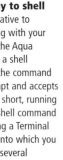

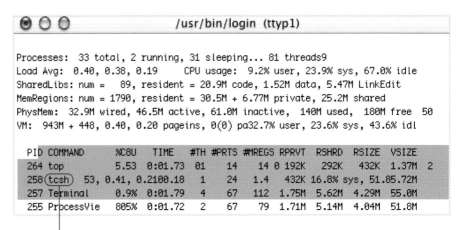

Gateway to shell
An alternative to interacting with your Mac via the Aqua interface, a shell displays the command line prompt and accepts input. (In short, running a single shell command or opening a Terminal window into which you can type several commands is a unique, and more controlled, way of telling your Mac what to do.)

Shell's your oyster
The shell is an application that interprets entered commands to Mac OS X's UNIX kernel. One of the first UNIX shells to be developed and still currently in active use is 'sh'. A number of backward compatible shells have since been developed. (This means that anything that works in 'sh' should work in any shell developed thereafter.) Darwin's default shell, 'tcsh', is derived from 'csh' (the C shell). In Mac OS X some major enhancements have been brought to 'tcsh' such as the ability to: • repeat previous commands without retyping; • fix typing errors and change commands and spelling suggestions in command line; and • more flexible prompts.

Finger fun
Commands typed on the command line will appear after the prompt. Pressing Return actions the system to confirm its response. Note: most commands are names of programs and when typed, will be launched by Darwin (an alternative to double-clicking a program in the OS X Finder.)

Standard prompt
When Terminal is launched, it displays your Mac's name, the directory you're in and your username.

Shortcut commands to get you going

Note: type bindkey at the command-line prompt
for a comprehensive list of command shortcuts.

Directory commands
~	home directory
.	current directory
..	parent directory to current directory
/	topmost or root directory

Command	Details
cal	prints a calendar for any year specified (1 to 9999)
cat	displays text file
cd	sets current default directory
cp	copies file
crypt	encodes files
df	displays free-space
diff	compares two files
du	disk utilisation
find	locates files in directory
grep	searches for strings or patterns

Command	Details
head	displays the first 20 lines of a file
ls	lists a directory,
man	extensive Mac OS X manual (see page 292)
mkdir	creates a directory
mv	moves/renames file or patterns
pwd	informs user of current directory
rm	deletes file
rmdir	removes a directory
tail	displays the last 20 lines of a file

SUMMARY

FREE OPEN-SOURCE APPLICATIONS
Thanks to open source technology, developers can
customise and enhance relevant applications using
Darwin. Some of these are freely available for
download, such as:
• Apache Web server;
• analog (for Web logs analysis);
• Samba file server for Windows; and
• mrtg to monitor and graph network activity.

Plan B

Your data is too important for you not to protect it with Plan B—
Plan Backup, that is. Dantz Retrospect Express is the most
popular backup program for the Macintosh. It is also available as
part of the Norton SystemWorks bundle.

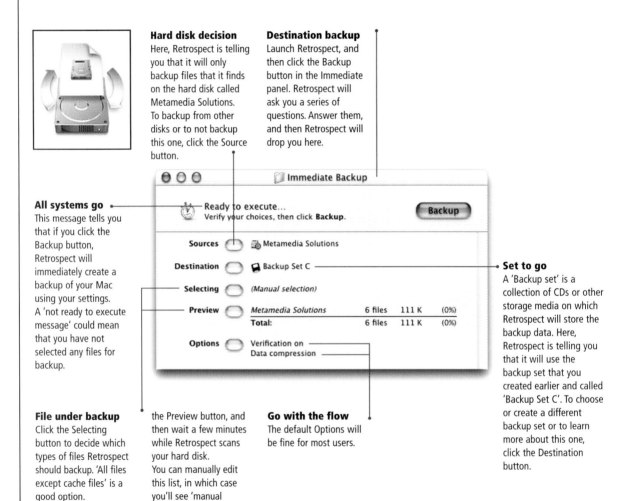

Hard disk decision
Here, Retrospect is telling
you that it will only
backup files that it finds
on the hard disk called
Metamedia Solutions.
To backup from other
disks or to not backup
this one, click the Source
button.

Destination backup
Launch Retrospect, and
then click the Backup
button in the Immediate
panel. Retrospect will
ask you a series of
questions. Answer them,
and then Retrospect will
drop you here.

All systems go
This message tells you
that if you click the
Backup button,
Retrospect will
immediately create a
backup of your Mac
using your settings.
A 'not ready to execute
message' could mean
that you have not
selected any files for
backup.

Set to go
A 'Backup set' is a
collection of CDs or other
storage media on which
Retrospect will store the
backup data. Here,
Retrospect is telling you
that it will use the
backup set that you
created earlier and called
'Backup Set C'. To choose
or create a different
backup set or to learn
more about this one,
click the Destination
button.

File under backup
Click the Selecting
button to decide which
types of files Retrospect
should backup. 'All files
except cache files' is a
good option.
To view the complete list
of files of this type, click

the Preview button, and
then wait a few minutes
while Retrospect scans
your hard disk.
You can manually edit
this list, in which case
you'll see 'manual
selection' in this window.

Go with the flow
The default Options will
be fine for most users.

While you were sleeping

Retrospect can automatically keep your backups up-to-date. To get to the 'Backup: EasyScript Backup' window, click on the Automate tab in Retrospect's main window, and then click the EasyScript button. Answer Retrospect's questions, then click the 'Open Script' button in the final window to arrive here, where you can revise your backup script if need be. Unlike the 'Immediate Backup' window, there is no Preview button in this window, as Retrospect cannot know what files will be on your Mac when it runs the backup script. Click the Schedule button to change when your backup script will run.

Backup hardware

Most Macs now come with built-in CD burners, which are great for personal backups. When you insert a blank CD-R disc, your Mac will ask if it can prepare the disc for use. Click the Ignore button, as you want Retrospect, not your Mac, to prepare the disc for holding backup files. Also, you might have to backup to non-rewritable CD-Rs, despite having a Mac that includes a CD-RW drive. For more details check: www.dantz.com/index.php3?SCREEN= osx_apple_opt_compat_dev

In command

Usually, we control our Macs with the mouse. We point and click, drag and drop, and enter commands by choosing them from menus. But Mac OS X also has an optional 'command line', where you can type sophisticated instructions. It's not as easy as using the mouse, but it's a lot more powerful and it can be faster too. What's more, mastering the command line is the only way to use many handy Unix programs, and sometimes it's the only way to fix a flaky Mac.

The open desktop.

Down in the depths
'Underneath' Mac OS X sits a UNIX-based operating system, called Darwin. You can access

Darwin's command line directly by running Terminal, which is in Utilities in Mac OS X's Applications folder.

Prompt service
Darwin presents you with a 'prompt' (everything up to and including the '%') to tell you that it's ready for you to start typing. The 'localhost' in the prompt is the default name of your Mac, 'john' is the short version of your Mac OS X username, '~' means that you are currently in your home directory, and '%' means that you are a normal user, not the all-powerful 'root' user. Now type 'pwd' (no quotes) and press the return key. This command tells Darwin to show you the 'path' to where your current location — John's home folder in your Mac's Users folder.

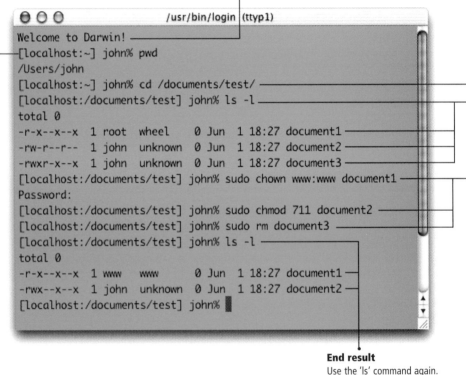

```
                    /usr/bin/login (ttyp1)
Welcome to Darwin!
[localhost:~] john% pwd
/Users/john
[localhost:~] john% cd /documents/test/
[localhost:/documents/test] john% ls -l
total 0
-r-x--x--x  1 root   wheel    0 Jun  1 18:27 document1
-rw-r--r--  1 john   unknown  0 Jun  1 18:27 document2
-rwxr-x--x  1 john   unknown  0 Jun  1 18:27 document3
[localhost:/documents/test] john% sudo chown www:www document1
Password:
[localhost:/documents/test] john% sudo chmod 711 document2
[localhost:/documents/test] john% sudo rm document3
[localhost:/documents/test] john% ls -l
total 0
-r-x--x--x  1 www    www      0 Jun  1 18:27 document1
-rwx--x--x  1 john   unknown  0 Jun  1 18:27 document2
[localhost:/documents/test] john%
```

End result
Use the 'ls' command again. Doc1 is now owned by 'www'. Doc2 now has 'rwx--x--x' privileges. Doc3 no longer exists.

	test	
Metamedia Solutions ▶	Applications ▶	document1
Network ▶	Applications (Mac OS 9) ▶	document2
	Documents ▶	document3
	Library ▶	
	Metamedia Solutions ▶	
	System ▶	

Installer Logs ▶
test ▶

Change directory
Type 'cd' (the change directory command) followed by the path to the folder to which you want to move. Include the 'preceding slash' (the first '/') to tell Darwin you have typed a full path to this folder, all the way from the root level of the hard disk. The prompt changes to show your new location.

Easy street
Use TextEdit to create blank text files called document1, document2 and document 3 in a folder called test in your Documents folder if you want to take these Terminal commands for a spin. These files will be owned by you and have 'rw-r--r--' privileges.

Superuser do
Use the 'chown' command to change the owner of document1 to 'www' (a hidden user that runs your Mac's web server, and which belongs to a group called 'www'). Type 'sudo' before the 'chown' command to give yourself 'superuser' abilities, such as the ability to change the file's owner. Give your password when prompted. Use the 'chmod' command to give 'read/write/execute' privileges (indicated by the number 7) to document2's owner, and 'execute only' privileges (indicated by the number 1) to everyone else. Use the 'rm' command to delete document3.

List directory contents
The 'list directory contents' command ('ls') shows all the files in the current directory. The '-l' flag requests additional information about these files. If we saw 'drwxrwxrwx' in the first column of our listing, we'd know that the file was actually a directory ('d'); that the file's owner was permitted to read the file (the first 'r'), write to it (the first 'w'), or execute it as a script or program (the first 'x'); that every member of the owner's group had the same freedoms (the next 'rwx'); and that everyone else had these freedoms (the last 'rwx'). By way of contrast, the first column of our directory listing shows that document1 is a file not a directory – only the file's owner may read it, no-one may write to it, and anyone may execute it. The all-powerful hidden user 'root' owns document1, 'john' owns the other two.

READ THE MANUAL
The UNIX layer included with Mac OS X comes with an extensive manual, called 'the man pages'. Access the manual with the 'man' command. For example, type 'man rm' to read the manual for the rm command.

HOT TIP

Speedway Macway

Every time you do something with your Mac, it writes data to your hard disk. If your Mac needs to write a 20Mb file, and the largest unbroken gap on your disk is 15Mb your Mac will break the file into two or more fragments. Over time, the fragmentation of your hard disk can slow your Mac and cause reliability problems. The solution is to defragment your disk using a tool like Speed Disk, which is part of Symantec Norton Utilities.

Color by numbers
Each type of file on your hard disk gets a different color. These colors don't form nice clean bands in this window because this hard disk is fragmented. Click the View button to see more information about the files that are represented by each color in this window.

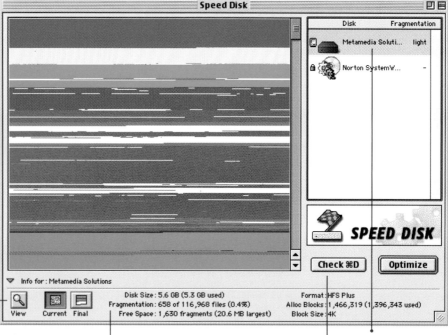

First things first
This window looks different to the Mac OS X windows throughout this book because we have to restart in Mac OS 9 to use Speed Disk. First, insert the Norton SystemWorks or Norton Utilities CD-ROM into your Mac. Next, open Mac OS X's System

Preferences, go to the Startup Disk panel, click on the icon representing this CD, and then click on the Restart button. If you don't see a Restart button, it's because you're using an out-of-date version of Mac OS X. Bring it up to date with Software Update (see pages 174, 175).

Just looking
Click the Check button to view the current level of fragmentation on your hard disk, or click the Optimize button to defragment your disk.

Small steps
0.4% is a very low degree of fragmentation, but as long as your files are backed up there is no harm in defragmenting your hard disk anyway.

Mission impossible
Select your hard disk—you can't defragment a CD-ROM.

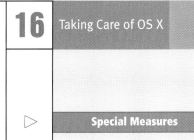

Just for Mac OS X

Speed Disk uses profiles to rearrange your files on your hard disk. To create a profile that puts Mac OS X's most important files on the fastest part of your hard disk, do this: Restart from the Norton Utilities CD-ROM and open Speed Disk Editor. Select New Profile from the Edit menu then double-click the profile to edit it. Name the profile 'Mac OS X' then select New Category from the Edit menu. Double-click this unnamed category to open it, name it 'System', and give it the highest priority: 255. Double-click in the 'Match

Specifications' window then select New Folder Spec from the Edit menu. Navigate to Mac OS X's 'System' folder (not Mac OS 9's 'System Folder' folder) and choose it. Return to your profile window and drag this category to the top of the Categories list. Repeat this process for as many categories as you choose. Choose Save from the File menu and save the profile to a folder on your hard disk. Open Speed Disk, then choose Add Profile from the 'Optimize For' menu. Navigate to and choose the folder that holds your profile. Now defragment your hard disk.

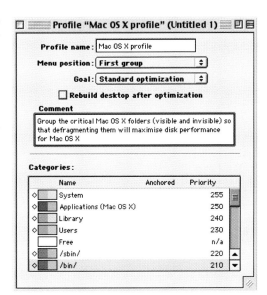

RED ALERT
Before you even think about defragmenting your hard disk, do the following:
- Backup all your files (see pages 290, 291).
- Check for and repair any file or disk damage using a tool like Norton Disk Doctor (see pages 238, 239 and pages 296, 297).
- Undertake any activities that will greatly alter the contents of your hard disk, such as installing
  large applications or archiving old projects
- Ensure your hard disk drivers are up-to-date by running Software Update (see pages 174, 175).

An Apple a day

When the internet catches a cold, the whole world sneezes. So, use an anti-virus program to keep the doctor away from your Mac by stopping viruses and other hostile software before they cause any damage.

Virus Protection

Mind your malware
Hostile programs—or 'malware'—come in many forms, including viruses, worms and trojan horses, though the term 'virus' is often used to describe all hostile software. The 'virus definition file' used by this copy of Norton AntiVirus describes more than 4,000 destructive programs, so it can spot them and stop them. Virus writers continually release new threats into the wild, which is why it's vital to keep your virus definition file up-to-date.

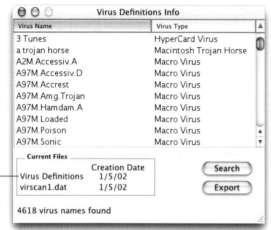

Shields up
There are few reasons why you would not tell Norton AntiVirus to automatically check every in-coming file or disk for viruses. That's why this is the default setting in the Preferences dialog box, and you need an administrator's password to change this setting. Note: there is not a separate preference for automatically scanning e-mail attachments in the Mac OS X version of Norton AntiVirus. Unlike some earlier versions of the program, this version always scans incoming email attachments if you set it to 'Autoprotect' your Mac.

Beyond the brand
Here we've shown how to use a few security products from Symantec, but this is only because this brand is quite popular. Many other companies produce software to help protect your Mac, and you can take many security measures that don't require any special software — such as not opening e-mail attachments when you don't know who sent them. The Secure Mac site can help you survey all your security options: securemac.com

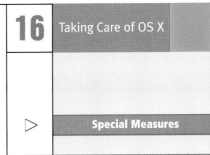

▷ **Special Measures**

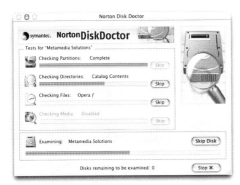

When catastrophe strikes

When a virus or a hacker or a cup of coffee damages your files or your entire hard disk, you will be horrified if you don't have a proper backup system (see 'Plan B', page 290). But Norton Utilities will give you a second chance. This program will attempt to repair damaged files and disks, though it can't fix everything. To use Norton Utilities to its greatest potential, insert your Norton Utilities CD-ROM, select it in the Startup Disk panel in Mac OS X's System Preferences, click the Restart button to restart in Mac OS 9, and then run Norton Utilities from the CD-ROM.

Always on, always vulnerable

If you have a broadband Internet connection (cable, DSL or satellite), viruses are not your only concern. You are always connected to the Internet, so you are always exposed to hackers. A firewall is your first line of defence. Luckily, Mac OS X

includes a firewall. For a guide to enabling it from the command line, open Terminal and type 'man ipfw' (no quotes). To control this firewall via a simpler point-and-click interface, try a program like Norton Personal Firewall (pictured) or the free Sun Shield: homepage.mac.com/opalliere/Menu3.html

Safety schedule

As long as you have an internet connection, Norton AntiVirus can automatically keep its virus definition files up-to-date. Just click on the Schedule button to go to the Norton Scheduler window. Here, we have also created schedules for periodically checking our entire hard disk for

viruses, for checking that all our Norton software is up to date, and for updating FileSaver data, which Norton Utilities might find useful if we ever ask it to attempt to repair a damaged file or disk.

To add a new schedule to this list, click one of the buttons along the top of this window.

Your Mac's autopilot

Whenever you find yourself completing simple tasks over and again, you can ask AppleScript — your Mac's autopilot—to take the controls. Just write a short script using AppleScript (which looks more like English than a programming language), or grab a free script that does exactly what you're looking for from a site like ScriptBuilders: www.macscripter.net/script-builder.t

Find fabulous fonts
Type 'The quick brown fox…' a few hundred times, and format each line with a different font so you can compare all your typefaces. Sound useful? Sounds boring and repetitive. Sounds like a job for AppleScript! Check out Apple's Font Sampler script, which is in the Example Scripts folder in AppleScript in Mac OS X's Applications folder (See also pages 192, 193).

Revisionism
What were you thinking? You didn't holiday in Tahiti in 1999—it was 2000. No problem, you can instantly change the name of every digital photo in a folder on your Mac using AppleScript. And this is just one of many uses for the handy 'Replace Text In Items Name' script, which is in the Example Scripts folder.

From scripting to programming
AppleScript is a very simple scripting language. In fact, many AppleScript scripts look like ordinary English sentences, and creating a new AppleScript using Script Editor is simpler than creating a new resume in Microsoft Word. But that doesn't mean that AppleScript is not powerful. If you install the contents of the optional Developer Tools CD-ROM that came with Mac OS X or your Macintosh, you'll find that AppleScript is one of the languages that you can use with Project Builder—Apple's fully fledged programming environment for the Macintosh. Apple calls this combination AppleScript Studio. If and when you are ready, you can use AppleScript Studio to turn your scripts into sophisticated programs, complete with dialog boxes and pull-down menus.

Give it a go
After taking Apple's sample AppleScripts for a spin, you're probably keen to create some scripts of your own. Just open Script Editor (in the AppleScript folder, in Mac OS X's Applications folder), type what you see here (without the colours or indentation), click the Check Syntax button, and then click the Run button. Your new script will open Internet Explorer and then go to Apple's 'AppleScript—Mac OS X' Web page.

AppleScript online
AppleScript and so-called 'XML Web Services' can exchange information over the Internet—an ability that's exploited by Apple's Translate English Phrase script, which you can download from: www.apple.com/applescript/macosx/script_menu
The text we entered in English was: 'Please translate this sentence into French using an "XML Web Service".'

In the red
Individual programs often come with their own handy AppleScripts. For example, if your Mac came with AppleWorks, you can open the program, create a spreadsheet, insert some data, and then run the Negative Cells Red script (by selecting it from AppleWorks' Script menu, in the menu bar). This script will show you if and where you're 'in the red'.

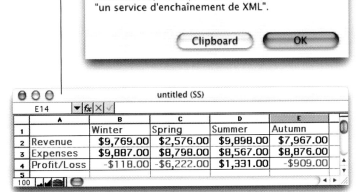

traduisez svp cette phrase en Français en utilisant "un service d'enchaînement de XML".

Clipboard   OK

	A	B	C	D	E
		Winter	Spring	Summer	Autumn
2	Revenue	$9,769.00	$2,576.00	$9,898.00	$7,967.00
3	Expenses	$9,887.00	$8,798.00	$8,567.00	$8,876.00
4	Profit/Loss	-$118.00	-$6,222.00	$1,331.00	-$909.00
5					

Talk, talk

The two most popular scripting systems for Mac OS X — AppleScript and UNIX shell scripting — can 'talk' to each other. Experienced AppleScript and UNIX users will instantly realize how powerful this combination could be. The UNIX command cron — which can be set to trigger any command at any time of the day, including a command that runs an AppleScript application — provides a gentle introduction to this awesome combination. To control 'cron', edit the crontab file.

Root of the problem
A crontab file tells your Mac when to automatically run certain UNIX commands. The system's crontab file belongs to the all-powerful root user, which is why we had to use the 'sudo' command to open it. If you don't want to execute these commands when other users are logged into your Mac, edit your own crontab file, not the system's file.

Take a Pico
Open the system's crontab file by launching Terminal (Applications > Utilities folder), typing 'sudo pico /private/etc/crontab', giving your admin

password when required. This opens the file in Pico, which is a very basic text editor for UNIX—like TextEdit is a text editor for Mac OS X.

Synchronise watches
Tell UNIX to execute the command at 1.10pm (24-hour clock) on every day of every month (as shown here), or on any other days or times that you choose. Press the Tab key to jump from column to column.

Perfect placement
Go to the Emulation panel in Terminal's Preferences dialog box and turn on the ability to place the cursor by Option-clicking. Then, hold down the Option key and click here to place the cursor. Press the Return key once, and start typing on a new line to create your new crontab entry.

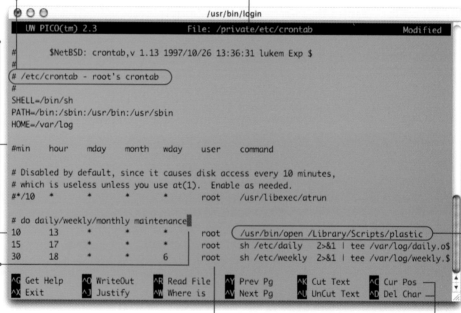

Privileged few
Keep in mind the consequences of asking cron to run your script as the root user, or as any other user. (See pages 248, 249.)

Keyboard commands
When you have typed your new crontab entry, press Control+O (that is, hold down the Control key while you press the O key) to WriteOut the file, then press the Return key when Pico's asks for confirmation. Last, press Control+X to Exit from Pico.

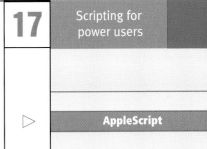

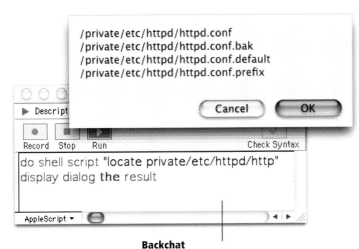

Backchat
The conversation can flow in the other direction, too. AppleScript's 'do shell script' command allows an AppleScript to execute any UNIX command and to receive the result. Here, the AppleScript has executed the UNIX command 'locate private/etc/httpd/http' and sent the result to a dialog box.

Interesting application
For simplicity's sake, save your script as an AppleScript application (not a compiled script) in the Scripts folder in Mac OS X's Library folder. (Our demonstration script is called 'plastic'.) Then, edit crontab so that it will use the Open command to launch this application at the times that you entered earlier. The '/usr/bin/' suffix is insurance against the possibility that cron won't know where to find the Open command.

Simplicity itself
Getting cron to automatically run a compiled AppleScript script is a challenge, which is why we saved our demonstration script 'plastic' as an AppleScript application. However, executing a compiled script from the command line is simple. Just resave the AppleScript application 'plastic' as a compiled script (in the same location), then open Terminal and type 'osascript /Library/Scripts/plastic'.

Light, camera, AppleScript

There are dozens of ways to launch an AppleScript in Mac OS X, and to be effective, those that you choose should be instantly accessible and easy to use. On these pages, we provide a few handy pointers and examples to choose from.

Rocket ride

Script Runner is in the AppleScript folder in Mac OS X's Applications folder. From the Script menu, choose Open Scripts Folder to go to the folder where you should put compiled scripts for your personal use. Or, add compiled scripts to the Scripts folder in the Library folder at the root level of your hard disk to make them available to anyone who uses your Mac.

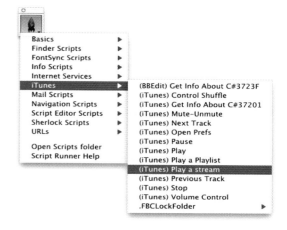

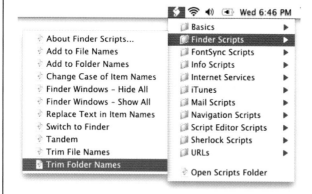

To the toolbar

You already knew you could add icons to your Finder window toolbars by selecting Customize Toolbar from the Finder's View menu, right? Well, you can drag AppleScript applications there too. (See also pages 47, 116 and 117.)

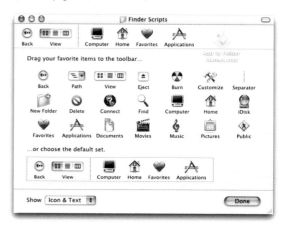

Pop-up pleasure

Add Script Menu to your menu bar for access to the same compiled scripts that you can access through Script Runner, as well as Perl and UNIX shell scripts. Download Script Menu (www.apple.com/applescript/macosx/script_menu/), put it somewhere for safe keeping, and then drag it to the menu bar. (Requires Mac OS X 10.1 or later.) To remove it, hold down the Command key and drag Script Menu off the menu bar.

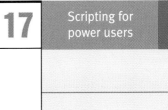
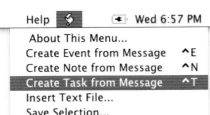

Special service

Smart programs include their own script menu where you can launch compiled scripts designed to work with that program in particular. Some programs will even let you attach an AppleScript to a keyboard shortcut. One of the Microsoft Entourage scripts shown here will automatically turn an e-mail message into an event in your calendar.

AppleScript speed

Running AppleScripts as compiled scripts is faster than running them as an application, because you don't have to wait for the application to launch. To turn an AppleScript application into a compiled script, open it in Script Editor, choose Save As, and then choose 'Compiled Script' in the Format pop-up menu. To turn a compiled script into an application, choose Application from this pop-up menu and put a tick in the Never Show Startup Screen checkbox. You will only be able to do this if the script's author has not saved it as Run Only.

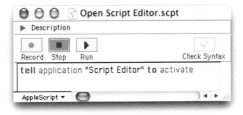

Ready, Set, Run

Script Editor, the program you use to write and edit AppleScripts, also includes a Run button for running scripts.

Drag and drop

Many AppleScripts that you have saved as double-clickable applications can also function as 'droplets' — AppleScripts that act on the files and folders that you drag onto them. Here, we are adding the Documents, Library, Music, Pictures and Public folders to our Favorites menu by dragging them onto Apple's '+favs' script, a free download from: www.apple.com/applescript/macosx/toolbar_scripts/

Imagine this

AppleScript is the ideal tool for manipulating hundreds of images in the same way — cropping or scaling them all to the same size, changing them all to black-and-white, or compressing them all for the Web. Here's how to get started with Photoshop, GraphicConverter and AppleScript.

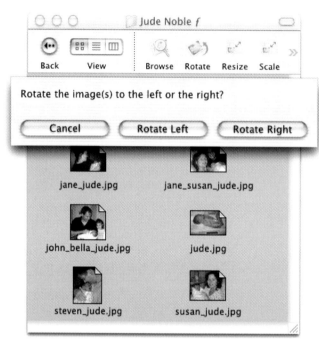

jane_jude.jpg   jane_susan_jude.jpg

john_bella_jude.jpg   jude.jpg

steven_jude.jpg   susan_jude.jpg

Built right in
Mac OS X includes a small program called Image Capture. This program has a few basic image-editing abilities that can operate in the background. If you download Apple's free Digital Camera scripts (www.apple.com/applescript/macosx/toolbar_scripts/) and install them in your Finder window toolbar, you'll be able to easily scale or rotate all the photographs in a folder. The scripts do this by harnessing Image Capture's basic image-editing abilities.

Ghostly thumbnails with GraphicConverter
Imagine that your Web site uses dark, brooding, thumbnail images to link to each page. It took just seconds to write this script, which tells the shareware program GraphicConverter to turn a photograph into an inverted, black-and-white, thumbnail. Write this script in Script Editor and then save it in the Scripts folder in the GraphicConverter folder, in Application Support, in Library, in your home directory. Restart GraphicConverter, and then open your image and select this script from the script menu whenever you want to use it. Other free AppleScripts for GraphicConverter can be found at:
www.lemkesoft.com/us_scripts.html

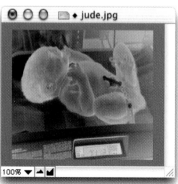

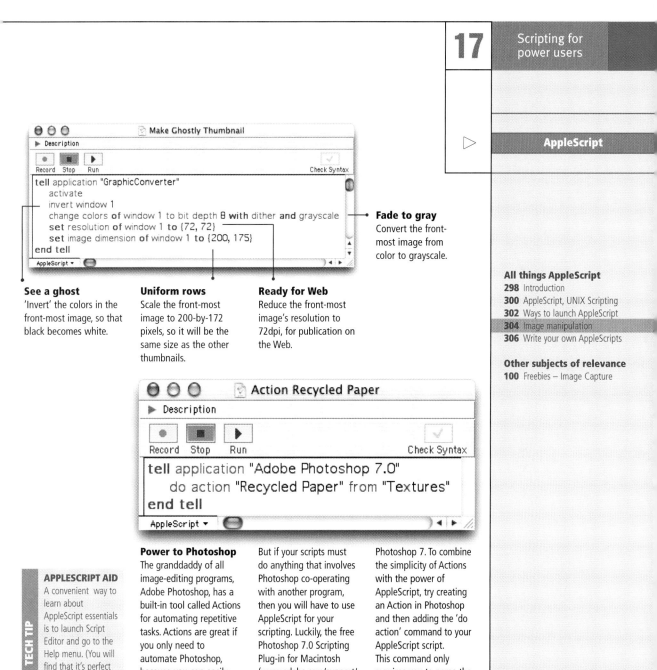

```
⊝ ⊝ ⊝          📄 Make Ghostly Thumbnail
▶ Description
[●] [■] [▶]                                    [✓]
Record Stop Run                        Check Syntax
tell application "GraphicConverter"
    activate
    invert window 1
    change colors of window 1 to bit depth 8 with dither and grayscale
    set resolution of window 1 to {72, 72}
    set image dimension of window 1 to {200, 175}
end tell
AppleScript ▾  ⊝                      ) ◀ ▶
```

Fade to gray
Convert the front-most image from color to grayscale.

See a ghost
'Invert' the colors in the front-most image, so that black becomes white.

Uniform rows
Scale the front-most image to 200-by-172 pixels, so it will be the same size as the other thumbnails.

Ready for Web
Reduce the front-most image's resolution to 72dpi, for publication on the Web.

```
⊝ ⊝ ⊝          📄 Action Recycled Paper
▶ Description
[●] [■] [▶]                                    [✓]
Record Stop Run                        Check Syntax
tell application "Adobe Photoshop 7.0"
    do action "Recycled Paper" from "Textures"
end tell
AppleScript ▾  ⊝                      ) ◀ ▶
```

TECH TIP

APPLESCRIPT AID
A convenient way to learn about AppleScript essentials is to launch Script Editor and go to the Help menu. (You will find that it's perfect for specific enquiries and easy to find your way around!)

Power to Photoshop
The granddaddy of all image-editing programs, Adobe Photoshop, has a built-in tool called Actions for automating repetitive tasks. Actions are great if you only need to automate Photoshop, because you can easily 'record' Actions using the Actions palette and convert them to droplets.

But if your scripts must do anything that involves Photoshop co-operating with another program, then you will have to use AppleScript for your scripting. Luckily, the free Photoshop 7.0 Scripting Plug-in for Macintosh (www.adobe.com/support/downloads/detail.jsp?ftpID=1477) brings AppleScript support to

Photoshop 7. To combine the simplicity of Actions with the power of AppleScript, try creating an Action in Photoshop and then adding the 'do action' command to your AppleScript script. This command only requires you to name the Action you wish to use and the Action group to which it belongs.

Write your own AppleScripts

Write your own AppleScripts using Script Editor, which is in the AppleScript folder in the Applications folder. You can also use Script Editor to modify other people's scripts — like this version of a script from Apple, which creates two parallel Finder windows to help you quickly moving files around you hard disk. If you catch the AppleScript bug, look to AppleScript Studio for greater possibilities including interface building tools.

Start at the start (5)
This Finder window will show the startup disk – rather than, say, a CD-ROM or a particular folder.

First things first
We invent three 'variables': monitor_width, monitor_height and startup_disk, and set the first two to 800 and 600 to match the dimensions of our display.
The 'path to' command sets startup_disk to the name and location of the startup disk, such as 'Macintosh HD:'.

Straight talking (1)
All the commands between the 'tell' and 'end tell' statements are directed to the Finder. The first such command, 'activate', makes the Finder the front-most, active program.

For good measure (2)
Create a similar Finder window in the top half of the screen using the same techniques.

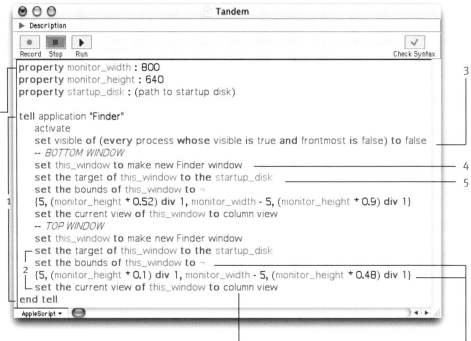

```
000                                    Tandem
▶ Description
 ●    ■    ▶                                              ✓
Record Stop  Run                                      Check Syntax
property monitor_width : 800
property monitor_height : 640
property startup_disk : (path to startup disk)

tell application "Finder"
    activate
    set visible of (every process whose visible is true and frontmost is false) to false
    -- BOTTOM WINDOW
    set this_window to make new Finder window
    set the target of this_window to the startup_disk
    set the bounds of this_window to ¬
    {5, (monitor_height * 0.52) div 1, monitor_width - 5, (monitor_height * 0.9) div 1}
    set the current view of this_window to column view
    -- TOP WINDOW
    set this_window to make new Finder window
    set the target of this_window to the startup_disk
    set the bounds of this_window to ¬
    {5, (monitor_height * 0.1) div 1, monitor_width - 5, (monitor_height * 0.48) div 1}
    set the current view of this_window to column view
end tell
AppleScript ▼
```

Hide and seek (3)
We hide ('set visible to false') every visible program ('every process whose visible is true') other than the front-most program ('and frontmost is false'), which is the Finder (see 'Straight talking').

Wish for a window (4)
We create a new Finder window, and decide that for the purposes of this AppleScript we will call it 'this_window'.

Colour by numbers
Position the Finder window so that its top-left corner is five pixels from the left edge of the screen and slightly more than half way down (52%). The bottom-right corner is five pixels from the right edge and 90% of the way down the screen. The "div 1" ensures the result of the calculation is a whole number, and the "¬" breaks the statement over two lines.

Neat, little rows
Tell the Finder window to use Column view.

The rulebook
Select Open Dictionary from Script Editor's Edit menu to read a 'dictionary' of the commands available within any AppleScript-aware program. For example, the Finder's dictionary tells us that the property 'frontmost' is boolean. This means that it's either true or false — rather than being a number between 1 and 100, for example. Either the Finder is in front of all other programs, or it is not.

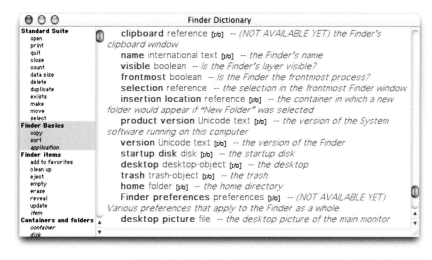

Essential reading
The complete guide to the AppleScript language is online at:
developer.apple.com/techpubs/macosx/Carbon/interapplicationcomm/
AppleScript/AppleScriptLangGuide/AppleScript.1.html.
This is not for beginners. There's a gentler introduction to
AppleScript at: www.apple.com/applescript/begin/pgs/begin_00.html,
but remember that this tutorial was written before Mac OS X.
An introduction to how AppleScript has changed with Mac OS X is
online at: www.apple.com/applescript/MacOSX_Overview/index.htm

Field Guide
search

A